# UNSPEAKABLE ACTS

# UNSPEAKABLE ACTS

TRUE TALES OF CRIME, MURDER, DECEIT, AND OBSESSION

## SARAH WEINMAN

*An Imprint of* HarperCollins*Publishers*

HarperCollins books may be purchased for educational, business, or sales promotional use. For information, please email the Special Markets Department at SPsales@harpercollins.com.

Ecco® and HarperCollins® are trademarks of HarperCollins Publishers.

FIRST EDITION

*Designed by Paula Russell Szafranski*

Library of Congress Cataloging-in-Publication Data has been applied for.

ISBN 978-0-06-283988-6

20 21 22 23 24  LSC  10 9 8 7 6 5 4 3

To those who find meaning, solace, catharsis,
and outrage in crime stories, which is all of us

# CONTENTS

---

## PART III: JUSTICE AND SOCIETY

# INTRODUCTION

BY PATRICK RADDEN KEEFE

When I was in fourth grade, kids told stories about a killer who was supposedly stalking the area. This was in Milton, Massachusetts, a suburb of Boston, in the mid-1980s. The man drove a Chevy Nova and carried a knife, my classmates said. He was known as the Milton Quincy Stabber. I don't have many specific recollections of fourth grade, but I can vividly remember walking out of art class, positively vibrating with terror. The stabber was at large, in our area, and would almost certainly stab again. I suddenly became attuned to the make and model of every approaching car, though the Milton Quincy Stabber was said to direct his violence only at women.

If I ever learned what became of the Milton Quincy Stabber, I have forgotten. Which is strange, when you think about it, because even as children, we are drawn to the puzzle of crime narratives, and if we read them compulsively it's often because we feel compelled to hunt for a solution. My favorite part of any Sherlock Holmes story was always the final scene, when the great detective reassembles the random clues into a coherent narrative that is legible only in retrospect. Was the stabber apprehended? If I bothered to find out as a kid, the memory hasn't lingered. What has stayed with me, indelibly, is that first vicarious brush with the concept of random murder: the whiff of mortal fear, the revelation that sometimes life doesn't stretch out before you in an unbroken path to old age. Sometimes it terminates, abruptly, when a stranger pulls over in his Chevy Nova.

A few years ago, I spent some time back in Massachusetts to report the story of an unrelated killing, and while I was there, I started thinking about the Milton Quincy Stabber. When I ran the phrase through Google, however, nothing came up. My mind flipped through a sequence of bizarre explanations. Had one of my fourth-grade classmates invented the stabber? This was a feature of childhood before the advent of the search engine: nobody fact-checked anything. Wild legends circulated, like the one about the untimely death of little Mikey, who made the suicidal mistake of mixing Coke and Pop Rocks. But could someone have invented a serial killer? Even as I weighed this possibility, a more troubling scenario presented itself: Could I have concocted the story myself? As a child, I had a febrile imagination—not a fantasy life per se, but the attention of an actuary to the probability of improbable catastrophes. I slept with the lights on for years. Could I have somehow fantasized the stabber?

I mention all this because the whole episode captures two distinct elements of our relationship with stories about real crimes. The first is that, from childhood, we are hardwired to be fascinated by danger, and by the dark potential of other humans.

When you read a Patricia Highsmith novel, the abyss of human depravity into which you peer runs only as deep as Highsmith's imagination. But a true story of human cruelty engages—and implicates—the reader in a more profound and unsettling way.

The story of the Milton Quincy Stabber was also a *story*, with the familiar contours of a fairy tale: a predator, a string of innocent victims, a hunting ground that children should avoid. If "true crime" is enjoying a renaissance at the moment, I think it is at least in part a function of narrative modalities: bingeable, long-form, serialized storytelling lends itself particularly well to tales of investigation. At the same time, any journalist seeking to incorporate the truth of an actual crime into some engaging narrative construct must contend with very real moral hazard. The most engaging crime stories often take the form of a mystery or a thriller. But if they're true, they are also, almost always, tragedies. The more lurid the story, the more likely the victims—and the real human costs of the crime—are to be forgotten.

For the crime reporter, certain forms of selection bias can also take hold. "Narrative" tends to mean characters—protagonists and antagonists, conflict and motivation—and crime writing has historically favored certain sorts of characters (white female murder victims, to take the most glaring example) to the exclusion of others. There's a subtler danger, too, when we focus on stories of individual characters and crimes, because the greatest crimes, now and always, have been systemic, and systemic stories are harder to tell. One conspicuous upside of the current boom in crime reportage is that it has created space and demand and recognition for writing about crime that is more representative—and for an approach to crime writing that grapples more overtly with these risks. On both counts, the collection you are about to read is exemplary and overdue.

As I was preparing to write this introduction, I searched one more time for the Milton Quincy Stabber, and found an article I'd missed when I looked before, a UPI story from January 1987, with the headline, "Hunt for Stabber Intensifies." Over a three-week period that winter, a man named William Marguetty stabbed four women in Milton and Quincy. They all survived, but before he was apprehended that March, he murdered a twenty-seven-year-old named Ann Gillietti. She was found stabbed to death in her apartment in a Roslindale housing project. In a typical failure of crime reportage, I could find hardly any information about Gillietti online, apart from the fact of her murder—and the terrible detail that she was not alone in the apartment when her killer arrived; her two-year-old daughter was with her and survived the attack.

Marguetty was eventually convicted of murder and attempted murder, and sentenced to life in prison. He had arrived in the United States on the Mariel boatlift in 1980, after being released from a prison in Cuba. "Victims have provided different descriptions of the attacker's car," the UPI reported. But two of the women said it might have been "a rust-colored Chevy Nova." I hadn't imagined the story, nor had my classmates. We just had the wrong dime-store nickname. In the press, Marguetty wasn't the Milton Quincy Stabber but the South Shore Stalker.

# EDITOR'S NOTE

True crime is having a moment. But then, one could say true crime has been having a moment for more than three centuries, since the New England–based minister Cotton Mather published his execution sermons for eager Puritan audiences, then, with an altogether different pamphlet, laid the groundwork for the Salem Witch Trials in 1692.

Lately, it's felt different. More highbrow. More participatory. More investigative. More in the public interest. More reflective, critical, even postmodern. The current state of the genre has broadened far past stories once reliably contained within the pages of mass-market paperbacks, covers with dripping fonts. Or tabloid-friendly tales slickly packaged into programs that air on Investigation Discovery, Oxygen, and Lifetime.

The new true crime moment dates to the fall of 2014, when the radio program *This American Life* presented the first series of its podcast spinoff, *Serial*. Sarah Koenig's week-by-week account of the 1999 murder of Hae Min Lee, the incarceration of Adnan Syed, and why his conviction could have been a wrongful one was not just a hit but a bona fide cultural phenomenon. Everyone who was anyone listened to *Serial*, even if they had never consumed—or knew they were consuming—true crime before then.

*Serial*'s astonishing success paved the way for even stronger, more superbly reported podcasts, such as *In the Dark*, *Bear Brook* (where victim and perpetrator identification led to the burgeoning field of forensic genealogy for cold cases), *Bundyville*, and *S-Town*. Television and streaming documentaries like *The Jinx* and *Making a Murderer* expanded the storytelling range so our appetites could handle the epic, Oscar-winning *O.J.: Made in America*. And the state of policing and criminal justice, then and now, yielded outstanding recent books like *Ghettoside* by Jill Leovy, *They Can't Kill Us All* by Wesley Lowery, *Killers of the Flower Moon* by David Grann, and *American Prison* by Shane Bauer.

The fascination with murder and illegality is a perennial one, because the shock of the deed creates a schism between order and chaos. We wish for justice, but even when we get it, the result rings somewhat hollow. We gorge on facts and innuendo but are then left with the hangover of trauma, the aftermath of a system that too often fails people. We crave a narrative that restores righteousness but are left with scraps of barely connected meaning.

The last few years of true crime storytelling have dwelled on the messiness. One important strand, as coined by WNYC's *On the Media* in 2017, is "true innocence," where convictions yield questions and possible exoneration. It's less who did it than why did she falsely confess, or what mistakes did the prosecutor or detective or lab technician make? Season two of *In the Dark*, the landmark podcast from American Public Media hosted by Madeleine Baran, uncovered so many inconsistencies in the case of Curtis Flowers, tried six times for an early-1990s quadruple murder in Winona, Mississippi, that its reporting helped lead the Supreme Court to reverse Flowers's most recent conviction.

The genre is also much more interactive. The proliferation of podcasts in particular creates communities of would-be amateur sleuths with a vested interest in seeing their pet cold (and not-so-cold) cases solved. Those communities are also spaces for finding friendship and comfort among those who love true crime, as the "Murderinos" who listen avidly to Georgia Hardstark and Karen Kilgariff's hit comedy podcast *My Favorite Murder* can attest.

Michelle McNamara's *I'll Be Gone in the Dark*, her posthumous 2018 blend of crime reporting and memoir on the Golden State Killer case, was as much a paean to the web of internet users equally invested in uncovering the killer's identity. That forensic genealogy—itself a discipline spearheaded by amateurs working outside law enforcement—brought about the identification and arrest of Joseph DeAngelo in April 2018, is as much a testament to nontraditional methods leading to the resolution of long-dormant cases.

That sense of interactivity helps explain the recent and parallel rise of the true-crime memoir. Those who have been directly affected by crime are giving voice to their own experiences in beautifully crafted works. Well-reported literary nonfiction such as *Down City* by Leah Carroll, *You All Grow Up and Leave Me* by Piper Weiss, *The Hot One* by Carolyn Murnick, and *After the Eclipse* by Sarah Perry, as well as podcasts like *The Ballad of Billy Balls* by iO Tillett Wright, illuminate how the violent death of a loved one causes lifelong ramifications that don't stop with the finished, produced work.

As I wrote for the *Guardian* in 2016: "a book or a documentary or a podcast is now seen as the continuation, even the beginning, of a crime story, not the end." Internet sleuths hold themselves up as better than professional detectives, and sometimes they prove to be right. The dichotomy of true crime is not about high versus low culture, but is between observer and participant. It's no longer enough to be horrified or morally outraged. Now, it seems, the perennial fascination that is murder has the power to make us act, even if our actions are futile.

IF TRUE CRIME IS HAVING A MOMENT, HOW BEST TO chronicle that moment? I am a creator and consumer of true crime. I've published true crime features and essays critiquing the genre. My own book, *The Real Lolita*, is a hybrid of crime investigation and literary criticism. I haven't read every single book, watched every documentary, or listened to every podcast—that would, quite simply, be impossible—but in our post-*Serial* world, it has been breathtaking to watch this genre I've loved my whole life grow and change, bend back upon itself, open itself up for serious criticism, and accept the possibility that its constraints can be crested.

The time seemed ripe for an anthology of recent writing about true crime across the broadest possible spectrum. Some years ago, there were annual anthologies under the banner of *The Best American Crime Reporting*, collections that affirmed to me that many of my favorite nonfiction writers journeyed into the land of crime and often stayed there for good. But in the years since those anthologies ceased to be, a new and fresh crop of crime writers has arrived.

They centered the victims as human beings rather than rely on the trope of beautiful white dead girls. They widened the storytelling lens far beyond the individual to the collective. They explored different subcultures and communities. They paid attention to stark topics like inequality, poverty, housing, and addiction, all of which affect and are affected by crime. They were women and people of color. They were unafraid to call out the problems inherent to what I think of as the "true crime industrial complex," which turns crime and murder into entertainment for the masses.

They are the present, and the future, of this genre. *Unspeakable Acts* includes a baker's dozen of these writers, separated into three broad categories.

The first section highlights more classic crime features. Pamela Colloff, indisputably among the great nonfiction crime writers of the twenty-first century, is here with one of her final features for *Texas Monthly*, where she worked for nearly two decades. Michelle Dean's BuzzFeed feature, the basis for the Hulu series *The Act* (which Dean cocreated), is here in print for the very first time. Rachel Monroe, author of the standout book of true crime criticism *Savage Appetites*, is here with a con artist tale that reflects, and stands apart from, the plethora of pieces on grifters, scammers, and frauds. And Canadian journalist Karen K. Ho blends personal history and dogged reporting with her stellar story on a girl expected to excel, with catastrophic results.

Section two gets more meta, looking at how true crime interacts with culture as well as itself. Author and documentary filmmaker Alex Mar compares and contrasts two stories of fatal girlhood friendship—one from the 1950s, one from a few years ago—and finds eerie parallels. Sarah Marshall, cohost of the wonderful *You're Wrong About* podcast, traces America's obsession with serial killer Ted Bundy and finds him, and us, profoundly wanting. Alice Bolin, author of the indispensable essay collection *Dead Girls*, takes direct aim at why we're in this true crime moment, and what it erases. Elon Green digs for the heartbreaking stories behind a legendary music video's photo montage of missing children. And my own contribution to the anthology is on the ill-fated bank robbery, and the fascinating woman involved in it, that inspired Barbara Loden's cult feminist film *Wanda*.

The third and final section widens the scope to broader issues of criminal justice and society. Jason Fagone embeds with a Philadelphia emergency-room doctor who is fed up at the number of shootings and the devastating human toll of gun violence. Emma Copley Eisenberg, author of *The Third*

*Rainbow Girl*, introduces us to a black transgender teenager named Sage Smith, and how her murder, and the neglect in solving the case, rippled across a town. Finally, Leora Smith profiles Herbert MacDonell, the so-called father of blood-spatter analysis, and how his methods inspired all manner of junk science in the courtroom.

Consuming and creating true crime is an ethically thorny endeavor, as it always was, and as it must be. But the pieces included in *Unspeakable Acts* go a long way to make the world a more just, more empathetic place.

# PART I

# NARRATIVE FEATURES

# Dee Dee Wanted Her Daughter to Be Sick, Gypsy Wanted Her Mom Murdered

## BY MICHELLE DEAN

For seven years before the murder, Dee Dee and Gypsy Rose Blancharde lived in a small pink bungalow on West Volunteer Way in Springfield, Missouri. Their neighbors liked them. "'Sweet' is the word I'd use," a former friend of Dee Dee's told me not too long ago. Once you met them, people said, they were impossible to forget.

Dee Dee was 48 years old, originally from Louisiana. She was a large, affable-looking person, which she reinforced by dressing in bright, cheerful colors. She had curly brown hair she liked to hold back with ribbons. People who knew her remember her as generous with her time and, when she could be, generous with money. She could make friends quickly and inspire deep devotion. She did not have a job, but instead served as a full-time caretaker for Gypsy Rose, her teenage daughter.

Gypsy was a tiny thing, perhaps five feet tall as far as anyone could guess. She was confined to a wheelchair. Her round face was overwhelmed by a pair of owlish glasses. She was pale and skinny, and her teeth were crumbling and painful. She had a feeding tube. Sometimes Dee Dee had to drag an oxygen tank around with them, nasal cannula looped around Gypsy's small ears. Ask about her daughter's diagnoses, and Dee Dee would reel off a list as long as her arm: chromosomal defects, muscular dystrophy, epilepsy, severe asthma, sleep apnea, eye problems. It had always been this way, Dee Dee said, ever since Gypsy was a baby. She had spent time in neonatal intensive care. She'd had leukemia as a toddler.

The endless health crises had taken a toll. Gypsy was friendly, talkative even, but her voice was high and childlike. Dee Dee would often remind people that her daughter had brain damage. She had to be homeschooled because she'd never be able to keep up with other kids. Gypsy had the mind of a child of seven, Dee Dee said. It was important to remember that in dealing with her. She loved princess outfits and dressing up. She wore wigs and hats to cover her small head. A curly blond Cinderella number seems to have been her favorite. She's wearing it in so many photographs of herself with her mother. She was always with her mother.

"We are a pair of shoes," Gypsy once said. "Never good without the other."

Their house, like everyone else's around them, had been built by Habitat for Humanity. It had amenities specially built for Gypsy: a ramp up to the front door, a Jacuzzi tub to help with "my muscles," Gypsy told a local television station in 2008. Sometimes, on summer nights, Dee Dee would set up a projector to play a movie on the side of her house, and the children of the neighborhood, whose parents usually couldn't afford to send them to a movie theater, came over for a treat. Dee Dee charged for concessions, but it was still cheaper than the local multiplex. The money was to go to Gypsy's treatments.

Dee Dee became particularly close with some people across the way, a single mother named Amy Pinegar and her four children. Over years of tea and coffee, Dee Dee would tell Pinegar her life story. She was originally from a small town in Louisiana, she said, but she'd had to flee her abusive family with Gypsy. It was her own father, Gypsy's grandfather, who'd been the last straw; he'd burned Gypsy with cigarettes. So she'd lit out from her hometown for good.

She told Pinegar that Gypsy's father was a deadbeat, an alcoholic drug abuser who had mocked his daughter's disabilities, called the Special Olympics a "freak show." As Pinegar understood it, he'd never sent them a dime, not even when Dee Dee and Gypsy had lost everything in Hurricane Katrina. It was a blessing that a doctor at a rescue shelter had helped them get to the Ozarks.

Sometimes, listening, Amy Pinegar found herself overwhelmed. "I wondered," Pinegar told me over the phone last fall, "keeping this child alive . . . Is she that happy?" All she could do was be a good neighbor and pitch in when she could. She'd drive Dee Dee and Gypsy to the airport for their medical trips to Kansas City, bring them things from Sam's Club. Ultimately, they did seem happy. They went on charity trips to Disney World, met Miranda Lambert through the Make-A-Wish Foundation. Looking back on it, Pinegar was sometimes even jealous of them.

It was a perfect story for a human-interest segment on the evening news: a family living through tragedy and disaster, managing to build a life for themselves in spite of so many obstacles. But the story wasn't over. One day last June, Dee Dee's Facebook account posted an update.

"That bitch is dead," it read.

IT WAS JUNE 14, A HOT SUNDAY AFTERNOON THAT had driven a lot of people indoors to the blessings of air-conditioning. The first few comments on the status are from friends expressing wild disbelief. Maybe the page had been hacked. Maybe someone should call. Does anyone know where they live? Should someone call the police, give them the address?

As they debated it, a new comment from Dee Dee's account appeared on the status: "I fucken SLASHED THAT FAT PIG AND RAPED HER SWEET INNOCENT DAUGHTER . . . HER SCREAM WAS SOOOO FUCKEN LOUD LOL."

Kim Blanchard, who lived nearby, was among the first to react. Though Kim had a similar last name to the Blanchardes, she wasn't a relative. She had met Dee Dee and

Gypsy in 2009 at a science fiction and fantasy convention held in the Ozarks, where Gypsy could wear costumes and not be particularly out of place. "They were just perfect," Kim said. "Here was this poor, sick child who was being taken care of by a wonderful, patient mother who only wanted to help everybody."

Kim called Dee Dee's number, but there was no answer. Kim's husband, David, suggested that they drive on over to the house just to make sure everything was all right. When they arrived, a crowd of worried neighbors was already gathering. Dee Dee and Gypsy had sometimes been unreachable before, off on medical trips without telling anyone. The windows had a protective film on them; it was hard to see in. Knocking on the doors brought no response. But everyone found it suspicious that Dee Dee's new cube van, which could easily transport Gypsy around in her wheelchair, was parked in the driveway.

Kim called 911. The police couldn't enter the house without a warrant, but didn't stop David from climbing through a window. Inside, he saw nothing amiss. All the lights had been turned off, and the air-conditioning was on high. There were no signs of a robbery, or any struggle. All of Gypsy's wheelchairs were still in the house. It was frightening to think about how helpless she might be without them.

The police began taking statements while they waited for a search warrant. Kim relayed information back to Facebook. Yes, they'd been to the house; yes, the police had been called. Dee Dee's online friends and acquaintances began bombarding Kim with questions. She answered as best she could, but the status was beginning to get shared around Missouri. "Here's the thing guys . . . I know everyone is very concerned," Kim wrote on Facebook. "We need to realize that whoever posted this can read all of this."

The search warrant didn't come through until 10:45 that night. The police found Dee Dee's body in the bedroom. She'd been stabbed and had been dead for several days. But there was no sign of Gypsy.

The next day, Kim organized a vigil and a GoFundMe account to take care of Dee Dee's funeral expenses—and possibly Gypsy's. Everyone feared the worst. All her life, Gypsy had evoked protective responses in people. She was so small and looked so helpless. Many people couldn't understand why this had happened to her. Who could prey on someone who had no defenses?

Meanwhile, the police were starting to sort things out. A young woman named Aleah Woodmansee had approached them. There were some things she knew, things that might be helpful. For example, she told them, Gypsy had a secret online boyfriend.

ALEAH WAS AMY PINEGAR'S DAUGHTER, A 23-YEAR-OLD who'd worked as a medical claims investigator. She felt like a big sister to Gypsy, and evidently Gypsy felt the same. But they were rarely alone together, as Gypsy's mother was constantly by her side. So when Gypsy confided in Aleah, it was through a secret Facebook account, under the name Emma Rose.

"This is my personal account my mom is still overprotective so she don't, know about this account," Gypsy wrote in October 2014. Then she confessed she'd met a man on a Christian singles site. She was in love with him, she told Aleah. Gypsy hadn't yet told her mother. She wrote that she knew Dee Dee wouldn't approve, that she wasn't allowed to date, though she longed to grow up and have a boyfriend like other girls her age.

"In the past I told my mom something mean I says I wished ur mom was my mom instead of my mom cus mrs Amy let Aleah date anyone she wanted so that hurt my mom," Gypsy wrote.

The new boyfriend's name, Gypsy revealed, was Nicholas Godejohn. They'd been communicating for over two years. He didn't care that she was in a wheelchair. And Gypsy planned to marry him. They were both Catholic. They had agreed on names for their children. She was cooking up an elaborate plan for Dee Dee to casually meet Nick at the local movie theater, after which Gypsy was hoping they could be open about their relationship.

This wasn't the first time Aleah had gotten clandestine messages from Gypsy about boys. She knew that Gypsy had tried to meet men online before, that in spite of what Dee Dee said about Gypsy's seven-year-old mind, thoughts about romance and sex were taking root anyway. But she was concerned. Gypsy had always seemed naïve to her. In October 2014, she wrote "I'm 18. Nick . . . is 24," which made Godejohn six years older.

Plus, the way she talked about the relationship was odd. "It was like some kind of magnificent fairy tale was unfolding," Aleah said over coffee in Springfield last fall.

She was worried, too, about Dee Dee, who'd confronted her in 2011 about her chats with Gypsy, telling her she was corrupting a child. "I'm not going to tell your mom about the things you said," she told Aleah. "But I don't want you talking to Gypsy like that." Dee Dee took away Gypsy's phone and computer for a time. Gypsy had always managed, nonetheless, to slip through some crack in her mother's attention, find some other way of getting to Aleah. But the two saw each other less and less, and after the messages about Nick Godejohn in the fall of 2014, Aleah didn't hear from Gypsy again.

Standing in front of the house half a year later with the crowd that had gathered, it occurred to Aleah that the police should know about all this. She showed them the Facebook messages, and they wrote the name down. The police also put a trace on the Facebook posts to Dee Dee's account. The IP address was registered to a Nicholas Godejohn in Big Bend, Wisconsin.

On June 15, a team of officers in Waukesha County, Wisconsin, were dispatched to Godejohn's house. The standoff was brief. Nick quickly surrendered. Luckily enough, Gypsy was with him, unharmed, in excellent health. Relief flooded everyone, at least for a moment.

"Things are not always as they appear," the Springfield sheriff said at a press conference the next morning.

It turned out that, in fact, Gypsy hadn't used a wheelchair from the moment she left her house a few days earlier. She didn't need one. She could walk just fine—there was nothing wrong with her muscles, and she had no medication or oxygen tank with her, either. Her hair was short and spiky, but she wasn't bald—her head had simply been shaved, all her life, to make her appear ill. She was well spoken, if shaken by recent events. The disabled child she'd long been in the eyes of others was nowhere to be found. It was all a fraud, she told the police. All of it. Every last bit. Her mother had made her do it.

"I just cried," Aleah said, her sheer disbelief about everything that had happened overwhelming her.

Kim Blanchard cried, too. "At that point it really became: 'I don't know anything about this person. What have I been believing? How could I have been so stupid?'"

"No one asked for any more documentation. No one raised an eyebrow," Amy Pinegar told me later. "Were they behind closed doors laughing at us"—she paused for a second—"suckers?"


DEE DEE'S LEGAL NAME WAS CLAUDDINE BLANCHARD. She'd used various aliases and misspellings over the years:

DeDe, Claudine, Deno. By the time she reached Missouri, she went by Clauddinnea and always added an "e" to her last name. Not all of her stories turned out to be false. She was, indeed, from Lafourche Parish, in the ball of Louisiana's foot. She had grown up in a town called Golden Meadow alongside five brothers and sisters, most still living. Her mother died in 1997, but her father is still alive.

So is Rod Blanchard, Gypsy's father. He still lives in the area, in Cut Off, not far from Golden Meadow. Gypsy has his nose. He has a laconic manner, sometimes stoic, sometimes funny. He met Dee Dee when he was still in high school, and they dated for four to six months. He was 17 to her 24 when she became pregnant, and at the time the only logical thing he thought he could do was marry her. "I woke up on my birthday, on my 18th birthday, and realized I wasn't where I was supposed to be," he told me recently. "I wasn't in love with her, really. I knew I got married for the wrong reasons." He left Dee Dee, and though she tried on more than one occasion to get him back, the marriage would not stick.

Gypsy Rose was born shortly after the couple separated, on July 27, 1991. Rod said Dee Dee liked the name Gypsy, and he was a Guns N' Roses fan. As far as he knows, neither of them knew about Gypsy Rose Lee, the 1920s vaudeville child star–turned-stripper whose early life was the basis for the Broadway musical *Gypsy*. That Gypsy had a controlling stage mother, too, one who lied about her daughter's age to make her seem younger, one who kept forcing her daughter to perform even though she didn't want to.

Gypsy was healthy at birth, Rod said. But when she was three months old, Dee Dee became convinced that her baby had sleep apnea, that Gypsy would stop breathing in the night. It was then that Dee Dee began taking her to the hospital. As Rod remembers it, the doctors couldn't find anything, in spite of three rounds of tests and a sleep monitor. The conviction that Gypsy was a sickly child took hold. She explained the increasingly bewildering array of problems to Rod by saying that Gypsy had a chromosomal defect. Many of Gypsy's health issues, she claimed, stemmed from that one thing.

It all spiraled so quickly. Dee Dee always had a new idea about what was wrong with Gypsy, a new doctor, a new drug. She had once worked as a nurse's aide; she had a knack for remembering medical terminology and spitting it back. The information overload acted as a kind of wall around mother and daughter. It always seemed that Dee Dee had things under control. She knew so much, and she was never troubled by questions—she always had an answer.

Rod eventually remarried and had two other children. He and his new wife, Kristy, saw Gypsy often over the first 10 years of her life, and can share pictures from various happy family outings right up until 2004. They remember going to the Special Olympics, too, but have good memories of it. "All smiles," Kristy said. They have a picture of Gypsy grinning widely with her father and brother there. In all those years, Gypsy never said a word against her mother or anything else.

Meanwhile, Dee Dee's relationship with her own family, never great to begin with, got worse. The cause isn't clear. (In spite of repeated attempts to contact her father, Claude Pitre, I was never able to speak to her family directly.) She'd begun to get in trouble with the law, usually for small misdemeanors, like writing bad checks. Eventually, Dee Dee simply moved away, to Slidell, two hours north and kitty-corner to New Orleans across Lake Pontchartrain.

Dee Dee and Gypsy spent their years in Slidell living in public housing and visiting doctors at the Tulane Medical Center and the Children's Hospital New Orleans. Dee Dee told doctors there that Gypsy had seizures every couple of months, so they put her on antiseizure medications. Dee Dee insisted to one doctor after another that her daughter had muscular dystrophy even after a muscle biopsy proved she didn't. There were problems with her eyes and ears, too, Dee Dee insisted, poor vision and frequent ear infections. Doctors dutifully operated on her. If Gypsy had a cold or cough, she was taken to the emergency room.

In 2005, Hurricane Katrina hit Slidell. The power was off for weeks. The pair turned up in a special-needs shelter in Covington, Louisiana, with pictures of their old apartment in rubble. She told the shelter staff she didn't have Gypsy's medical records with her because they'd been destroyed in the flood.

One of the doctors at the shelter, Janet Jordan, was from the Ozarks. (She declined to be interviewed for this article.) She was charmed by Gypsy in the shelter: "When I first met her, I had to cry a little bit, and she goes, 'It's okay, you're only human,'" Jordan told a local news station in 2005. It was, apparently, she who suggested the Blanchards move to Missouri.

The story of a mother and disabled daughter left without anything proved irresistible to local press. It worked on charities, too. Dee Dee and Gypsy were airlifted to Missouri in September 2005, where they rented a house in Aurora. They lived there until the Habitat for Humanity house on West Volunteer Way in March 2008.

While Gypsy had been involved with charities for children with disabilities from the time she was quite small—Dee Dee often stayed at Ronald McDonald houses—this was obviously the largest benefit Dee Dee had managed to arrange. It seemed to give her an appetite for more. While in Springfield, they'd benefit from free flights from a volunteer pilots organization, stays at a lodge for cancer patients, free trips to Disney World through various charity organizations. (None of the organizations with which the Blanchards had confirmed links returned requests for comment.)

Dee Dee kept Rod updated on his daughter's whereabouts and medical circumstances. She did this even as she told doctors and new friends in Missouri that he was a drug addict who had abandoned his daughter. Meanwhile, Rod and Kristy spoke to Gypsy pretty often. They always planned to visit, but "for one reason or another, it would never work out," Rod said.

Rod continued to send, as he always had, $1,200 a month

in child support to a New Orleans bank account. He also sent the occasional gifts Dee Dee asked for, television sets and a Nintendo Wii. He continued to send these things even after Gypsy turned 18, because Dee Dee said Gypsy still required full-time care. "There was never a question whether or not I was going to stop paying," he said.

There were, occasionally, small signs of deception. When Rod called Gypsy to talk on her 18th birthday, he said, he was excited to make all the jokes dads make to their daughters about becoming an adult. But Dee Dee intercepted the call, he said, to remind him that Gypsy didn't know her true age. "She thinks she's 14," Dee Dee said. She asked that he not upset Gypsy by claiming otherwise. Rod heeded the instruction.

"I think Dee Dee's problem was she started a web of lies, and there was no escaping after," Rod said. "She got so wound up in it, it was like a tornado got started, and then once she was in so deep that there was no escaping. One lie had to cover another lie, had to cover another lie, and that was her way of life." They never saw all the local news stories about Dee Dee and Gypsy that had been written and filmed up in Missouri. They knew nothing of any charity drives and trips except what Dee Dee told them, which was very little.

That all changed last June when Rod called Kristy, sobbing, in the middle of a workday. Dee Dee's sister had called him; Dee Dee was dead and Gypsy was missing. "I was in hysterics thinking she got brought somewhere and was left to die," Kristy said. And if Gypsy was found, she continued, "how could I take care of her when Dee Dee knew every-thing on how to take care of her?"

The first time Rod saw his daughter walk as an adult was in a news report on Gypsy's arraignment hearing in Wisconsin. No one had prepared them; Kristy had spotted the video on Facebook. Rod was so confused when he saw it that he said his first reaction was "I was really happy that she was walking."

When Gypsy's attorney showed them Dee Dee's autopsy report, Kristy said she stared for a while at the portion about Dee Dee's brain. The lawyer asked her why.

"I want to know what the hell was going through her mind," Kristy said. "What is in that brain of hers that triggered all of this shit?"

DEE DEE WON'T EVER BE ABLE TO ANSWER ANYONE'S questions. All there will be is Gypsy's story. And Gypsy doesn't know all of it herself. From the time she was arrested to my more recent talks with her in prison in Missouri, she is confused about details large and small. For example: when she was arrested, Gypsy told the police that she was 19. Rod and Kristy were able to straighten that out by giving authorities Gypsy's birth certificate. She was actually 23.

Parents make your world, and Dee Dee made Gypsy's into one where she did, indeed, have cancer. Gypsy told me her mother said some of the medications were related to it. Even as she grew older, she wasn't sure how to question it. There are lingering questions, in fact, about exactly what medications Gypsy was given over the years. Some of them may never have been prescribed to Gypsy at all; her attorney, for example, suspects Dee Dee gave Gypsy some kind of tranquilizer.

The pile of bogus diagnoses, the confusing lists of drugs: it all points to a syndrome called Munchausen syndrome by proxy. Munchausen syndrome was first identified by a British psychiatrist named Richard Asher in 1951. A successor, Roy Meadow, identified Munchausen syndrome by proxy in 1977. It has been in the *DSM*, the diagnostic manual used by psychiatrists, since 1980. (In the latest version, the *DSM-V*, it goes by the name "factitious disorder," but for clarity's sake I'll stick to the Munchausen nomenclature.) In short, a person with the syndrome either feigns or induces physical and psychological symptoms for no obvious benefit other than attention and sympathy. If the person does this to themselves, it's plain Munchausen syndrome; when the symptoms are feigned or induced in others, it's called Munchausen syndrome by proxy. The *DSM-V* recommends distinguishing Munchausen syndrome from what is called "malingering," that is, faking or inducing symptoms of illness where there is some hope of material benefit. Malingering isn't considered to be a mental illness. It's just plain fraud.

While most with the syndrome are mothers, there are also documented cases of fathers doing this to their children, husbands doing this to their wives, nieces doing this to their aunts. And doctors often don't detect it for months or years. In fact, it's difficult to say just how prevalent Munchausen is in the general population. By its very nature, it hides in plain sight.

That doctors often miss Munchausen seems counterintuitive, but the doctor-patient relationship is a bond of trust that goes both ways. "As health-care providers," said Caroline Burton, a doctor at the Mayo Clinic in Florida who's treated cases of Munchausen where the proxy is an adult, "we rely on what a patient tells us." Even if a doctor suspects his or her patient is lying, there isn't much incentive to refuse treatment based on the doubt. What if the doctor is wrong and the patient suffers for it? "You have to be careful not to overlook organic disease," Burton said. "You've really gotta go through quite a lot of diagnostic hurdles."

A diagnosis of Munchausen syndrome by proxy is attached to the perpetrator, not to the victim. Because Dee Dee is dead, it's impossible to diagnose her. She didn't leave behind a diary or some other documentation of her intentions. She did keep a binder of medical information in which she seemed to be sorting through the different information she'd given to various doctors. And she did fit certain parameters that doctors often cite as red flags for Munchausen syndrome: for example, she had some medical training. The number of doctors she took Gypsy to see over the years, and her propensity for changing locations so there was no clear medical trail, are also common. So are the concerns over sleep apnea, which is one way Munchausen often seems to begin in the various documented cases.

It is also not unusual, as Burton told me, for extended

family members—and even sometimes immediate ones—to be totally unaware of the feigning of illness. "The perpetrators are very intelligent people," she said. "They know how to manipulate other people."

They manipulate their victims, too, and the longer it goes on, the higher the chances are that the actual patient might collude with the perpetrator. The desire to please a parent can be enough to enlist a child in the deception. But even in adult cases, there can be some kind of emotional attachment keeping the patient in on the lie. "The relationship that develops between the two is so unhealthy," Burton told me of the adult cases she had treated. And no source I consulted had ever heard of a case where the abuse went on for this long, into the child's adulthood. One thing seems certain: for the patient in a Munchausen by proxy case, the truth becomes corroded.

GYPSY'S MEDICAL RECORDS ARE SOBERING. ALL THE way back in 2001, doctors at Tulane Medical Center tested Gypsy for muscular dystrophy. Her tests came back negative. In fact, all scans of her brain and spine were relatively clear. The records of all those tests survived Katrina. Nonetheless, Dee Dee continued to insist to doctor after doctor in Louisiana and Missouri that Gypsy had muscular dystrophy. Most doctors appear from these records to have taken her assertion at face value and didn't probe. Instead, they proceeded to treat Gypsy for various vision, hearing, sleep, and salivation problems that were presumed to flow from the muscular dystrophy. (The records I reviewed for this article appeared to cover only some of Gypsy's care. It's impossible to say how many other relevant records might exist.)

Some interventions were surgical. Gypsy's eye muscles were repeatedly operated on for alleged weakness. Tubes were put in her ears for alleged ear infections. She was given a feeding tube and ate very little by mouth, surviving on cans of the meal replacement PediaSure well into her twenties. Her salivary glands were first injected with Botox, then removed because her mother complained that she drooled too much. Gypsy's teeth rotted out and had to be extracted, though whether that was because of poor dental hygiene or a mixture of medications and severe malnutrition, it's hard to say.

The repeated invasions of Gypsy's body in the name of these illnesses she turned out not to have were, in short, serious and prolonged. It is difficult to say now whether any of it was medically needed at all. What is not difficult to say is that all of it began when Gypsy was impossibly young and could hardly have been expected to challenge authority figures—her mother or her doctors—about how she was feeling.

For their part, doctors did not pick up on innumerable hints that Dee Dee's stories did not add up—not even the sleep doctor, Dr. Robert Beckerman, who saw Gypsy both in New Orleans and in Kansas City. Instead, he featured his treatment of Gypsy in the hospital newsletter and mentioned repeatedly in the medical files that she and Dee Dee were his "favorite mother, daughter patient." (Beckerman did not reply to requests for comment for this story.)

There was one exception. In 2007, a pediatric neurologist named Bernardo Flasterstein, consulting on the case in Springfield, became suspicious. In a recent phone conversation, Flasterstein told me he had his doubts from the first time he saw Dee Dee and Gypsy. Dee Dee's stories about Gypsy's myriad illnesses didn't fly with him. In his notes to Gypsy's primary care doctor after the first visit, he wrote, in bold, underlined type, "The mother is not a good historian."

There was an "unusual distribution" to Gypsy's weakness for a muscular dystrophy patient, he wrote in his notes. Still, Flasterstein says, he gave the case the "benefit of the doubt" and sent Gypsy for all the usual tests, the MRIs and the blood work. It all came back normal. "I remember having her stand up," he told me, "and she could hold her own weight!" He said he told Dee Dee, "I don't see any reason why she doesn't walk."

In between his visits with Gypsy, Flasterstein tracked down a doctor who had seen Gypsy in New Orleans. That doctor told him that the muscle biopsy in New Orleans had been negative for muscular dystrophy, and that Gypsy's previous neurologist had explained that to Dee Dee. When confronted with the problem, Dee Dee simply stopped seeing those New Orleans doctors.

"Analyzing all the facts, and after talking to her previous pediatrician," Flasterstein wrote in the file, "there is a strong possibility of Munchausen by proxy, with maybe some underlying unknown etiology to explain for her symptoms." Dee Dee stopped seeing him after that visit. "I assume she got my notes," Flasterstein says. He said nurses told him later that on the way out of his office on that last visit, Dee Dee was complaining that he didn't know what he was talking about.

Flasterstein never followed up. He told me that in the network of Springfield doctors Dee Dee saw, "everyone bought their story." He remembers being told to treat the pair with "golden gloves." He says he thought that if he reported it to social services, they wouldn't believe him, either.

Thinking about it now, Flasterstein regrets not doing more. He says this was only the second case of Munchausen he'd seen in his decades-long career. He heard about the murder when a former nurse in his office wrote him about it last year. "Poor Gypsy," he told me. "She suffered all those years, and for no reason." He wishes he "could have been more aggressive."

It was not the only missed opportunity for authorities to intervene. In the fall of 2009, someone made an anonymous call to the Springfield Police Department, asking for a wellness check. The person said that they had doubts that Gypsy was suffering from all the ailments her mother described. (Flasterstein says it was not he who made that call.) The police drove over to the house, but Dee Dee put their fears to rest. She told them that the reason she sometimes used inconsistent birth dates and spellings of her name was to hide from an abusive husband. No one called Rod Blanchard or checked on these claims. The police accepted the explanation. Gypsy "does suffer from some type of mental handicap," they wrote in their report. The file was closed.

Gypsy also tried, once, to escape her mother. She met a man at the science fiction convention that Kim Blanchard and her husband also attended. Gypsy and this man began communicating online. At the time, in February 2011, Gypsy and Dee Dee were leaving everyone with the impression that she was 15. (She was actually 19.) According to Kim, the man in question was 35. He took Gypsy back to his hotel room. Through conventioneer intelligence—"We were all overprotective of her," Kim Blanchard said—Dee Dee found them. She apparently knocked on the hotel room door with papers that showed Gypsy was a minor, and the man let Gypsy leave. (He could not be reached for comment.)

After that incident, Dee Dee was furious to the point of public spectacle. She smashed the family computer with a hammer, cursed the internet to her friends. When she eventually replaced it, Gypsy was allowed to use the internet only with Dee Dee's supervision. And for months afterward, Kim Blanchard said, Gypsy was subdued, though "she wasn't acting any differently than a normal child who was in trouble at that point."

The whole situation has left bystanders in Springfield with feelings of guilt. "I just wish she would have come to me," Aleah Woodmansee told me. A lot of people feel that way. If Gypsy had, just once, stood up and walked across the room, the spell would have been broken. But plainly it wasn't that easy for her. In a way, that makes sense. She slipped, as people are fond of saying, through just about everyone's cracks. She had no reason to believe that her life would change. Until, apparently, she met Nick Godejohn.

UNDER OTHER CIRCUMSTANCES, A TALE OF CHILD ABUSE as long and as involved as what Gypsy experienced might have inspired public sympathy. But something about the fraud element deeply offended people, particularly those who hadn't known Gypsy or Dee Dee at all. Evidently there are a lot of people who are worried that others who are sick and disabled don't deserve their generosity. So Facebook groups began to spring up. They splintered on whether Gypsy could be said to be blamed, whether Rod and Kristy were in some way in on the fraud. Some groups ballooned to over 10,000 members, some of them posting every day about the crime, voicing unfounded theories about what had happened.

If their speculation had been confined to private forums, it might have been one thing. But more than a few of these amateur detectives were not satisfied with online discussion. They wanted to affect the case in real time. A St. Louis–based *Thought Catalog* writer named Meagan Pack was keeping track of "tips" she'd gotten from Facebook about Gypsy and Dee Dee's crimes and posting them to a much-referenced post. Pack told me she called the police detective to inform him of all she'd learned. Random observers on Facebook also called the police with their various speculations. Then, when the court hearings began, they came to those, too. One even showed up to Dee Dee's house when the initial "That bitch is dead" Facebook post went viral in Springfield. She hadn't known Gypsy or Dee Dee at all. She was shooed away from the crime scene by the neighbors and the police.

The result was informational chaos. Kim Blanchard's GoFundMe became a flash point for online sleuths. When Dee Dee's financial fraud was revealed by the sheriff, Kim shut it down, but not before the groups had taken it upon themselves to investigate Kim herself. Several thought Kim and David Blanchard were lying about their involvement with Gypsy and Dee Dee, and assumed they were relatives because of their last name.

Kristy Blanchard, meanwhile, was still gathering a lot of the news about her stepdaughter from Facebook. That's when she discovered that many thought she and Rod were in on Dee Dee's plans. Others thought Rod must have been a neglectful father who didn't financially support his own child. "They don't understand that I've always been supportive," he said. "In every way," Kristy chimed in. In fact, if anything, Dee Dee may have had so much money—Gypsy and Nick had escaped with about $4,000 from Dee Dee's safe—because they were receiving his support checks. (Dee Dee died intestate, without a will, and apparently without meaningful assets other than that cash.)

Kristy tried, at first, to defend herself and Rod to these groups, but it turned out they were hard to convince. "It was hell," she said. She withdrew from all the groups and asked friends and family to stop accepting new friend requests, which were pouring in.

The neighbors in Springfield also had this problem. "It was like, 'Forget you!'" Amy Pinegar said of the few attempts she made to correct the online sleuths on their factual errors. The obsessives ended up piling confusion onto the already confusing situation Dee Dee had created. And they proved quite resilient. At the hearing I attended in September 2015, two people from the largest Facebook group were there. After the hearing, they made a beeline for the local television crew and started talking to them. Gypsy's attorney, Michael Stanfield, saw them, too, and tried to hurry out of the courtroom to confront them.

"Who were those people?" he asked the television crew. "What did they say?"

FOR A WHILE, IT SEEMED LIKE GYPSY'S CASE WOULD, eventually, go to trial. The prosecutor declined to go for the death penalty, but both Gypsy and Nick were charged with first-degree murder. As the investigation into the crime continued, it turned up text messages between the two that appeared to discuss and plan Dee Dee's death. "Honey, you forget I am ruthless, and my hatred of her will force her to die," Godejohn texted Gypsy. "It's my evil side doing it. He won't mess up, because he enjoys killing." Prosecutors also said they found social media evidence of Gypsy directly asking Godejohn to kill her mother, though these have never been made public. Documents from pretrial discovery show him telling a friend about Gypsy's desire to murder her mother as early as May 2014.

Godejohn referred to his "evil side" because he and Gypsy had constructed an elaborate online fantasy life, mostly through a jigsaw puzzle of Facebook accounts. They were into BDSM imagery. They had specific names and roles for each other. They took pictures of themselves in costumes, Gypsy dressing up at one point as the comic book character Harley Quinn, posing with a knife. Reality and fantasy blended quite a lot, for both of them. Even now, it's not clear why Godejohn participated in this scheme. He had no history of violence. (Reached by telephone, Godejohn's attorney Andrew Mead declined to comment on the case.) His only prior arrest was for lewd conduct in 2013 at a McDonald's, where he had been watching pornography on a tablet. But both he and Gypsy told police he was the one to wield the knife. She said that while her mother was being stabbed, she was in the other room, listening. One of the taxi drivers who'd carted the pair around Springfield after the murder told interviewers they thought Gypsy was the ringleader.

Gypsy's attorney, Michael Stanfield, is a public defender. In an average year, he told me, he handles over 270 individual cases. He drew Gypsy's case at random and had no idea what he was in for. "I think this is probably the most complicated case I'll ever get," he said. The Greene County public defender's office was somewhat lucky in that they were also able to pull a former leading public defender, Clate

Baker, out of retirement for the case. Stanfield also had an investigator and a paralegal working on it. Kristy and Rod had no money to hire a private attorney, though they told me repeatedly as I reported this story that they would never have told Gypsy to switch attorneys because they found Stanfield so capable and reassuring.

The process of figuring out what had happened was, in a word, complex. Stanfield went down to Louisiana and dredged up some elements of Dee Dee's past. It took him months to get Gypsy's own medical records, because Dee Dee had set up a power of attorney over Gypsy's medical decisions after Gypsy turned 18. The hospitals refused to help, even though the power of attorney did not surrender Gypsy's rights to look at her own medical documents.

When the records finally arrived, though, they were so damning, Stanfield called the prosecutor without needing to investigate further. A plea deal was worked out. On July fifth, Gypsy pleaded guilty to second-degree murder. The judge gave her the minimum sentence: 10 years. With the year she's served, she'll be eligible for parole in about seven and a half years, at the end of 2023. By then she will be 32 years old.

For his part, Godejohn is still scheduled for trial in November. It was not, Stanfield told me, a listed condition of Gypsy's plea bargain that she testify against him. At a recent hearing in mid-July, he looked bewildered and lost, a beard concealing most of his face. His family never seems to come to hearings.

———

GYPSY IS NOW AN INMATE BEING PROCESSED AT THE Women's Eastern Reception, Diagnostic and Correctional Center in Vandalia, Missouri. Her hair is long, her skin clear and healthy, and she wears proper adult glasses. She's off all her medications, and there have been no health problems in the year she's been out of her mother's control. "Most of my clients lose weight in prison," Stanfield pointed out, because the food is so bad. Gypsy gained 14 pounds in the 12 months she spent in Greene County Jail before her plea.

Kim Blanchard, who visited Gypsy once in jail, told me, "She looked much more like the person that she was, which was the complete opposite of the person that I knew, and it was like she had a costume on that whole time and then took it off."

But obviously, there are lingering effects. When I last checked her inmate record, it still had her last name misspelled, bearing the extra "e" that her mother somehow thought was a good disguise. In the Greene County Jail, Gypsy had a therapist she saw once a week. It remains to be seen if she'll have one in her new home, or if that therapist will be trained to attend to the specifics of her unique situation.

Rod and Kristy saw Gypsy not too long after the plea bargain. It has been a relief to know what's going to happen to her. They don't know if they're going to sue the hospitals or doctors that Gypsy saw all her life. They'll decide that after everything has settled down, after they can properly talk to Gypsy. While the case was pending, they never discussed the crime with her; the prosecutor forbade it. Now there will be more to talk about. They're hoping to get up to her new facility two or three times a year. It's a long drive, and there's still the matter of money.

Months ago, Rod and Kristy told me they still catch Gypsy in small lies about her life, things she's clearly afraid to be frank with them about. It worries them. "Of course we want her to get better about that," Kristy said.

When I spoke to them more recently, Rod's voice was sagging a little. He sounded older. He said he'd started to wonder what exactly Dee Dee had told Gypsy about him all those years. He had only begun to pose those questions. He was wondering lately, he said, how Dee Dee had managed to be so friendly on the phone all those years if she hated him so much. He asked Gypsy about it.

"She said, 'Keep your enemies close,'" Gypsy told him.

FOR MOST OF THE YEAR I SPENT REPORTING THIS ARTI- cle, the case was pending and I wasn't able to speak to Gypsy herself. After the plea deal, that changed. I sent her a note. She called me from prison in Missouri to talk in short con- versations broken up over a few days.

Her voice is still high-pitched, though now that we know what we know, it no longer seems unusually high at all. People heard what they wanted to. Gypsy speaks in long, beautiful sentences. She is sometimes so eloquent in conversation that it is hard to believe anyone could ever have spoken with her and thought her "slow," as some put it. It reminded me of all the doctors who wrote in her files that in spite of Gypsy's alleged cognitive defect, she had a "rich vocabulary."

She was eager to talk, barely able to contain herself once she started. She wants people to know, she said, that this wasn't a situation where a girl killed her mom to be with her boyfriend. This was a situation, she said, of a girl trying to escape abuse. In prison she's hoping to join all sorts of programs, to help people. She wants to write a book to help others in her situation.

I asked her what I'd long been waiting to ask her: When did she realize her life was different, that there was something wrong? "Whenever I was 19," she said. She meant the time when she ran away with the man at the convention in 2011. When her mother came to take her back, she began to wonder why she wasn't allowed to be alone, to have friends.

About her mother, her opinion seems to waver. "The doctors thought that she was so devoted and caring," Gypsy said. "I think she would have been the perfect mom for someone that actually was sick. But I'm not sick. There's that big, big difference."

Gypsy still doesn't feel she actively deceived anyone. "I feel like I was just as used as everybody else," she said. "She used me as a pawn. I was in the dark about it. The only thing I knew was that I could walk, and that I could eat. As for everything else . . . Well, she'd shave my hair off. And she'd say, 'It's gonna fall out anyway, so let's keep it nice and neat!'" Gypsy said her mother told her she had cancer, too, and would tell her that her medication was cancer medication. She just accepted it.

As for a childlike demeanor, Gypsy grew defensive when I asked her about it. "It's not my fault. I can't help it. This is my voice."

Often, it didn't occur to her to question any of it, and when it did, she worried about hurting her mother's feelings. It often seems to Gypsy, even now, that Dee Dee really thought she was sick. "I was afraid that we were gonna get in trouble," Gypsy said. "The line between right and wrong . . . was kinda blurred, 'cause that's the way I was taught. I just grew up that way.

"When I think about it now," she added, "I wish I would have reached out to somebody and told somebody before I told Nick."

She mostly used the internet late at night, when her mother was asleep. Nick, she said, was the first person who had offered her real protection. She believed him. Ultimately, after everything that happened, she said she thinks he has "anger issues." She repeatedly takes responsibility for the murder: "What I did was wrong. I'll have to live with it." But she said Nick is the one who took "a plot between us both" and "made it into action." Gypsy was the one who had the idea to post about the murder on Facebook, so that the police would come check on her mom. She recalled asking Nick, "Can we please just post something on Facebook, something alarming, that would make people call the police?" But she said he told her what to write.

I asked, repeatedly: Are you angry? With your mom? With the doctors? She will admit only to frustration. "It makes me frustrated that none of the other doctors could see that I was perfectly healthy. That my legs were not skinny, like someone who was [really] paralyzed. That I can't . . . I don't need a feeding tube. Stuff like that." In jail, Gypsy had access to tablet computers. She looked up the definition of Munchausen, after hearing the word so often used to describe her situation. Her mother matched every symptom, she told me.

Every once in a while, I'd get Gypsy explaining some element of her abuse in such detail that something in me would break. Once, feeling speechless but aware that the clock was ticking on her phone time, I blurted out, "I'm so sorry this happened to you." Gypsy immediately switched into the girl she was back in those feel-good local news interviews. "It's okay. I mean, honestly, it's made me a stronger person, because I truly believe that everything happens for a reason."

Even on the subject of her prison sentence, Gypsy is a model of radical acceptance. She's told people she feels freer in prison than she did when living with her mom. "This time is good for me," she said to me. "I've been raised to do what my mother taught me to do. And those things aren't very good.

"She taught me to lie, and I don't wanna lie. I want to be a good, honest person."

Originally published on *BuzzFeed News*, August 2016

# The Reckoning

## BY PAMELA COLLOFF

### [ 1 ]

In the spring of 1967, when Claire Wilson was a freshman at the University of Texas, she went to the library one afternoon to track down an old copy of *Life* magazine. Thumbing through a stack of back issues, she scanned the dates on their well-worn covers. Finally, she arrived at the one she was looking for, and she slid it off the shelf. On the cover was a stark black-and-white photograph of a fractured store window, pierced by two bullet holes; in the distance loomed the UT Tower. Above the university's most iconic landmark were three words in bold, black letters: "The Texas Sniper."

Claire sat down and studied the large, color-saturated pictures inside, turning the pages as if she were handling a prized artifact. She read how Charles Whitman, an architectural engineering major, had brought an arsenal of weapons to the top of the Tower on August 1, 1966, and trained his rifles on the students and faculty below, methodically picking them off one by one. She pored over the images of people crouching behind cars as the massacre unfolded, and the aerial photo of campus dotted with red Xs showing where Whitman had hit his intended targets.

On the list of those killed, she located the name of her boyfriend, Thomas Eckman. Her gaze fell on Tom's picture, in which he sat in the formal pose of all midcentury yearbook photos, smiling broadly, his tie tucked into his V-neck sweater. Claire stared into his eyes, tracing the contours of his face. Holding the magazine in her hands, she felt some reassurance that what she had witnessed on campus that day had actually happened.

Not that she needed proof: above her left hip was a gnarled indentation, not yet healed, where one of Whitman's bullets had found its mark. She had been hospitalized for more than three months after the killing spree, spending what was supposed to have been the fall semester of her freshman year learning how to walk again. But by the time she returned to UT, in January, the tragedy had become a taboo subject on campus. Absent were the protocols that would later come to define school shootings: the grief counselors, the candlelight vigils, the nationwide soul-searching. Whitman's crime—decades before Columbine, Virginia Tech, and Newtown became shorthand for on-campus depravity—was unprecedented, and there was no language for it yet. The mass shooting was an obscenity whose memory stained the university, an aberration to be forgotten, and in the vastness of that silence, Claire found herself second-guessing what she remembered. The few times her friends tiptoed around the subject, they referred to it as "the accident."

The person Claire longed to talk with most was gone. She had known Tom for only a few months, but they had been inseparable. They had met as summer-school students in May 1966, when she was five months pregnant and single—a scandalous state of affairs for a middle-class girl from Dallas, though Claire had never cared much for social conventions. Tom, who was also 18 and new to Austin, had moved in with her on the spot. Claire had had no interest in getting married—the institution was an anachronism, as far as she was concerned—and Tom, whose parents had divorced when he was little, felt the same way.

Like her, Tom attended Students for a Democratic Society meetings and saw himself as a foot soldier in the civil rights movement, once driving with her to the Rio Grande Valley to stand in solidarity with striking farmworkers. The two passed whole afternoons on the screened-in porch they used for a bedroom in their house off campus, quoting favorite passages to each other from the novels they were reading: he, Joyce Cary's *The Horse's Mouth*, and she, Lawrence Durrell's *The Alexandria Quartet*. Sometimes Tom pressed his hand to her belly to see if he could feel the baby move.

In the wake of the shooting, Claire tried to hold moments like these in her mind. But her thoughts often wandered back to that August morning, when she and Tom had set out across the South Mall—and then she would be there again, on that blisteringly hot day, walking on the wide-open stretch of concrete beside him.

The anthropology class they were taking had let out early, some time after eleven o'clock. Claire and Tom walked to the Chuck Wagon, the cafeteria inside the student union where campus leftists and self-styled bohemians held court, and happened to run into an old friend of Tom's from junior high. Eager to catch up, the ex-classmate suggested that they go to the student lounge to shoot some pool. Tom explained that he and Claire had to feed the parking meter first; downing his coffee, he promised they would be right back.

Tom and Claire stepped out into the thick midday heat and headed east under a canopy of live oak trees. Tom was sporting a short-sleeved plaid shirt and his first mustache. Claire was wearing a brand-new maternity dress Tom had picked out: a beige shift with a flowery ribbon around the yoke. She was eight months along by then, and she could feel the weight of the baby as she walked. When they reached the upper terrace of the South Mall, the live oaks receded, and they were suddenly out in the open, exposed under the glare of the noon sun.

To their left stood the Tower, the tallest building in Austin after the Capitol; to their right stretched the mall's green, sloping lawn. As was often the case, they were deep in conversation; they had just begun a discussion about Claire's spartan eating habits and Tom's concern that the baby was not getting proper nutrition. Claire was in the middle of saying that she had, in fact, had a glass of orange juice that morning when a thunderous noise rang out. An instant later, she was falling, her knees buckling beneath her. Bewildered, Tom turned toward her. "Baby," he said, reaching for her. "What's wrong?" Then he too was knocked off his feet.

The two teenagers collapsed onto the pavement beside each other. Claire was flat on her back, the arc of her abdomen rising up in front of her. She felt as if a white-hot electric current were coursing through her. Tom lay to her left, close enough to touch, his head turned away from her. She called out to him, but he did not answer.

At first, no one on the South Mall seemed to realize what was happening. A man in a suit and tie ordered Claire and Tom to get up, ignoring her pleas for a doctor as he breezed by. She realized he thought it was a stunt—guerrilla theater or an antiwar protest, maybe, judging from his contempt. Moments later, she heard screams and the frantic cries of other students as they scattered, ducking for cover.

Bullets rained down from above, dinging balustrades, shattering windows, kicking loose concrete. A dozen yards from her and Tom, a physics professor was felled in mid-stride as he descended the stairs to the mall's lower terrace; his body would remain there, sprawled across the steps beside the bronze statue of Jefferson Davis, as students crouched behind the trees and hedges nearby. On the lawn, a young woman in a blue dress with nowhere to hide cowered behind the concrete base of a flagpole. Claire looked up at the Tower, where every now and then the nose of a rifle edged over the parapet, followed by the crack of gunfire and a wisp of smoke. She wondered if the Vietnam War had somehow come to Texas.

Every fifteen minutes, the Tower's bell would chime, but it was nearly half an hour before the sound of sirens neared, and even then, no help came. A police officer who was advancing behind a stone railing, service revolver drawn, was swiftly shot in the neck. Unable to lift herself, Claire remained where she had fallen, marooned. Blood pooled beneath her, saturating her dress. She played dead as the sound of gunshots reverberated around her, echoing off the red tile roofs and limestone walls. Dozens of students had run home to retrieve their deer rifles, and the echo of return fire rang out as they came back to take aim at the gunman.

It was nearly one hundred degrees by then, and she ached to get off the concrete, which scorched her bare legs. When the heat became unbearable, she bent her right knee just enough to lift her calf, half expecting to be torn apart by gunfire. She did not know whether to feel relief or dread when she was not. She feared that Tom was dead, and that her child was lost, too; instead of the thrumming energy she usually felt inside her, the baby had become still.

A young woman with long red hair suddenly ran into her field of vision, offering to help. "Lie down quick so we don't get shot," Claire pleaded. The woman dropped to the pavement and, from the spot where she lay, a few feet away, tried to keep Claire conscious by peppering her with questions. "What classes are you taking? Where did you grow up?" Claire whispered a few words back, struggling to answer.

Finally, more than an hour after the shooting had begun, three young men bolted from their hiding places and sprinted toward her and Tom. One grabbed Claire's arms, the other her ankles, and together they ran as her body dangled between them. The third man hoisted Tom's wilted frame into his arms, steadying himself under the weight of the teenager's lifeless body before following close behind.

As they raced across the mall, Claire did not feel the penetrating pain of her injuries or realize that she was losing copious amounts of blood. She could not make sense of what had just happened, much less begin to fathom how the jagged path of one bullet had, in a single moment, redrawn her life's course forever. She knew only that if she was lucky, she might live.

[ II ]

Growing up, Claire had never thought of guns as something to fear. As a kid she had taken riflery at summer camp in East Texas, where she had delighted in the thrill of target practice. Her parents kept guns in their house in East Dallas—her father, a bird hunter and ex-marine, stashed his long guns in the closet, where they leaned up casually against the wall. Guns were intertwined in her family history; they had made Texas passable for her Tennessee-born ancestors, who received a land grant from Stephen F. Austin in the 1820s. At age twelve, her maternal grandfather had used the proceeds from his initial cotton harvest in Brazoria County to buy his first rifle.

Even when President Kennedy was assassinated, Claire did not blame gun violence but rather the culture of intolerance that gripped her hometown. She knew all too well what it meant to be an outsider in Dallas: at a time when the John Birch Society and archconservative oil magnate H. L. Hunt held sway over the city, her father, John, had dedicated his legal career to representing clients, many of them black, in worker's compensation cases. Her mother, Mary, was the local precinct chair for the Democratic Party, so consumed by her work championing various liberal causes that Claire came to measure time in election cycles.

Though the Wilsons lived only one block from the Lakewood Country Club, they refused to join, leaving Claire and her four siblings to make the long walk to the municipal pool—which was also closed to blacks but at least welcomed their Jewish friends. Not wanting Claire, the eldest, to be oblivious to the injustices beyond their privileged, all-white enclave, her father drove her on more than one occasion through West Dallas, then home to a toxic lead smelter and slums that lacked sewage systems and running water. When she was twelve, her father took her to see Martin Luther King Jr. speak at the Majestic Theater in Fort Worth, where few whites were present; at a private reception afterward, he led her up to the young minister to shake his hand.

At the time, in the late fifties, the unspoken rules of segregated society seemed immutable to Claire. When her parents went out to dinner one night with a black couple they knew, she watched, frozen, as the four drove off in her parents' Cadillac, convinced they would all be murdered. By the time she was a teenager, however, she had grown impatient with the pace of change. Each day for a month during the summer of 1964, she donned a dress, hat, and white gloves and headed downtown with her mother to take part in the protests outside the Piccadilly Cafeteria, a popular restaurant that refused service to blacks. Claire was arrested and booked into the city jail, but the charges were dismissed. She was ridiculed for being a "nigger lover" when she returned that fall to Woodrow Wilson High School, an epithet she doubled down on when she spent the following summer in the Mississippi Delta working as a volunteer with the Student Nonviolent Coordinating Committee. So immersed did she become in the SNCC's effort to get black residents registered to vote that she stayed on until October, content to miss her senior year.

Late that fall, she ran into John Muir, an acquaintance who had come home to Dallas unexpectedly from his sophomore year at Columbia University. Muir was wrestling with whether to drop out of college and devote himself to the civil rights movement. A graduate of the elite St. Mark's School of Texas, Muir was charismatic and well read, and though he was white, he had served as vice president of the local NAACP Youth Council. Claire had gotten to know him during the summer of the Piccadilly protest, when a multiracial group of teen activists had regularly gathered at her parents' house. During those unhurried afternoons, Muir had introduced her to the works of E. E. Cummings and

Joseph Heller and played her the first Bob Dylan album she had ever heard, but it was not until Christmas week in 1965, after Claire had returned from Mississippi, that they slept together.

Muir decided to return to Columbia after the holidays, but first he agreed to help Claire move to Austin. Her parents, whose marriage had been foundering for years, had recently divorced, and she saw no compelling reason to stay in Dallas. Before long, Claire had landed a job waiting tables in her new city and enrolled for night classes at Austin High. She felt at home in the sleepy capital, a place of cheap rent, psychedelic rock, and nascent political activism. Her involvement in the civil rights movement quickly won her respect and friends, and she fell in with a group of like-minded UT students who were ablaze with new ideas.

It was in the midst of this happy-go-lucky time—when she was finally free from the judgments of racist classmates and the near-constant threat of violence she had felt in Mississippi—that Claire discovered she was pregnant. Muir dutifully made a trip to Austin after she told him the news, but during their discussions about how to move forward, he never suggested they make a life together. While she had no desire to get married, Claire felt bruised by the rejection. Muir returned to Columbia, leaving behind the then-considerable sum of $200 so she could have an abortion.

On the advice of friends, Claire met with a woman who knew how to procure the illegal—and, at that time, often perilous—procedure. But she could not bring herself to go any further. Though her decision to keep the baby would have meant certain exile from most social circles, in her group of free-thinking friends, her pregnancy was of little concern. Privately, the idea of having a child thrilled her, but it was not until she met Tom that May that someone shared in her joy.

"I was really, truly happy for the first time in my life," Claire told me. "I was out on my own, and I was in love, and I had so many friends. We were revolutionizing the world, and Tom and I were at the front of it."

Whitman hit his targets with terrifying precision. Across a crime scene that spanned five city blocks, the former marine sharpshooter managed to strike his intended victims with ease, felling them from distances well beyond 500 yards. His arsenal included a scoped 6mm Remington bolt-action rifle; a .35-caliber pump rifle; a .357 Magnum Smith & Wesson revolver; a .30-caliber M1 carbine; a 9mm Luger pistol; a Galesi-Brescia .25-caliber pistol; a 12-gauge shotgun with a sawed-off barrel; and about seven hundred rounds of ammunition. His rampage dragged on for more than an hour and a half before Austin police officers Ramiro Martinez and Houston McCoy reached him on the Tower's observation deck and shot him dead. By the time it was all over, Whitman had succeeded in killing 16 people and wounding 31.

Claire's rescuers miraculously avoided being hit as they ran headlong toward the western edge of the mall, spiriting her to the shelter of the Jefferson Davis statue. From there, five bystanders took over, carrying her to Inner Campus Drive, where they loaded her into a waiting ambulance.

She would be one of 39 gunshot victims delivered to Brackenridge Hospital's emergency room in the span of 90 minutes. Many of them were bleeding out quickly, and doctors and nurses shouted back and forth as they tried to discern who should be sent into surgery first. Claire and a 17-year-old high school student named Karen Griffith, who had been shot in the lung, were lying on gurneys beside each other, waiting to be X-rayed, when a doctor intervened. "There's no time for X-rays," he yelled, directing his staff to prep them both for surgery.

Claire was still conscious when a medic began cutting off her blood-soaked dress, and she begged him to stop, not wanting to lose the garment Tom had picked out for her. Though she clung to the delusion that she had only been shot in the arm, her magical thinking did not extend to Tom, whom she felt certain was dead. She had seen his inert body as she was lifted away.

Claire was put under general anesthetic, and her doctors set to work. The full extent of the damage was not evident until they made a lengthy incision down her torso, from sternum to pubic bone. The bullet had torn into her left side just above the hip, splintering the tip of her pelvis, puncturing her small intestine and uterus, lacerating an ovary, and riddling her internal organs with shrapnel. A C-section was performed, but the baby—a boy—was stillborn. A bullet fragment had pierced his skull.

The operation took twelve hours. Not long after Claire regained consciousness, she was wheeled down a corridor to the ICU. Standing along the walls on either side were her friends, who had waited at the hospital until past midnight to learn if she had made it out of surgery. "We love you, Claire!" they called out.

She spent the next seven weeks in the ICU in a fog of Demerol and Darvon. All told, she would endure five operations at Brackenridge to repair the damage done to her. To distract herself from the pain, she would belt out protest songs from her bed, delivering renditions of "Which Side Are You On?" and "We Shall Overcome" at the top of her lungs. With no TVs or even visitors, besides family members, allowed inside the ICU, she had few distractions and little information about life outside Brackenridge. Despite being a victim in a tragedy that had made headlines around the world, she never saw or heard a single news report about the shooting.

Her life narrowed to her hospital bed and the green floor-to-ceiling curtains the nurses drew tightly around her, past which she could sometimes catch sight of a tree and a sliver of sky. Intravenous lines extended from all four of her limbs, and her left leg, which was in traction, was suspended above her. Every two hours, in an excruciating ritual she came to dread, a nurse would turn her, rolling her onto one side and then the other. Her mother, who tried to project an image of strength, often sat at her bedside, chatting with the doctors and offering Claire words of encouragement. Refusing to give in to the chaos that the shooting had wrought, she was always immaculately dressed, often wearing a two-piece knit suit from Neiman Marcus, her blond hair pulled into a French twist.

If Claire's mother or her doctors ever explicitly told her that her baby was stillborn, she struck it from her memory. No one, as far as she could recall, ever spoke aloud the fact that her child had died. That the baby was a boy and that a burial plot had been secured for him were the only details she gleaned. Claire did not ask questions because she already knew; she felt his absence. She was startled when her milk came in days after the C-section, leaving her breasts engorged, and relieved when it dried up and her baby weight fell away. Her body settled back into its old contours, her belly flat, as if the pregnancy had never happened.

Without the chance to hold the baby in her arms, Claire did not know how to mourn his loss; she had not yet chosen a name, and he felt like an abstraction, his face unknowable. But her grief for Tom, and their abbreviated summer together, only metastasized once the fall semester got under way. She was tormented by the fact that she had not been able to attend his funeral. "I learned more in those [months with Tom] than perhaps in any other period of my life," she wrote in a four-page condolence letter to his father. "The sort of things that were between Tom and me happen so rarely in this world that most people don't even understand the language."

Most of the shooting victims who had been admitted to

Brackenridge were discharged; some, like Karen Griffith, did not survive. Only Claire stayed on, her presence noted every now and then in the local paper, which ran a two-sentence squib on September 16 announcing that she was the last of Whitman's victims to remain hospitalized.

The myriad complications of abdominal gunshot wounds, including the threat of infection and sepsis, made Claire's condition tenuous. By the time her surgeries were complete, several feet of her intestine had been removed, as well as an ovary and the iliac crest of her pelvic bone. Daily physical therapy sessions allowed her to gradually regain the ability to walk. After she was moved out of the ICU, she became adept at using a cane, and at night, when she was unable to sleep, she would maneuver her way to the nurses' station to visit with the women in starched white uniforms who cared for her, some of whom were not much older than she was.

Claire was finally released the first week of November. She was 19 by then, though she felt a thousand years old. She returned to campus in January, and in the early spring, she made the first of several visits to the library to page through the August 12 issue of *Life*. She had no pictures of Tom, and though the yearbook photo featured in the magazine failed to capture his spirit, she liked to study it all the same.

The confirmation she sought about the massacre—that she had not dreamed or invented it—was muddled by the fact that *Life*, like most publications at the time, omitted her preterm baby from the official tally of the dead. And so rather than avoid the South Mall on her way to class each day, she purposely walked past the spot where she and Tom had been hit, intensely curious, as if her proximity to the crime scene would render it more vivid. When the Tower's observation deck was reopened that June, she visited it by herself, riding the elevator to the 27th floor and then taking three short flights of stairs to the top, just as Whitman had with his arsenal. She looked over the balustrade down at the mall, as he had, and crouched down to peer through the downspouts where he had rested the barrel of his gun.

Austin was a place that had brought her so much happiness, but as she surveyed campus and the city that spread out beyond it, she felt an overwhelming sense of dislocation. How would she ever recover from the enormity of her loss, she wondered, or navigate the years ahead? "I was so lonely and so longing for some sort of physical contact," Claire said. "All I wanted right then was for somebody to put their arms around me and hold me tight."

[ III ]

Ten years after the shooting, on a warm July afternoon in 1976, Claire stood in a phone booth in northern Colorado, not far from the rugged peaks of the Continental Divide, with the receiver pressed to one ear. She had agreed to speak to an Austin *American-Statesman* reporter named Brenda Bell who was interviewing survivors of the shooting for an article that would mark its 10-year anniversary. With the help of Claire's father, Bell had tracked Claire down in the foothills of the Rocky Mountains, outside the small town of Loveland. Claire had never spoken about the shooting publicly, and her voice was soft as she answered the reporter's questions.

After she had been shot, she told Bell, she was "basically mixed up—confused about life in general." Only once she started reading the Bible in the years that followed had she found some peace. Scripture, she explained, "started effecting a lot of changes in my life." She had found a group of Seventh-day Adventists who worked as medical missionaries around Loveland, where they tried "to help other young people physically, mentally, and spiritually," she said. Her time there, immersed in nature and the gospel, had been restorative. "I'm so thankful," she told Bell before she hung up. "I'm glad to be alive."

Claire had spent five years living and working at the Eden Valley Institute, a spiritual retreat accessible only by unpaved roads and bounded by jaw-dropping panoramas of the snow-capped Rockies. Its clean-living, Adventist doctrine rejected not just smoking, drinking, and sex outside marriage but also the distractions of popular culture. In an era defined by the loosening of social mores, it was a monastic existence; Claire did not watch the evening news, listen to the radio, or go to the movie theater. While some women worked on the institute's farm, which yielded much of their food, or helped with the cooking and childcare, her main occupation was teaching the residents' school-age children. (Her father approvingly told her on his first visit that the self-sustaining community was "the closest thing to Red China" he had ever seen.) Though newspapers could be found at Eden Valley, Claire steered clear of them, preferring to spend her free time taking long walks through the backcountry. She was unaware of the Watergate hearings or the fall of Saigon. "It was very healing to be way out, deep in the mountains, apart from the rest of the world," Claire told me.

She had tried at first to heal herself in more conventional ways, visiting UT's University Health Services as early as 1967 for the talk therapy she believed she urgently needed. But after her first session, during which she felt that the psychologist had made a pass at her, Claire abandoned the idea. At her father's urging, she transferred to the University of Colorado at Boulder that fall, leaving the near-constant reminders of the shooting behind, but she was homesick there, and she returned to UT the following year.

To her friends, she had seemed fine—"Nice and sunny," recalled one—but not long after her return, she landed at the student health center again when she abruptly stopped eating. The psychiatrist who evaluated her, Claire thought, showed more interest in her admission that she had taken LSD before than in her obvious depression. He put her on Thorazine, a powerful antipsychotic, and though her hair began falling out and she struggled to concentrate in class, her treatment was not adjusted. "Questioning doctors was just not done then, so I was an obedient patient," she told me. "There never was any talk therapy. He only wanted to discuss my past drug experiences, which were so few." In 1969, at the end of her spring semester, she dropped out and moved back to Colorado.

It was that same year that Claire began to feel the stirrings of belief. "After the shooting, I'd started wondering what forces were at work in the universe," she said. "I felt strongly that there was a force I couldn't see, and I was interested in finding out what it was." She escaped to the mountains outside Boulder with a University of Colorado student named Ernie, with whom she lived in a rough-hewn house in the woods with no indoor heat or plumbing. They immersed themselves in nature and back-to-basics living, warming themselves by a coal stove and hauling water from a well.

Just down the road from them and the other hippies who had taken up residence in Lefthand Canyon was an 82-year-old woman named Emma Spencer, whom her neighbors called "Ma." A Seventh-day Adventist, she grew her own food, wove rugs by hand, and strictly observed the Sabbath. To Claire, the child of nonbelievers, she was a source of fascination. Ma gave her a Bible, which she began to read, and one afternoon, Claire found herself kneeling in prayer beside the older woman, searching for words as she tried to communicate with God. She had cried for Tom many times, but as she knelt on the knobby rag rug in Ma's log cabin, she felt, as she would later recall, an "unbidden and unexpected" grief surface for the baby. For the first time, Claire began to weep for her lost son.

Her desire for "a sincere, authentic, Christian life," as she called it, took her to Eden Valley in 1971. She would remain there until she was thirty, not striking out on her own until the winter of 1977. Her friends in Texas and Colorado, who heard from her infrequently during this time, if at all, were stunned that the girl they knew, who delighted in skinny-dipping and challenging the status quo, had suddenly gotten religion. "I don't know what combination of PTSD, spiritual yearning—which was very much of the moment—depression, and epiphany led her to the strict regime of the Seventh-day Adventist utopia," observed Tim Coursey, a childhood friend. "But I do remember thinking, 'Well, how about that? She walked right through the looking glass.'"

The dream, which Claire first had in her twenties, always began the same way: she would look down and discover her baby, bright-eyed, in her arms. He was never as small as a newborn—he would be a few months old, perhaps, or a toddler, even, old enough to meet her gaze—and she would be flooded with relief as she stared back at him in wonder. Then she would glance away, or walk into another room, her attention wandering for no more than a second, and when she looked back, her son would be gone.

Claire did not have the dream frequently, but when she did, in the peripatetic years that followed her time at Eden Valley, she awakened with a start, a deep ache in her chest. As she moved from Colorado to other states in the West—New Mexico, Texas, and Wyoming—she would occasionally stop in a public library to see if she could find the old *Life* magazine, anxious for something concrete upon which to anchor her longings. In those analog days, before it was possible to conjure up information about anything with a few keystrokes, her personal history was relegated to microfilm reels and hardbound magazine volumes, and there, alone among the stacks, she would scrutinize Tom's photo again. People she met had sometimes heard she was the victim of gun violence—one rumor at Eden Valley placed her at the 1970 Kent State shootings—but she rarely shared her story.

After Eden Valley, Claire made a brief sojourn to another religious community in upstate New York and then headed to New Mexico, where her sister, Lucy, was working as a psychologist at a residential facility for developmentally disabled adults. It was there that Claire met her first husband—an easygoing teacher who ran the facility's art therapy program—and they wed in 1979. She never discussed the shooting with him, and he never showed any interest in discussing it. "I really just wanted to be married and have a baby, and that was more important to me than whether we were a good match," Claire said. They were not, and within two years they had divorced.

Claire packed her belongings and headed to Stephenville, Texas, where she moved in with her grandmother and enrolled in Tarleton State University, determined to finally finish college. She did so two years later, in 1983, with honors, when she was 35 years old. Armed with a degree in education, she then made her way to Wyoming, where she taught at a private Seventh-day Adventist school in the town of Buffalo, in the shadow of the Bighorn Mountains. Like many rural Adventist schools, it was modeled on a one-room schoolhouse, and she was its only teacher. Her life in Wyoming suited her well—the school was out in the country, and she had fewer than a dozen students, ranging in grades from first to eighth—but even as she devoted herself to the children, Claire found she could not shake her recurring thoughts about her baby. She wanted to have a child of her own, before she ran out of time, and her dreams about holding her son took on a new intensity.

Claire had sought psychological help at Tarleton with little success, and two years after moving to Wyoming, she tried again. Soon she met a bright, empathetic local therapist who listened without judgment as she described the anger that sometimes felt as if it might consume her. She began to see him in twice-weekly sessions in his comfortable office just off Main Street, where she finally spoke freely—nearly two decades after the fact—about having lost Tom and the baby. "It was the first time I'd been given permission to talk about what had happened and to mourn in any sort of meaningful, sustained way," said Claire.

Her therapist told her about post-traumatic stress disorder, a then-new medical diagnosis that he said described the array of symptoms some trauma victims, many of them veterans of war, experienced in the wake of catastrophic violence. PTSD, he explained, was characterized by nightmares, emotional detachment, rage, and a strong desire to avoid people and places that might trigger memories of the trauma. It was a diagnosis Claire reflexively resisted, because to accept it "felt cheap, since I hadn't earned it," she said. "I had never seen the horrors of Vietnam."

The incremental progress she was making was cut short when, six months into counseling, her therapist transferred her into group therapy, and Claire found herself surrounded by people with substance-abuse problems—many of whom had been mandated, by court order, to attend—who had little insight into her state of mind. At loose ends, she abandoned the group and took up with a 19-year-old ranch hand and Wyoming native named Brian James. Then 38, she had little in common with the soft-spoken high school graduate, but in him she saw a kindred spirit with a curious and unconventional mind. Each afternoon, after she had dismissed her students, they talked for hours, hiking through the canyons and dry creeks that he had grown up exploring. Eight months after they met, they decided to get married.

When they wed, in August 1986—a full 20 years after the UT tragedy—Brian was just two years older than Claire had been when she was shot. "I think she was still trying to recover all that she had lost at eighteen," her sister, Lucy, told me. They moved to Arizona, where Lucy had already put down roots, and rented a house in Patagonia, near the border town of Nogales. Claire taught elementary school and Brian worked construction jobs, and their marriage was a happy one at first, though they would never delve into the defining event of her life. "I knew Claire had been shot, and that she had lost her boyfriend and her baby, but we never had a deep conversation about it," Brian told me. "It wasn't something I asked her about, and it wasn't something she seemed eager to discuss."

Instead, Claire tried to get pregnant, but she was met with disappointment. Though her doctors in 1966 had assured her that she would still be able to have children despite being left with one ovary and a uterus that had been stitched back together, she often wondered if Whitman, who had already robbed her of so much, had also stolen her ability to conceive.

She had all but given up by 1989, when she was 41, and her mother called with an improbable offer. Mary Wilson was by then on her third marriage and had reinvented herself as a successful New York City real estate agent. She was animated on the phone as she laid out her proposal for Claire: a realtor who worked for her, who had emigrated from Ethiopia, had introduced her to a good friend of his from Addis Ababa. The friend had been allowed into the United States a year earlier so that his young son could undergo emergency surgery for a congenital heart defect that had left him near death. The boy had remained in the States so he could receive follow-up medical care, but he and his father had overstayed their visas, and if they returned to Ethiopia, he would not have access to the pediatric cardiologists he needed.

The father had already embarked on the long and complex process of seeking asylum, her mother continued, but his and his son's legal status was precarious. Would Claire and Brian consider adopting the boy, she asked, so he could remain in the country? The first step would be to take legal guardianship of him, an effort that his father supported. The boy was four years old, added her mother, and his name was Sirak.

That June, after Claire had studied every book she could find at the library on the subject of adoption, she and Brian packed up their hatchback and embarked on a cross-country road trip to New York to meet the little boy who would become their son. "He was an incredible gift," Claire said. "A gift I didn't expect."

[ IV ]

Sirak had not seen his mother since he had left Addis Ababa as a toddler, and from the moment he caught sight of Claire in her mother's house in Riverdale, he brightened. "I can't remember a time when I didn't know her," Sirak told me. On their first day together, his father and Brian set out to go sightseeing around the city, leaving Sirak and Claire to become acquainted with each other. For the next three days, she fed him, bathed him, sang to him, read to him, and tucked him in at night. He was cheerful and playful in return, and from the first day, he called her Mommy in his accented English.

When it was finally time to load his meager belongings— two shirts, two pairs of shorts, and a toy school bus—into the hatchback and head home to Arizona, his father walked him to the car and buckled him in. "His dad was very loving, but he didn't make a big deal out of saying goodbye," Claire said. "He made it seem like Sirak was going on a long trip, on a big adventure." Sirak's father could travel inside the United States while his application for asylum was under review, and he promised the boy that he would come see him soon.

As Brian drove, Claire and Sirak sat together in the back seat, watching as the Manhattan skyline faded from view. The boy cried quietly to himself for a few minutes, but he became more animated as they moved farther from the city, and he was insistent on Claire's undivided attention. If she pulled her book out and started to read—she was in the middle of James Michener's *Alaska*—he would stick his head between her and the page, grinning. If she lay down and stretched out across the back seat, he would sprawl on top of her until his face hovered just above hers. They remained that way for hours, talking and laughing and staring up at the flat, blue summer sky.

Though they could not have looked any more different, they each bore a similar scar: a long, vertical line along the torso where a surgeon's scalpel had once traced a path. Hers began below the sternum, while his was located higher up, closer to his heart. Years later, when he was old enough to understand, Claire would tell him what had happened to her in 1966 and he would listen, carefully considering her story, before adding that he would always think of the baby she had lost as his brother.

Despite the fact that Sirak had been born with a ventricular septal defect, or a hole in his heart, he thrived. He was a healthy, if slight, little boy, and when Claire took him to see his pediatric cardiologist every three months for his check-ups, he was usually given a clean bill of health. As the only dark-skinned person in their community, he was a source of fascination to the kids who reached out to touch his hair. But Sirak embraced the very thing that set him apart, beaming when his father—who made biannual visits to Arizona—stood before his classmates and spoke about their African heritage. From the start, Sirak was quick to make friends and an exuberant presence. "Teach me!" he exhorted one teacher the summer before he started kindergarten.

Claire and Brian formally adopted him when he was six years old, shortly after they moved west to the unincorporated community of Arivaca. Sirak's father continued to make the trek out to see them, and each time he left, the boy would take the snap-brim cap his dad had worn during his visit and bring it to bed with him, resting it on the pillow. On nights when the stars shone so brightly above their desert outpost that they illuminated the canyons below, Claire, Brian, and Sirak would roll out their sleeping bags on the flat portion of their roof and lie side by side, staring up at the constellations.

Still, the area between the two lower chambers of Sirak's heart remained fragile, and at the age of seven, he was rushed into surgery after an echocardiogram suggested that his aorta had narrowed and was impeding blood flow to his brain. (The operation was called off after another round of tests.) Afterward, Claire found herself preoccupied with the possibility that something cataclysmic might happen. Even a nick in the mouth—sustained during a dental exam, say, or while playing with other kids—could allow bacteria into his bloodstream and have fatal consequences. Claire girded herself, carrying supplies of antibiotics in her purse at all times, but she could not shake her fear that, at any moment, she could lose Sirak. Once, she dreamed that she watched him board a bus that then abruptly pulled away, and she chased after it, calling out for the boy and waving her arms wildly, before losing sight of him.

Claire did her best to keep her worry to herself. Harder to hide was the anguish she had carried since the shooting, which would surface unpredictably despite how fortunate she felt about finally having a family. "I still had so much anger," Claire told me. She was moody and short-tempered, often lashing out at Brian, who grew distant, spending more and more time away from home. In 1996, when Sirak was eleven, Claire accepted a teaching position at a Seventh-day Adventist school in Virginia and took their son with her. Three years later, she and Brian divorced.

And then, just like that, Claire was a single mother, scratching out a living, ashamed by her cardinal failure, as she saw it, to keep her family intact. Her restlessness ensured that she and Sirak did not stay in Virginia long; they moved to Nebraska in 1999, when he started high school, and then to Kansas two years later. Though her pay as a teacher was barely enough to get by on, she and Sirak were resourceful, baking their own bread and gathering windfall apples. In

Virginia, where they lived next to a public housing project, Claire sometimes treated herself to a 25-cent copy of the *Washington Post*, and she and Sirak took turns reading the restaurant reviews aloud at the kitchen table, imagining that they, too, were dining in a white-tablecloth establishment.

What little Claire scraped together she put into piano lessons for her son, who was captivated by classical music. Once, when she reached to turn down the volume of a Beethoven symphony they were listening to in the car, Sirak had signaled for her to stop. "No," he said, smiling, as if transported. "We were just getting to the exciting part." He spent hours at the piano each day practicing Chopin's Études, and he played wherever he could find an audience, from their church to local nursing homes.

Then one day, at age 14, he started complaining of blinding headaches. His physician initially believed he had meningitis, but after further testing, he was diagnosed with Guillain-Barré syndrome, a rare disorder in which the body's immune system attacks the nervous system, often causing temporary paralysis. Sirak was rushed to the hospital, where he soon found himself unable to walk. Seeing Sirak confined to a hospital bed—so weak, at first, that he could not play the keyboard his teacher had brought him—Claire was seized by terror. As she sat vigil at his bedside, she closed her eyes and bowed her head, silently pleading with God not to take this son from her, too.

The syndrome, exotic-sounding and mercurial, eventually ebbed with treatment, and Sirak returned to the ninth grade a month later, shuffling behind a walker. No sooner was his body strong again than he faced another ordeal; during his hospitalization, doctors had discovered he needed open-heart surgery to repair his aorta, this time unequivocally. The operation, performed in the spring of 2000, was a success, though it would be another three years—when his cardiologist told Claire that his heart had fully healed—before she felt any sense of relief. Sirak, who was 18 by then, would be a healthy adult, the doctor explained.

Sometimes, in those days after Sirak's recovery, Claire thought back to an epiphany she'd had years before, while on a hike in Wyoming. She had come across a tree whose trunk bent at a dramatic angle at its midway point, forming a curvature that resembled the letter "C." Something catastrophic—lightning? drought?—had diverted it from its path, but the tree, resilient, had righted itself and grown straight again.

[ V ]

Claire was still living in Virginia in the spring of 1999 when one word—Columbine—became synonymous with mass murder. Because she did not own a TV, she was not subjected to the disturbing footage that seemed to play on every channel, in which petrified teenagers streamed out of their suburban Denver high school, hands over their heads, frantic to escape the carnage inside. Still, when she saw the headlines, she felt her pulse race. She scoured the newspaper for details—about the pair of teenagers who had come to school armed with bombs and guns; about the 12 students and the teacher who had been slaughtered; about the 21 gunshot victims who had survived. Even as she grieved for them, Claire was taken aback by the attention the shooting commanded. As the victim of a crime that was still cloaked in silence and shame, she felt strangely envious. "So much of what had happened to me was still a mystery," she said. "Every single detail that revealed itself was precious."

In fact, Claire had begun to reconstruct parts of her story the previous Thanksgiving. That week, she had stopped in a bookstore in Dulles International Airport, where she was waiting for a flight that would take her to Arizona to see her sister. Sirak was staying with friends for the holiday, and Claire, who was rarely apart from him, was on her own. Someone she knew had recently mentioned an item in the *Washington Post* on a new book called *A Sniper in the Tower*, by Texas historian Gary Lavergne, and Claire, who was curious to see it, eyed the shelves. Though pop culture had elevated Charles Whitman to near-mythic status in the intervening decades through both film and music—Harry Chapin's 1972 song "Sniper" cast him as a misunderstood antihero—the tragedy itself had received scant attention, save for the obligatory anniversary stories that ran in Texas newspapers.

Claire finally spotted the book, whose cover featured an old black-and-white yearbook photo of Whitman wearing a wide grin. Rather than start at the beginning, she flipped to the end and scanned the index, where she was startled to see her name. Turning to the first citation, on page 141, she skimmed the text and then came to a stop. "Eighteen-year-old Claire Wilson . . . was walking with her eighteen-year-old boyfriend and roommate, Thomas F. Eckman," she read. "Reportedly, both were members of the highly controversial Students for a Democratic Society. She was also eight months pregnant and due for a normal delivery of a baby boy in a few short weeks."

Claire could feel her heart thumping in her chest at what came next:

"Looking down on her from a fortress 231 feet above, Whitman pulled the trigger. With his four-power scope he would have clearly seen her advanced state of pregnancy. As if to define the monster he had become, he chose the youngest life as his first victim from the deck. Given his marksmanship, the magnification of the four-power scope, an unobstructed view, his elevation, and no interference from the ground, it can only be concluded that he aimed for the baby in Claire Wilson's womb."

Claire stood still, the frenetic energy of her fellow travelers receding into the background. What astonished her more than the notion that Whitman had deliberately taken aim at her child—an idea she could not yet fully grasp—was the simple fact that what had happened to her more than three decades earlier was written down in a book that she could hold in her hands. Though she had no money to speak of at that particular moment—her father had purchased her plane ticket for her—she did not hesitate before handing over her last $20 to buy the book, which she devoured on her flight to Tucson.

The act of reclaiming her history would come afterward in fits and starts, beginning one summer night in 2001, when Claire sat at her computer and used a search engine for the very first time, carefully typing out the words "UT Tower Shooting." She had only a dial-up connection, and the results were slow to load, but the first link that appeared led to a blog written by an Austin advertising executive named Forrest Preece, who had narrowly escaped being shot by Whitman. Preece had been standing across the street from the student union, outside the Rexall drugstore, on the morning of the shooting, when a bullet had whizzed by his right ear. As Claire read his account of the massacre—"Every year, when August approaches, I start trying to forget . . . but as any rational person knows, when you try to forget something, you just end up thinking about it more"—she felt strangely comforted. Each detail he described—the earsplitting gunfire, the bodies splayed on the ground, the onlookers who stood immobilized, wild with fright—was one she had carried with her all those years, too.

Claire initiated a sporadic correspondence with Preece as she continued her itinerant existence—first heading to New York, to take care of her ailing mother after Sirak left for college, and then moving back to Colorado in 2005, and Wyoming two years later, to teach in Adventist schools. In each place, she felt the strange pull of the shooting tug at her. Once, in a sporting goods store in the Rocky Mountains, she decided to stop at the gun counter and ask the clerk if she could look at a .30-06. (Whitman had in fact shot her with a 6mm bolt-action rifle, but Claire had been told otherwise.) The clerk laid the .30-06 out on the glass counter and Claire studied the weapon, finally reaching out to touch its stock, before pulling her hand back a moment later, unsure what she had come to see. Another time, while driving through the Denver area, she chose to take a detour through Columbine, even circling around the high school. She could not say exactly what she had gone looking for "except for some deeper understanding," she told me, that went unsatisfied.

Claire had stayed away from Austin for nearly forty years, but in 2008, when Preece asked her to attend a building dedication for the law enforcement officers and civilians who had helped bring Whitman's rampage to an end, she felt compelled to return. The previous year, a student at Virginia Tech had armed himself and opened fire, killing 32 people and injuring 17, and Claire, rattled by yet another tragedy, craved human connection.

At the ceremony, which took place at a county building far from campus, she fumbled for the right words as she tried to convey her thankfulness to Houston McCoy, one of the police officers who had shot Whitman. When she later joined him, Preece, and several former officers on a visit to UT, she was dismayed to find that the only reference to the horror that had unfolded there was a small bronze plaque on the north side of the Tower. Set in a limestone boulder beside a pond, it was easy to miss. As Claire surveyed the modest memorial, an industrial air-conditioning unit that sat nearby cycled on and a dull roar broke the silence. "I had heard about the memorial and had taken solace in thinking that it was a lovely place," she told me. "I was so disappointed to find no mention of Tom, the baby, or any of the victims."

Afterward, at his home, Preece showed her old news footage that TV cameramen had shot on the day of the tragedy, looking out onto the South Mall. As she watched, Claire was startled to realize that she was looking at a grainy image of her younger self, lying on the hot pavement. When she saw two teenagers dash out from their hiding places and run headlong toward her, she leaned closer, dumbstruck. Local news stations had aired the footage in the aftermath of the shooting and on subsequent anniversaries, but Claire had never seen any of it, and witnessing her own rescue was revelatory. She had always known the name of one of the students who saved her; James Love, a fellow freshman, had been in her anthropology class, and she had stopped him on campus once in 1967 to thank him for what he had done, but he had seemed ill at ease and eager to break free from the conversation. His partner, a teenager in a black button-down shirt and Buddy Holly glasses, had remained unknown to her, so much so that she had half wondered, until she saw the black-and-white footage, if he had been an angel.

Preece helped her solve the mystery in 2011, after he spotted a headline in the *American-Statesman* that read "Man Who's the Life of the Party Has Brush with Death." Below it, the article detailed how a local performance artist named

Artly Snuff, a member of the parody rock band the Uranium Savages, had survived a near-fatal car accident. Born John Fox, Snuff had graduated from Austin High and been weeks away from starting his freshman year at UT when Whitman opened fire. Though the article never referenced the shooting, the mention of Snuff's name jogged Preece's memory, and he recalled an *American-Statesman* column on Snuff years earlier in which he was praised for having helped carry a pregnant woman in the midst of the massacre.

Preece tracked down Snuff on Facebook, and in 2012, he put Snuff and Claire in touch. "To finally hear her voice was stunning, because I'd wondered what had happened to her so many times," Snuff told me of their first phone call, which spanned hours. "For both of us, just talking was a catharsis. I'd seen things no seventeen-year-old should ever have to see, and I'd carried those memories with me, and Claire understood."

Snuff told Claire how he had crouched behind the Jefferson Davis statue with Love—a friend of his from high school whose life was later cut short by bone cancer—as gunfire erupted around them. They had agonized about what to do, he explained, as they looked onto the South Mall and saw her lying there, still alive. Too terrified to move, they had initially stayed put—Snuff's own cowardice, as he saw it, measured in 15-minute increments whenever the Tower's bells chimed on the quarter hour. In a voice thick with emotion, he told her that he had always regretted taking so long to work up the courage to help her.

Claire assured him that he owed her no apologies, saying that she loved him and would always think of him as her brother. She said so again when they saw each other in Austin in 2013, wrapping her arms around him in the entrance of the Mexican restaurant where they had agreed to meet. Oblivious to everyone else, they embraced for several minutes. "It was so affirming to finally say thank you," Claire told me.

Around them, a national debate about gun control had just erupted with new force. Three months earlier, in Newtown, Connecticut, a disturbed young man had fatally shot 20 children, none more than seven years old, and six adults, at Sandy Hook Elementary School. In a forceful speech at a memorial service for the victims, President Barack Obama had pushed for tighter regulation of firearms, warning that the cost of inaction was too great. In response, many gun owners had bristled at the notion that fewer licensed weapons, and more government regulation, would keep anyone safe. In Texas, where the legislature was in session that spring, lawmakers had proposed several "campus carry" bills, which sought to upend the long-standing state law banning firearms at public universities. If passed, concealed handguns would be permitted on university grounds, in dorms, and in college classrooms.

Claire had returned to Austin because Jim Bryce, a lawyer and gun-control activist whom she had met when they were both students at UT, had asked if she, as a victim of campus gun violence, would testify at the Capitol. Though she had not engaged in any activism since the sixties—the Seventh-day Adventist Church advocates strict political neutrality—she felt that she could not turn down Bryce's invitation. And so on March 14, 2013, Claire appeared before the Homeland Security & Public Safety Committee, one among scores of people who had come to voice their support or opposition to the bills. No longer the campus radical she had once been, she did not stand out in the overflow crowd; at 65, everything about her—from her chin-length silver bob to the reading glasses she slid on when it was her turn to speak to her comfortable shoes—was muted and sensible.

Like the other speakers, Claire was allotted three minutes. Compressing the totality of her experience into a few sound bites seemed impossible, but once at the microphone, she tried. "I never thought about somebody using a gun to kill themselves or others until August 1, 1966, when I was walking across the campus of the University of Texas," she said, her voice clear and steady. She sketched out what had happened to her in a few unadorned sentences—"I was eighteen and eight months pregnant"—and when she reached the end of her story, she added, "I was not able ever again to have a child."

She expressed her reservations, as both an educator and a sixth-generation Texan who had grown up around guns, about the proposed bills, arguing that the legislature's objective should be to prevent future attacks, not arm more civilians. "A campus is a sacred place," she said. Then her time was up.

That fall, Claire received an email from Gary Lavergne,

with whom she had met and corresponded after reading *A Sniper in the Tower.* The email told of an astounding discovery. "My Dear Friend, Claire," it began. "A few years ago, while working on my last book, I downloaded a database of grave sites located in the Austin Memorial Park. (My purpose was to locate the graves of some of the persons I had written about in *Before Brown*.) It wasn't until this past weekend that, while browsing among the almost 23,000 entries in that dataset, I noticed an entry for a 'Baby Boy Wilson.'"

Lavergne went on to explain that the burial date for the child was listed as August 2, 1966—the day after the massacre. Records showed that the unmarked plot had been purchased by a Lyman Jones, a man whose name Lavergne did not recognize. Claire did, immediately; a veteran journalist who had written for the *Texas Observer* during the '50s and '60s, Jones was her mother's second husband, and Claire's stepfather at the time of the shooting.

Claire had always been aware that the baby had received a proper burial, but she had not pressed her mother for details until her later years, when her mother's memory was failing and she could no longer summon them. The small plot, she now learned from Lavergne, was located in a section of the cemetery mostly devoted to infants and stillborn babies. "Claire, I hope this gives you comfort," he wrote, explaining that he had gone to Austin Memorial Park to find the burial place. "Attached is a picture I took of the grave site. Your son is buried beneath the flowers I placed there so that you can see the exact spot."

Claire read and reread the email in silence, brushing away tears. *Your son. Buried beneath the flowers.*

She would visit the cemetery the following August, after Lavergne and his family had a headstone made, with Claire's blessing. Below the image of a cross, it read:

Baby Boy Wilson

August 1, 1966

It stood near the perimeter of the cemetery, on a sun-burned stretch of grass near a single hackberry tree. When Claire found it, she knelt down and gathered a handful of soil, placing it inside a folded sheet of paper for a keepsake. Then she prostrated herself, pressing her forehead against the marble marker, which was cool even in the blazing August sun. She thought about Tom and about the baby's father, John Muir, whom she had called and spoken with, after a decades-long estrangement, before he had passed away that June. As she lay there, she was acutely aware of the baby's presence, of the molecules somewhere below the earth's surface that belonged to him. Claire stayed for a long time and prayed. "I felt not so hollow," she said. "I felt close to God."

[ VI ]

Claire lives in Texas now, having finally, after all her years of wandering, come home. Six years ago, she moved to Texarkana—which, with some 37,000 residents, is the most densely populated place she has lived for some time. An Adventist school had needed a teacher, and so, as she had done more than a dozen times before, she started over. Not since Eden Valley has she remained in one place for so long.

When I went to visit her earlier this year, we met at her white double-wide trailer, which sits on the pine-studded western edge of town. Her bedroom window looks out onto a pasture, and though the view lacks the grandeur of the Rockies or the Great Plains, it allows her to imagine that she still lives in the wilderness, far from civilization. A few steps from her front door, in raised beds she built herself with wood, she had planted a winter garden. Collard greens and kale flourished next to fat heads of cabbage, and despite a recent freeze, a few stalwart strawberry plants thrived. As we talked, Claire bent down and tore off a few sprigs of mint, handing me some to taste. "Isn't it wonderful?" she said, her pale blue eyes widening.

When Claire told friends about her life in Texarkana, she focused on the happy things: her garden; the Nigerian family she had befriended; her students, many of whom lived below the poverty line, who hugged her waist and called her Miss Claire. She did not share her worry about Sirak, who was standing beside her on that January morning. He wore a cheerless expression, a black wool hat pulled down to his eyebrows, his shoulders squared against the cold. He had moved back in with her in August, not long after his thirtieth birthday, but he bore little resemblance to the young man she had sent off to college. Unless prodded to talk, he said little, and his speech was slow and leaden. Every now and then, as Claire and I chatted, he would smile at the mention of a childhood friend or a story about his and Claire's days in the Arizona high desert. Except for those moments, he seemed to have taken up residence in a world of his own.

For Claire, the first clue that something was not right with Sirak came in 2007. Then a month shy of graduating with a music degree from Union College, in Nebraska, Sirak had called her late one night. "Mom, my thoughts are racing and I can't make them stop," he confided, adding that he had not been sleeping much. Claire offered reassurance, certain these were the typical jitters of a graduating senior. But that July, shortly before he was set to begin a prestigious teaching fellowship in the University of Nebraska's music program, he called again and begged her to take him home. Rather than try to reason with him, she made the 10-hour drive from Colorado. When she arrived, she found Sirak standing in the parking lot of his apartment complex, wide-eyed and on edge. He refused to step foot inside his apartment by himself. "He was terrified, shaking, talking so fast," she told me. "That's when I knew something was really wrong."

At home, his behavior only grew more erratic. Sirak, usually a modest person, would walk to the mailbox at the end of their driveway in nothing but his underwear. He slept little and was reluctant to venture far from the house. Once, after he and Claire ate out, he told her he was sure that the restaurant's staff had put laxatives in their food. She took Sirak to see a series of mental health professionals, but no one could offer a definitive diagnosis; a prescription for Lexapro, a popular antidepressant, did little to lessen his anxiety. Sometimes he would slip into a manic state, and Claire would coax him into her car and head for the emergency room. "At the hospital, I always got the same question: 'Is he threatening you or trying to hurt himself?'" she said. "And I would say, 'No,' and they would tell me that they couldn't help me."

Rather than face his descent into mental illness alone, Claire reached out to his biological father, who had been granted asylum in 1999. (Her ex-husband, Brian, had remarried and largely receded from Sirak's life.) The rest of Sirak's family—his mother, two brothers, and two sisters—had immigrated when Sirak was thirteen and settled with his father in Atlanta. Sirak had visited them nearly every summer since, and he and his siblings had forged an easy bond. Claire believed that Atlanta, with its big-city mental health resources, would be a better place for him than rural Colorado, and in 2008, it was agreed that he would go live with his Ethiopian family.

In Atlanta, a psychiatrist finally diagnosed Sirak with bipolar disorder and prescribed him lithium, a mood stabilizer. During long, discursive phone conversations with Claire, Sirak assured her that he was taking his medication, but despite his sincere longing to get well, he never consistently followed his treatment protocol. Though he managed to hold a number of menial jobs—he bagged groceries, worked as a drugstore clerk, cleaned out moving trucks, delivered auto parts—his employment was often cut short when a manic episode overtook him. By 2012, during one of many voluntary commitments to Georgia Regional, a large, state-run hospital with a psychiatric ward, his diagnosis was modified to reflect his worsening condition. "I have Bipolar One, manic severe, with psychotic features," Sirak explained to me matter-of-factly, referring to the most severe form of the disorder.

When Claire saw Sirak on a visit last July, she was stunned. His doctors had put him on a powerful antipsychotic drug to keep his most serious symptoms in check, but it was plain that he was overmedicated. Sirak absently raised his feet, walking in place where he stood, and looked unfocused, his clothes rumpled, his hair uncombed. When he sat, he sometimes drifted off to sleep, and when he spoke, his voice was a curious monotone. "I'm not enjoying being alive very much right now," he told her. Eager to find a way to dial back his medications, she moved him to Texarkana the following month and gave him her spare bedroom. She found a psychiatrist to fine-tune his prescriptions and arranged for weekly talk therapy sessions. The change of scenery seemed to help him, at least at first. "Today Sirak told me he no longer wants to die," Claire emailed a handful of close friends in late August. "Rejoice with me."

By the time of my visit, he had lapsed back into a depression, and he announced that he wanted to return to Atlanta. (Several weeks later, he did.) Though he had once devoted hours each day to the piano—in 2012 he even went to New York to audition for the master's program at Juilliard—he had stopped playing, he told me, because he had lost his passion for music. "My doctor said I have something called anhedonia," he said. "It's like hedonism, but the opposite. It means I don't feel pleasure anymore."

He brightened only when he changed the subject to an obsession of his: his conviction that he will one day be reborn as a "child of prophecy," or a sort of modern-day messiah. As he described the superpowers he would possess when the prophecy came to fruition, he grew elated, his face alight. Beside him, Claire sat in silence, staring down at her clasped hands.

What if Whitman's bullet had never found her? Claire sometimes thinks about the intricate calculus that put her in his sights that day. What if her anthropology class had not let out early? What if Tom had lingered over his coffee one minute longer before they had gone to feed the parking meter? Such deliberations have never satisfied her, because each shift in the variables sets in motion other consequences. If she had not been shot, she might never have found God. If she had given birth, she would not have known the exhilaration, at 41, of becoming a mother, or the hard-won joy of raising Sirak. Sometimes she finds herself calculating the age of her first child, had he lived, and the number always astonishes her. She wrote it in my notebook one afternoon, carefully forming each numeral: 49. He would probably be a father by now, she observed, and she a grandmother.

She rarely gives much thought to Whitman, who remains, in her mind, remote and inscrutable. "I never saw his face, because we were separated by so much distance," Claire said. "So it's always been hard to understand that he did this—that a person did this—to me." Paging through *Life* on her library visits all those years ago, she studied the photos of him, and one particular image—taken at the beach when Whitman was two years old—has always stayed with her. In the picture, he is standing barefoot in the sand, grinning sweetly at a small dog. Two of his father's rifles are positioned upright on either side of him, and Whitman is holding on to them the way a skier grips his poles.

"That's how I see him—as that little boy on the shore, still open to the world, just wanting his father's love and approval," Claire said. She cannot grasp how, in such a short span of time, "he became so twisted and decided to do what he did," she said. "But I've never felt it was personal. How could I? He didn't know me, I didn't know him."

It will have been fifty years since the shooting this summer, an anniversary that, for Claire, has brought the tragedy into clearer focus. A documentary that tells the story of the day of the massacre from the perspective of eyewitnesses and survivors, with an emphasis on Claire's ordeal, premiered at the South by Southwest Film Festival in Austin in March; directed by Austin-based filmmaker Keith Maitland, *Tower* will air nationally on PBS later this year. (The documentary is loosely based on a 2006 *Texas Monthly* oral history; I served as one of its executive producers.) The film, and recent efforts to plan a memorial for August 1, have reconnected Claire to people she thought she would never see again. "I felt so isolated by the years of silence," she wrote to Maitland during filming. "Now I feel restored to the community from which I was ripped."

Last spring, Claire found herself at the Capitol once again to testify against legislation that would allow concealed handguns on college campuses. While the bills she opposed in 2013 had ultimately failed, this time her testimony did little to deter gun-rights advocates, who succeeded in passing a campus carry bill by a two-to-one margin. Though supporters argued that the measure would make universities safer, Claire was heartened when protests erupted at UT, where an overwhelming majority of students, professors, and administrators balked at the legislature's actions. In what Claire sees as a grotesque insult, the law will go into effect on August 1, half a century to the day that Whitman walked onto the Tower's observation deck and opened fire.

Like many survivors of the shooting, Claire will return to campus to mark the anniversary. The university, now a sprawling, multibillion-dollar institution whose shiny new research facilities dominate the landscape, is drastically different from the one she entered in 1966, but the unsettled legacy of that summer remains. Though the gaping bullet holes left by Whitman's rampage were quickly patched over, not every scar was filled, and anyone who takes the time to look closely at the limestone walls and balustrades that line the South Mall can still make out tiny divots where his bullets missed their mark.

Claire longs to lie down in the shadow of the Tower, on

the precise spot where she was shot. "It's beyond me why I would feel comforted there," she told me. "But I want to lie down, and remember the heat, and remember Tom, and remember the baby." That wide-open stretch of concrete is the last place they were all together.

Originally published in *Texas Monthly*, March 2016

# Jennifer Pan's Revenge

BY KAREN K. HO

Bich Ha and Huei Hann Pan were classic examples of the Canadian immigrant success story. Hann was raised and educated in Vietnam and moved to Canada as a political refugee in 1979. Bich (pronounced "Bick") came separately, also a refugee. They married in Toronto and lived in Scarborough. They had two kids, Jennifer in 1986 and Felix three years later, and found jobs at the Aurora-based auto parts manufacturer Magna International, Hann as a tool and die maker and Bich making car parts. They lived frugally. By 2004, Bich and Hann had saved enough to buy a large home with a two-car garage on a quiet residential street in Markham. He drove a Mercedes-Benz and she a Lexus ES 300, and they accumulated $200,000 in the bank.

Their expectation was that Jennifer and Felix would work as hard as they had in establishing their lives in Canada. They'd laid the groundwork, and their kids would need to improve upon it. They enrolled Jennifer in piano classes at age four, and she showed early promise. By elementary school, she'd racked up a trophy case full of awards. They put her in figure skating, and she hoped to compete at the national level, with her sights set on the 2010 Winter Olympics in Vancouver until she tore a ligament in her knee. Some nights during elementary school, Jennifer would come home from skating practice at 10 p.m., do homework until midnight, then head to bed. The pressure was intense. She began cutting herself—little horizontal cuts on her forearms.

As graduation from grade eight loomed, Jennifer expected to be named valedictorian and to collect a handful of medals for her academic achievements. But she received none, and she wasn't named valedictorian. She was stunned. What was the point in trying if no one acknowledged your efforts? And yet, instead of expressing her devastation, she told anyone who asked that she was perfectly fine—something she called her "happy mask." A close observer might have noticed that Jennifer seemed off, but I never did. I was a year behind her at Mary Ward Catholic Secondary in north Scarborough. As far as Catholic schools go, it was something of an anomaly: it had the usual high academic standards and strict dress code, mixed with a decidedly bohemian vibe. It was easy to find your tribe. Bright kids and arty misfits hung out together, across subjects, grades, and social groups. If you played three instruments, took advanced classes, competed on the ski team, and starred in the school's annual International Night—a showcase of various cultures around the world—you were cool. Outsiders were embraced, geekiness celebrated (anime club meetings were constantly packed) and precocious ambition supported (our most famous alumnus, Craig Kielburger, pretty much ran his charity, Free the Children, from the halls of Mary Ward).

It was the perfect community for a student like Jennifer. A social butterfly with an easy, high-pitched laugh, she mixed with guys, girls, Asians, Caucasians, jocks, nerds, people deep into the arts. Outside of school, Jennifer swam and practiced the martial art of wushu.

At five foot seven, she was taller than most of the other Asian girls at the school, and pretty but plain. She rarely wore makeup; she had small, round wire-frame glasses that were neither stylish nor expensive; and she kept her hair straight and unstyled.

Jennifer and I both played the flute, though she was in the senior stage band and I was in junior. We would interact in the band room, had dozens of mutual acquaintances and were friends on Facebook. In conversation, she always seemed focused on the moment—if you had her attention, you had it completely.

I discovered later that Jennifer's friendly, confident persona was a façade, beneath which she was tormented by feelings of inadequacy, self-doubt, and shame. When she failed to win first place at skating competitions, she tried to hide her devastation from her parents, not wanting to add worry to their disappointment. Her mother, Bich, noticed something was amiss and would comfort her daughter at night, when Hann was asleep, saying, "You know all we want from you is just your best—just do what you can."

She had been a top student in elementary school, but midway through grade nine, she was averaging 70 percent in all subjects—with the exception of music, where she excelled. Using old report cards, scissors, glue, and a photocopier, she created a new, forged report card with straight As. Since universities didn't consider marks from grades nine and ten for admission, she told herself it wasn't a big deal.

Hann was the classic tiger dad, and Bich his reluctant accomplice. They picked Jennifer up from school at the end of the day, monitored her extracurricular activities, and forbade her from attending dances, which Hann considered unproductive. Parties were off-limits and boyfriends verboten until after university. When Jennifer was permitted to attend a sleepover at a friend's house, Bich and Hann dropped her off late at night and picked her up early the following morning. By age 22, she had never gone to a club, been drunk, visited a friend's cottage, or gone on vacation without her family.

Presumably, their overprotectiveness was born of love and concern. To Jennifer and her friends, however, it was tyranny. "They were absolutely controlling," said one former classmate, who asked not to be named. "They treated her like shit for such a long time."

The more I learned about Jennifer's strict upbringing, the more I could relate to her. I grew up with immigrant parents who also came to Canada from Asia (in their case Hong

Kong) with almost nothing, and a father who demanded a lot from me. My dad expected me to be at the top of my class, especially in math and science, to always be obedient, and to be exemplary in every other way. He wanted a child who was like a trophy—something he could brag about. I suspected the achievements of his siblings and their children made him feel insecure, and he wanted my accomplishments to match theirs. I felt like a hamster on a wheel, sprinting to meet some sort of expectation, solely determined by him, that was always just out of reach. Hugs were a rarity in my house, and birthday parties and gifts from Santa ceased around age nine. I was talented at math and figure skating, though my father almost never complimented me, even when I excelled. He played down my educational achievements, just like his parents had done with him—the prevailing theory in our culture being that flattery spoils ambition.

JENNIFER MET DANIEL WONG IN GRADE 11. HE WAS A YEAR older, goofy and gregarious, with a big laugh, a wide smile, and a little paunch around his waistline. He played trumpet in the school band and in a marching band outside of school. Their relationship was platonic until a band trip to Europe in 2003. After a performance in a concert hall filled with smokers, Jennifer suffered an asthma attack. She started panicking, was led outside to the tour bus, and almost blacked out. Daniel calmed her down, coaching her breathing. "He pretty much saved my life," she later said. "It meant everything." That summer, they started dating.

Of Jennifer's friends, I knew Daniel best. We met in my grade-nine year at Mary Ward, and he would come over to my house nearly every day after school to watch TV and play *Halo* on my Xbox. He would often stick around and eat dinner with my family. Dan spoke to my parents in Cantonese, and my dad would regularly buy him Zesty Cheese Doritos—his favorite. When Daniel was in his final year at Mary Ward, we drifted apart, and midway through the year, he transferred to Cardinal Carter Academy, an arts school in North York. He was falling behind at Mary Ward, and, unbeknownst to me, he had been charged with trafficking after cops found half a pound of weed in his car.

Jennifer's parents assumed their daughter was an A student; in truth, she earned mostly Bs—respectable for most kids but unacceptable in her strict household. So Jennifer continued to doctor her report cards throughout high school. She received early acceptance to Ryerson, but then failed calculus in her final year and wasn't able to graduate. The university withdrew its offer. Desperate to keep her parents from digging into her high school records, she lied and said she'd be starting at Ryerson in the fall. She said her plan was to do two years of science, then transfer over to U of T's pharmacology program, which was her father's hope. Hann was delighted and bought her a laptop. Jennifer collected used biology and physics textbooks and bought school supplies. In September, she pretended to attend frosh week. When it came to tuition, she doctored papers stating she was receiving an OSAP loan and convinced her dad she'd won a $3,000 scholarship.

She would pack up her book bag and take public transit downtown. Her parents assumed she was headed to class. Instead, Jennifer would go to public libraries, where she would research on the Web what she figured were relevant scientific topics and fill her books with copious notes. She'd spend her free time at cafes or visiting Daniel at York University, where he was taking classes. She picked up a few day shifts as a server at East Side Mario's in Markham, taught piano lessons, and later tended bar at a Boston Pizza, where Daniel worked as a kitchen manager. At home, Hann often asked Jennifer about her studies, but Bich told him not to interfere. "Let her be herself," she'd say.

In order to keep the charade from unraveling, Jennifer lied to her friends, too. She even amplified her dad's meddling ways, telling one friend, falsely, that her father had hired a private investigator to follow her.

After Jennifer had pretended to be enrolled at Ryerson for two years, Hann asked her if she was still planning to switch to U of T. She said yes, she'd been accepted into the pharmacology program. Her parents were thrilled. She suggested moving in with her friend Topaz downtown for three nights a week. Bich sympathized with Jennifer's long commute each day and convinced Hann that it was a good idea.

Jennifer never stayed with Topaz. Monday through Wednesday, she stayed with Daniel and his family at their home in Ajax, a large house on a quiet, tree-lined street. Jennifer lied to Daniel's parents as well, telling them her parents were okay with the arrangement and brushing off their repeated requests to meet Hann and Bich over dim sum.

After two more years, it was theoretically time to graduate from U of T. Jennifer and Daniel hired someone they found online to create a fake transcript, full of As. When it came to the ceremony, Jennifer told her parents that the extra-large class size meant there weren't enough seats—graduating students were allowed only one guest each, and she didn't want one of her parents to feel left out, so she gave her ticket to a friend.

Jennifer developed a mental strategy to deal with her lies. "I tried looking at myself in the third person, and I didn't like who I saw," she later said, "but rationalizations in my head said I had to keep going—otherwise I would lose everything that ever meant anything to me."

Eventually, Jennifer's fictional academic career began to collapse. While supposedly studying at U of T, she had told her parents about an exciting new development: she was volunteering at the blood-testing lab at SickKids. The gig sometimes required late-night shifts on Fridays and weekends. Perhaps, she suggested, she should spend more of the week at Topaz's. But Hann noticed something odd: Jennifer had no uniform or key card from SickKids. So the next day, he insisted that they drop her off at the hospital. As soon as the car stopped, she sprinted inside, and Hann instructed Bich to follow her. Realizing she was being tailed by her mom, Jennifer hid in the waiting area of the ER for a few hours until they left. Early the next morning, they called Topaz, who groggily told the truth: Jennifer wasn't there. When Jennifer finally came home, Hann confronted her. She confessed that she didn't volunteer at SickKids, had never been in U of 'T's pharmacology program and had indeed been staying at Daniel's—though she neglected to tell them that she'd never graduated high school and that her time at Ryerson was also complete fiction.

Bich wept. Hann was apoplectic. He told Jennifer to get out and never come back, but Bich convinced him to let their daughter stay. They took away her cell phone and laptop for two weeks, after which she was only permitted to use them in her parents' presence and had to endure surprise checks of her messages. They forbade her from seeing Daniel. They ordered her to quit all of her jobs except for teaching piano and began tracking the odometer on the car.

Jennifer was madly in love with Daniel, and lonely, too. For two weeks, she was housebound, her mother by her side nearly constantly—though Bich told Jennifer where her dad had hidden her phone, so she could periodically check her messages. In February 2009, she wrote on her Facebook page: "Living in my house is like living under house arrest." She also posted a note: "No one person knows everything about me, and no two people put together knows everything about me . . . I like being a mystery." Over the spring and summer, she snuck calls with Daniel on her cell phone at night, whispering in the dark.

Eventually, she was allowed some measure of freedom, and she enrolled in a calculus course to get her final high school credit. Still, in defiance of her parents' orders, she visited Daniel in between piano lessons. One night, she arranged her blankets to look like she was asleep, then snuck out to Daniel's house. But she forgot that she had her mother's wallet. In the morning, Bich went into the room to get it and discovered Jennifer was gone. Bich and Hann ordered Jennifer to come home immediately. They demanded that she apply to college—she could still be a pharmacy lab technician or nurse—and told her that she had to cut off all contact with Daniel.

Jennifer resisted, but Daniel had grown weary of their secret romance. She was 24 and still sneaking around, terrified of her parents' tirades but not willing to leave home. He told her to figure out her life, and he broke off their relationship. Jennifer was heartbroken. Shortly thereafter, she learned that Daniel was seeing a girl named Christine. In an attempt to win back his attention and discredit Christine, she concocted a bizarre tale. She told him a man had knocked on her door and flashed what looked like a police badge. When she opened the door, a group of men rushed in, overpowered her, and gang-raped her in the foyer of her house. Then a few days later, she said, she received a bullet in an envelope in her mailbox. Both instances, she alleged, were warnings from Christine to leave Daniel alone.

IN THE SPRING OF 2010, JENNIFER RECONNECTED WITH Andrew Montemayor, a friend from elementary school. According to Jennifer's later evidence in court, he had boasted about robbing people at knifepoint in the park near his home (a claim he denies). When Jennifer told him about her torturous relationship with her dad, Montemayor confessed that he'd once considered killing his own father. The notion intrigued Jennifer, who began imagining how much better her life would be without her father around. Montemayor introduced Jennifer to his roommate, Ricardo Duncan, a goth kid with black nail polish.

Over bubble tea in between her piano lessons, according to Jennifer, they hatched a plan for Duncan to murder her father in a parking lot at his work, a tool and die company called Kobay Enstel, near Finch and McCowan. She says she gave Duncan $1,500, earnings from her piano classes, and they agreed to connect later by phone to arrange the date and time of the hit. But Duncan stopped answering her calls, and by early July, Jennifer realized she had been ripped off. (Duncan says she called him in early July, hysterical, requesting that he come and kill her parents. He said he felt offended and said no, and that the only money she gave him was $200 for a night out, which he promptly returned.)

According to the police, it was at this point that Daniel and Jennifer, who were back in contact and exchanging daily flirty texts, devised an even more sinister plan: they'd hire a hit on Bich and Hann, collect the estate—Jennifer's portion totaling about $500,000—and live together, unencumbered by her meddling parents. Daniel gave Jennifer a spare iPhone and SIM card, and connected her with an acquaintance named Lenford Crawford, whom he called Homeboy.

Jennifer asked what the going rate was for a contract killing. Crawford said it was $20,000, but for a friend of Daniel's it could be done for $10,000. Jennifer was careful to use her iPhone for crime-related conversations and her Samsung phone for everything else. On Halloween night, Crawford visited the Pans' neighborhood—probably to scout the site. Kids in costume streaming up and down the street provided the perfect cover.

On the afternoon of November 2, the plan took an unexpected turn. Daniel texted Jennifer, saying that he felt as strongly about Christine as she did about him. Suddenly, everything was thrown into question. She texted Daniel: "So you feel for her what I feel for you, then call it off with Homeboy." Daniel responded, "I thought you wanted this for you?" Jennifer replied to Daniel, "I do, but I have nowhere to go." Daniel wrote back: "Call it off with Homeboy? You said you wanted this with or without me." Jennifer: "I want it for me." The next day, Daniel texted, "I did everything and lined it all up for you." It seemed Daniel wanted out of the arrangement. But within hours, they'd reverted to their old ways, texting and flirting. Later that day, Crawford texted Jennifer, "I need the time of completion, think about it." Jennifer wrote back, "Today is a no go. Dinner plans out so won't be home in time." Over the following week, there was a flurry of text and phone conversations between Jennifer, Daniel, and Crawford. On the morning of November 8, Crawford texted Jennifer: "After work ok will be game time."

That evening, Jennifer watched *Gossip Girl* and *Jon & Kate*

*Plus Eight* in her bedroom while Hann read the Vietnamese news down the hall before heading to bed around 8:30 p.m. Bich was out line dancing with a friend and a cousin. Felix, who was studying engineering at McMaster University, wasn't home. At approximately 9:30 p.m., Bich came home from her line dancing class, changed into her pajamas, and soaked her feet in front of the TV on the main floor. At 9:35 p.m., a man named David Mylvaganam, a friend of Crawford's, called Jennifer, and they spoke for nearly two minutes. Jennifer went downstairs to say good night to Bich and, as Jennifer later admitted, unlock the front door (a statement she eventually retracted). At 10:02 p.m., the light in the upstairs study switched on—allegedly a signal to the intruders—and a minute later, it switched off. At 10:05 p.m., Mylvaganam called again, and he and Jennifer spoke for three and a half minutes. Moments later, Crawford, Mylvaganam, and a third man, named Eric Carty, walked through the front door, all three carrying guns. One pointed his gun at Bich while another ran upstairs, shoved a gun at Hann's face, and directed him out of bed, down the stairs, and into the living room.

Upstairs, Carty confronted Jennifer outside her bedroom door. According to Jennifer, Carty tied her arms behind her using a shoelace. He directed her back inside, where she handed over approximately $2,500 in cash, then to her parents' bedroom, where he located $1,100 in US funds in her mother's nightstand, and then finally to the kitchen to search for her mother's wallet.

"How could they enter the house?" Bich asked Hann in Cantonese. "I don't know. I was sleeping," Hann replied. "Shut up! You talk too much!" one of the intruders yelled at Hann. "Where's the fucking money?" Hann had just $60 in his wallet and said as much. "Liar!" one man replied, and pistol-whipped him on the back of the head. Bich began weeping, pleading with the men not to hurt their daughter. One of the intruders replied, "Rest assured, she is nice and will not be hurt."

Carty led Jennifer back upstairs and tied her arms to the banister, while Mylvaganam and Crawford took Bich and Hann to the basement and covered their heads with blankets. They shot Hann twice, once in the shoulder and then in the face. He crumpled to the floor. They shot Bich three times in the head, killing her instantly, then fled through the front door.

Jennifer somehow managed to reach her phone, tucked into the waistband of her pants, and dial 911 (despite, as she later claimed, having her hands tied behind her back). "Help me, please! I need help!" she cried. "I don't know where my parents are! . . . Please hurry!" At the 34-second mark of the call, the unexpected happens: Hann can be heard moaning in the background. He had awoken, covered in blood, with his dead wife's body next to him, and crawled up the stairs to the main floor. Jennifer yelled down that she was calling 911. Hann stumbled outside, screaming wildly, and encountered his startled neighbor, who was about to leave for work, in the driveway next door. The neighbor called 911. Police and an ambulance arrived at the scene minutes later, and Hann was rushed to a nearby hospital, then airlifted to Sunnybrook.

York Regional Police interviewed Jennifer just before 3:00 a.m. She told them that the men had entered the house looking for money, tied her to the banister, and taken her parents to the basement and shot them. Two days later, the police brought her in again to give a second statement. At their request, she showed how she'd contorted her body to get her phone—a flip phone—out of her waistband to place a call while tied to a banister.

Holes began to emerge in Jennifer's story. For instance, the keys to Hann's Lexus were in plain view by the front door. If it were indeed a home invasion, why did the intruders not take the car? And why didn't they have a crowbar to get in, or a backpack to carry the loot, or zip ties to restrain the residents? And most important: Why would they shoot two witnesses but leave one unharmed? The police assigned a surveillance team to monitor Jennifer's movements.

By November 12, Hann had woken up from his three-day induced coma. He had a broken bone near his eye, bullet fragments lodged in his face that doctors couldn't remove, and a shattered neck bone—the bullet had grazed the carotid artery. Remarkably, he remembered everything, including two troubling details: he recalled seeing his daughter chatting softly—"Like a friend," he said—with one of the intruders, and that her arms were not tied behind her back while she was being led around the house.

On November 22, the police brought Jennifer in for a

third interview. This one developed a different tone: the detective, William Goetz, said that he knew she was involved in the crime. He knew that she had lied to him, and said it was in her best interest to fess up. Jennifer, hunched over and sobbing, asked repeatedly, "But what happens to me?"

Over nearly four hours, Jennifer spun out an absurd explanation. She said the attack had been an elaborate plan to commit suicide gone horribly wrong. She had given up on life but couldn't manage to kill herself, so she hired Homeboy, whose real name she claimed not to know, to do it for her. In September, however, her relationship with her father had suddenly improved, and she'd decided to call off the hit. But somehow wires got crossed, and the men ended up killing her parents instead of her. Police arrested Jennifer on the spot. In the spring of 2011, relying on analysis of cell phone calls and texts, they also nabbed Daniel, Mylvaganam, Carty, and Crawford, and charged all five with first-degree murder, attempted murder, and conspiracy to commit murder.

THE TRIAL BEGAN ON MARCH 19, 2014, IN NEWMARKET. IT was expected to last six months but stretched for nearly 10. More than 50 witnesses testified, and more than 200 exhibits were filed. Jennifer was on the stand for seven days, bobbing and weaving in a futile attempt to explain away the damning text messages with Crawford and Daniel and the calls with Mylvaganam, and desperately trying to convince the jury that while she had indeed ordered a hit on her father in August 2010, three months later she had wanted nothing of the sort.

Before the jury delivered the verdict, Jennifer appeared almost upbeat, playfully picking lint off her lawyer's robes. When the guilty verdict was delivered, she showed no emotion, but once the press had left the courtroom, she wept, shaking uncontrollably. For the charge of first-degree murder, Jennifer received an automatic life sentence with no chance of parole for 25 years; for the attempted murder of her father, she received another sentence of life, to be served concurrently. Daniel, Mylvaganam, and Crawford each received the same sentence. Carty's lawyer fell ill during the trial, and his trial was postponed to early 2016. The judge granted two noncommunication orders, one banning communication among the five defendants until Carty's trial is complete, and a second between Jennifer and her family, at the latter's request, effectively preventing Jennifer from speaking to her father or brother ever again. Her lawyer addressed the order in court. "Jennifer is open to communicating with her family if they wanted to," he said.

Hann and Felix both wrote victim impact statements. "When I lost my wife, I lost my daughter at the same time," Hann wrote. "I don't feel like I have a family anymore. [ . . . ] Some say I should feel lucky to be alive but I feel like I am dead too." He is now unable to work due to his injuries. He suffers anxiety attacks, insomnia, and, when he can sleep, nightmares. He is in constant pain and has given up gardening, working on his cars, and listening to music, since none of those activities bring him joy anymore. He can't bear to be in his house, so he lives with relatives nearby. Felix moved to the East Coast to find work with a private technology company and escape the stigma of being a member of the Pan family. He suffers from depression and has become closed off. Hann is desperate to sell the family home, but no one will buy it. At the end of his statement, Hann addressed Jennifer. "I hope my daughter Jennifer thinks about what has happened to her family and can become a good honest person someday."

THIS WAS A DIFFICULT STORY FOR ME TO WRITE. IT'S complicated to report on a murder when you were once friends with the people involved. Late last year, I drove up to the correctional facility in Lindsay a few times to see Daniel. In the harsh, white, empty halls of the massive building, even separated from me by a large pane of Plexiglas, he still seemed so familiar—a little pudgy, happy, cracking jokes. His favorite color was always orange, but he tugged on his bright pumpkin jumpsuit and said he'd cooled on the color lately, then broke into a big laugh. He asked how I was doing, and I told him my parents had recently separated, and how it had been tough on me. He said that if he ever got out, he would give my dad relationship advice.

I asked him if he ever wonders whether, if even little things had gone just slightly differently, he wouldn't be in prison. He shook his head and said thinking like that could drive a person mad. He said the best thing for him was to focus on reality: that he was in jail, and he had to make the best of it. Daniel said he'd bonded with the Cantonese speakers in his block and was helping them adjust to life inside. When I asked him about the case, he clammed up, citing limitations set by his lawyer. He intends to appeal, as do Jennifer, Mylvaganam, and Crawford. Presuming they lose, they'll be eligible for parole in 2035. Jennifer will be 49, Daniel 50.

A number of questions linger. Was Jennifer mentally ill? A chemical imbalance would certainly make the ordeal easier to understand. But her lawyers didn't attempt to present her as unfit to stand trial. That leaves a harder conclusion: that Jennifer was in complete control of her faculties. That she wanted Bich and Hann dead and put a plan into action to make it happen. That the guilt of years of her snowballing lies and the shame when it all came out drove her to murder.

It's not that simple, though. I believe that on some level, Jennifer loved her parents. "I needed my family to be around me. I wanted them to accept me; I didn't want to live alone [ . . . ] I didn't want them to abandon me either," she said on the stand. She was hysterical on the phone when she called 911 and teared up in the courthouse while describing the sound of her parents being shot. Yet how do you believe a liar? Jennifer lied in all three statements she gave to police. Under oath, she was repeatedly caught in tiny half-truths.

Some think her parents were to blame. "I think they pushed her to that point," a friend of Jennifer's told me. "I honestly don't think Jennifer is evil. This is just two people she hated." In February, I submitted separate formal requests to interview Jennifer and Daniel about the trial itself, the judgment, and the sentence. They declined. The result is the purgatory of not knowing what my former schoolmates were thinking, feeling, and hoping for. And it's likely I never will.

Originally published in *Toronto Life*, July 2015

# The Perfect Man Who Wasn't

## BY RACHEL MONROE

By the spring of 2016, Missi Brandt had emerged from a rough few years with a new sense of solidity. At 45, she was three years sober and on the leeward side of a stormy divorce. She was living with her preteen daughters in the suburbs of St. Paul, Minnesota, and working as a flight attendant. Missi felt ready for a serious relationship again, so she made a profile on Ourtime.co.uk, a dating site for people in middle age.

Among all the duds—the desperate and depressed and not-quite-divorced—a 45-year-old man named Richie Peterson stood out. He was a career naval officer, an Afghanistan veteran who was finishing his doctorate in political science at the University of Minnesota. When Missi "liked" his profile, he sent her a message right away and called her that afternoon. They talked about their kids (he had two; she had three), their divorces, their sobriety. Richie told her he was on vacation in Hawaii, but they planned to meet up as soon as he got back.

A few days later, when he was supposed to pick her up for their first date, Richie was nowhere to be found, and he wasn't responding to her texts, either. Missi sat in her living room, alternately furious at him (for letting her down) and at herself (for getting her hopes up enough to be let down). "I'm thinking, *What a dumbass I am. He's probably at home, hanging out with his wife and kids*," she says.

At 10 p.m., she sent him a final message: *This is completely unacceptable*. A few minutes later, she got a reply from Richie's friend Chris, who said Richie had been in a car accident. He was okay, thank God, but the doctors wanted to do some extra testing, since he'd suffered head trauma while in Afghanistan. Chris sent Missi a picture of Richie in a hospital bed, looking a little banged up but grinning gamely for the camera. Missi felt a wave of relief, both that Richie was okay and that her suspicions were unwarranted.

When she finally did meet him in person, her relief was even more profound. Richie was tall and charming, a good talker and a good listener who seemed eager for a relationship. He could be a little awkward, but Missi chalked that up to his inexperience—he told her he hadn't been with a woman in eight years. Plus, dating him was fun. Richie had a taste for nice things—expensive restaurants, four-star hotels—and he always insisted on paying. He kept a motorboat docked at a nearby marina, and he'd take Missi and her daughters out for afternoons on the water. The girls liked him, and so did the dog. Richie mentioned that his cousin Vicki worked for the same airline as Missi. The two women didn't work together regularly, but they knew each other. Missi thought it was a fun coincidence. "Don't mention us to her," Richie said. "One day we'll show up together to some family event and surprise her; it'll be great."

A few months into their relationship, she missed a shift at work and got fired. Richie leapt into provider mode. He told her that he'd take care of her bills for the next four months, that she should relax and take stock of her life and spend time with the kids. Maybe he could put her and the girls on his university insurance. Maybe, he told her, with the benevolent confidence of a wealthy man, she wouldn't have to work. The offer wasn't all that appealing to Missi—"I didn't want to be a stay-at-home mom again," she says—but she took it as a sign that things were getting serious.

The longer they kept dating, though, the more problems cropped up. Richie liked to say he didn't "do drama," but drama seemed to follow him nonetheless. It got to feel as if every text from him was an announcement of some new disaster: he had to check his daughter Sarah into rehab; he had to put his beloved shih tzu, Thumper, to sleep. Richie had lingering medical problems from his time in the service, and Missi was constantly having to drop him off at or pick him up from the hospital. He was always canceling plans, or not showing up when he was supposed to. When Missi got fed up—*Why did I get out of a crappy marriage just to be in this crappy relationship?*—some new tragedy would happen (his mother died; he was in a motorcycle accident), and she'd be roped back in.

One day in early August, driven by a feeling she couldn't quite pinpoint, Missi took a peek at Richie's wallet. Inside was a Minnesota state ID with a photograph that was unmistakably Richie's, but with an entirely different name: Derek Mylan Alldred. The wallet also contained a couple of credit cards belonging to someone named Linda. Missi's heart sank. She'd had a nagging sense that something wasn't right in her relationship, but she'd shaken it off as her being untrusting. These mysterious objects in his wallet, though, seemed to affirm that Richie was engaged in some larger form of deceit, even if she didn't understand all the details just yet.

When Missi googled Derek Alldred, half a dozen mug shots of Richie—Derek—popped up, alongside news articles with alarming phrases such as *career con man* and *long history of deception*. Missi sat down on the couch and slowly read every word of every article she could find: Derek Alldred had posed as a firefighter and scammed hospitals out of drugs. Derek Alldred had dated a woman in California under false pretenses and drained her bank account of almost $200,000. Derek Alldred had married a woman, pretended to pay the bills on their home, then vanished after it was foreclosed on. Derek Alldred had posed as a surgeon, checked into the posh Saint Paul Hotel with a woman and her two daughters, racked up nearly $2,000 in charges, then skipped out on the bill (and the woman).

As she read, Missi began to feel sick, as if her body was having trouble physically assimilating the idea that her boyfriend was not a scholar and war hero, but rather a serial con man. And those credit cards kept nagging at her: "There is someone else out there who is being completely fricking screwed right now," she remembers thinking. It took a bit of detective work, but eventually Missi tracked Linda down on Facebook and sent her a message. "You're probably going to think I'm crazy," it began.

WHEN LINDA DYAS, AGE 46, GOT MISSI'S MESSAGE, SHE was in the house she shared with Rich Peterson, her boyfriend of seven months. Linda, who is tall and blond and funny, had been going through an ugly divorce when she'd met Rich on Ourtime.co.uk, and he'd seemed almost too good to be true: a Christian, a military vet, a fellow conservative. On their first date, after the server set down their plates, Rich closed his eyes and said a beautiful prayer. "I was blown away by that," Linda told me when we met at a wine bar in St. Paul over the summer. "Here I was on a first date, and he's actually going to stop and say a prayer in a restaurant. It was touching." Linda was smitten. "Head over heels, you know?" she said. "Within two weeks, he was at my house all the time."

After a few months, Linda lost her job with a financial

services company, but Rich made it seem okay. He found them a house to rent in an upscale suburb of St. Paul, one she wouldn't have been able to afford on her own, and she and her six-year-old son moved in. Linda hung her clothes next to Rich's navy uniforms; he displayed the framed certificates for his military honors—a Purple Heart, a Silver Star—on the walls. One day she stumbled onto paperwork for a $100,000 college fund he had secretly started for her son, and her heart surged.

Recently, though, the relationship had been rockier. Rich drank a lot, and his constant trips to the hospital—which he blamed on the persistent effects of his war wounds—were exhausting. When Linda received Missi's message, she initially dismissed it as the rantings of a jealous ex. But for a few weeks she'd had a vague sense that things between her and Rich were askew in some fundamental way. When, a couple of days later, she finally opened the links Missi had sent, she realized why. "My first instinct was, *How do I get him out of the house?*" she recalled. He solved that problem for her, announcing that he was once again in so much pain, he needed to go to the emergency room. Linda dropped him off and then called the police on her way home. She sat up for hours. At three in the morning, Derek told her he would catch an Uber home, and Linda alerted the police. When she saw the red-and-blue lights through her window, she sent Missi a message, letting her know that Derek was in custody.

Linda eventually figured out that Derek Alldred had not only been lying about his name, his job, and his past—he'd been depleting her savings to bolster his fake life. As she went over her bank statements, she said, she began to piece it together: how he had stolen her emergency credit cards out of her jewelry box and ordered new cards in her name, then used those cards to fund fancy dinners and trips to Hawaii with her and other women; how he'd siphoned money from her retirement savings to pay off the credit-card bills, and to buy a boat and two motorcycles he'd ostensibly given her as gifts; how he'd ask her to drop him off at the hospital, only to get Missi to pick him up as soon as she was gone; how her name was somehow the only one on the house's lease, and she was now on the hook for rent she couldn't afford.

The night after Derek's arrest, Missi came over so Linda wouldn't have to be alone. When Linda's dog trotted into the room, Missi laughed. "Thumper!" she said. "I thought you were dead." (Derek's mother, they later learned, was also still alive.) On the surface, the two women didn't seem to have much in common—Missi is grounded and easygoing, with a yin-yang symbol tattooed on her big toe, while Linda is a conservative navy vet with a drawl that betrays her Texas roots—but they bonded over the absurdity of their shared situation.

The next day, Washington County police were at Linda's house taking her statement when a delivery arrived, addressed to Rich Peterson. Linda handled the package gingerly; it felt like a missive from an alternate reality. One of the police officers told her she might as well open it: "It's not like he's a real person." The box contained whiskey and chocolate and a sweet get-well-soon note from a woman whose return address was just a few neighborhoods away.

Linda texted Missi, who compiled a dossier of news articles documenting all of Derek's misdeeds and dropped it off with the third woman, Joy (who asked to be identified by her middle name). That weekend, Joy stopped by Linda's, and the two women split a bottle of wine, trying to piece together how they'd been taken so thoroughly. Joy, a 42-year-old IT director, had also met "Rich" on Ourtime.co.uk, in February. He'd told her he was a professor who volunteered at a homeless shelter downtown. (The women later found out that he had actually been living at the shelter before he moved in with Linda.) They'd dated for a few months, until "he started having just a ton of drama in his life," Joy says. She broke it off with him but stayed friendly. On the Fourth of July, he sent her a picture of himself looking tan and happy, his arms around Missi and her kids on the boat that Linda had paid for. *I bought a boat and took my sister and her kids out on it today,* he wrote. *My life has calmed down—want to try again?* Joy decided to give him another chance. She later found that he'd stolen almost $8,000 worth of jewelry, her passport, and her birth certificate.

The false life that Derek—it was still hard not to slip and call him Rich—had constructed for himself was thorough: He had a University of Minnesota email address and an ID card that allowed him to swipe into university buildings. He would FaceTime the women from UM classrooms between classes. He had hourlong phone conversations—ostensibly with his admiral, his faculty supervisor, or his daughter Sarah, three people who turned out not to exist—during which Linda could hear a voice on the other end of the line. He had uniforms and medals and a stack of framed, official-looking awards: a Purple Heart and a Silver Star, a SEAL Team One membership, a certificate of completion for a naval underwater demolition course. There were just so many props bolstering Derek's stories that even when doubts had started to bubble up, the women had repressed them down—*There's no way it could all be fake*, they'd told themselves. *That would be crazy.*

The three women's conversations had another recurring theme: "We also knew there had to be more victims," Linda told me.

AMERICANS LOVE A CON MAN. IN HIS INSOUCIANCE, HIS blithe refusal to stick to one category or class, his constant self-reinvention, the confidence man (and he is almost always a man) takes one of America's foundational myths—You can be anything you want to be!—to its extreme. The con man, the writer Lewis Hyde has argued, is "one of America's unacknowledged founding fathers."

Con men thrive in times of upheaval. "Transition is the confidence game's great ally," Maria Konnikova writes in *The Confidence Game*, an account of how swindlers manipulate human psychology. "There's nothing a con artist likes better than exploiting the sense of unease we feel when it appears that the world as we know it is about to change." The first great era of the American scam artist—the period when the confidence man got his name—began in the mid-19th century. The country was rapidly urbanizing; previously far-flung places were newly linked by railroads. Americans were meeting more strangers than ever before, and thanks to a growing economy, they had more money than previous generations. All of those strangers, all of that cash, resulted in an era powered by trust, one that Mark Twain and Charles Dudley Warner satirized in *The Gilded Age* for its "unlimited reliance upon human promises."

The age of the internet, with its infinitude of strangers and swiftly evolving social mores, has also been good for con men. The FBI's Internet Crime Complaint Center, which tracks internet-facilitated criminal activity, received nearly 300,000 complaints in 2016, reporting total losses of more than $1.3 billion. Of those, more than 14,500 were for relationship fraud, a number that has more than doubled since 2011. In 2016, relationship scams were the second-most-costly form of internet fraud (after wire fraud), netting scammers nearly $220 million. By comparison, Americans lost only $31 million to phishing scams, about $2.5 million to ransomware attacks, and $1.6 million to phony charities.

The FBI warns that the most common targets of dating scams "are women over 40 who are divorced, widowed, and/or disabled." In many cases, women are courted online by men who claim to be deployed in Afghanistan or tending an offshore oil rig in Qatar. After weeks or months of intimate emails, texts, and phone calls, the putative boyfriend will urgently need money to replace a broken laptop or buy a plane ticket home. Some, like Derek or "Dirty John" Meehan—whose romance scam was exposed last year by the *Los Angeles Times*—escalate an online relationship to an in-person con, going as far as living with their victims or even marrying them. Derek stands out for how remarkably prolific he was: He often had two or three separate relationship scams going at a time. When one woman discovered the truth, he'd quickly move on to another.

According to the Department of Justice, only 15 percent of fraud victims report the crimes to law enforcement, largely due to "shame, guilt, embarrassment, and disbelief." "You feel really crappy about yourself," Missi told me, then slipped into a tone that sounded like the mean voice that lives inside her head: "I'm a stupid woman; I'm a dumb, dumb dumbass."

But Derek's victims didn't let their shame stop them from coming forward. Many of them did report him—only to discover that by drawing them so deeply into his con, he had paradoxically made it less likely that he'd face consequences.

THE POLICE RELEASED DEREK AFTER 48 HOURS, TELLING Linda they wanted to build a stronger case. (A police spokeswoman told me the county attorney had concluded that fraud charges probably wouldn't have held up in court. Because Linda's and Derek's lives were so entwined, it would have been too difficult to determine which credit card charges were fraudulent and which were authorized.) Seven months later, the police department finally issued a warrant for Derek's arrest, on one misdemeanor charge of impersonating an officer. By then he was long gone.

While Linda sorted through her finances, her sister-in-law delved into old news articles about Derek, looking for any information that might be useful in bringing him to justice. Most of the women quoted were anonymous, or referred to only by their first names. A woman named Cindi Pardini, however, had used her full name. A tech professional living in San Francisco, she said Derek had stolen hundreds of thousands of dollars (and 660,000 airline miles) from her over the course of a few months in 2013. Linda sent Cindi a Facebook message and soon learned that Cindi was a kind of unofficial point person for Derek's accusers. Because her name was one of the only searchable ones linked to his, women who'd been scammed by Derek reached out to Cindi through Twitter, Facebook, and LinkedIn. She was in touch with about a dozen victims.

Cindi wasn't always easy to deal with. On the phone with the other victims, she'd ramble for hours about Derek and the trouble he'd brought into her life, how he'd drained her bank account, ruined her credit score, and undermined her sense of reality. "I was not in a good place," Cindi admits. "This has taken over my life for the past five years. My friends and family are like, 'Why are you still going after this? It's killing you.'"

But Cindi's single-mindedness also made her the case's most diligent detective. She kept careful track of news reporting on Derek's exploits and made sure police were informed.

She also contacted Derek's college-age daughter, who Cindi learned was estranged from her father. (The second daughter, Sarah, was a fabrication.) And she talked with one of his childhood friends, who said that Derek, who had grown up in a wealthy suburb of San Francisco, was trouble from an early age. He'd often discussed his family with Missi, and at least some of what he told her appears to have been true. "He'd talk about how they were such good people, and how he was such a black sheep in his family," Missi says. Cindi was in touch with one of his earliest victims, a woman who had met Derek in the early 1990s and had been convinced that he was a medical student conducting important cystic fibrosis research.

Cindi added Linda to a group text with several other victims, and Linda found some comfort in swapping stories with them, and in seeing that they were far from stupid. If anything, Derek seems to have preferred intelligent women; his victims included a doctor and a couple of women who worked in tech. Linda herself was an engineer at a nuclear power plant. But the other women's stories of trying to hold Derek to account for his crimes were not encouraging.

JoAnn, a 43-year-old from Minneapolis who asked that her last name not be used, met "Derek Allarad" on Match .com in August 2014. He told her he was a lawyer with a big downtown firm; in reality, he was hiding out from a warrant for defrauding the Saint Paul Hotel. Derek racked up about $23,000 on JoAnn's credit cards during the three months they were together. When she reported him to the police, she was told that legal action would likely be a waste of her time and money. "The fraud detective told me it would cost me way too much money to get a lawyer and sue him in civil court," JoAnn says. "He said they'd say I was just blaming my ex-boyfriend because I'm bitter. He said, 'If I were you, I'd let it go.'" Six months and many phone calls later, the credit card company finally reversed the charges. But JoAnn still regrets not taking Derek to court. "Just because of how many women he hurt since me," she says.

All together, Derek seems to have scammed at least a dozen women out of about $1 million since 2010. He used different names and occupations, but the identities he took on always had an element of financial prestige or manly valor: decorated veteran, surgeon, air marshal, investment banker. Con artists have long known that a uniform bolsters an illusion, and Derek was fond of dressing up in scrubs and military fatigues. He tended to look for women in their 40s or 50s, preferably divorced, preferably with a couple of kids and a dog or two. Many of his victims were in a vulnerable place in their lives—recently divorced, fresh out of an abusive relationship, or recovering from a serious accident—and he presented himself as a hero and caretaker, the man who would step in and save the day. Even women who weren't struggling when they met Derek soon found their lives destabilized by the chaos he brought—they lost jobs, had panic attacks, became estranged from family members.

Yet, as far as the growing group of Derek's victims could

ascertain, he had never been charged for a crime against any of the women he'd scammed, only for defrauding businesses. Derek seems to have counted on the fact that credit card abuse is often not taken all that seriously by law enforcement when the victim and the perpetrator know each other. Even in instances where the police pursued Derek, he'd typically serve a short sentence. Or he'd just skip town—like he did in November 2014, after he was caught racking up thousands of dollars in fraudulent charges at luxury hotels. When he was finally captured and brought back to Minnesota, prosecutors lobbied to escalate the charges and hold him on $100,000 bail.

"That's a little harsh, don't you think?" the judge asked.

"Judge, if I may," the assistant county attorney replied, "the defendant is a con man. He conned a number of victims within the state of Minnesota. He's been all over the world pretending to be people he's not, and taking money from people who don't have money to spare."

The judge denied the motion. About six months later, Derek was released. Shortly afterward—and despite the fact that his parole mandated that he stay in Minnesota—he was sitting on a beach in Hawaii with another woman who thought she'd met the perfect man.

FOR YEARS, DEREK HAD EVADED PUNISHMENT BY MOVing around; local police had limited ability to chase him across state lines. But the women he'd victimized had no jurisdictional limitations. They began tracking his progress across the country, using social media to share updates and information—and to warn others.

Missi reached out to her former coworker at the airline, Vicki, who was Derek's cousin-in-law—that part of his story, at least, wasn't a total lie. After Missi explained what Derek had done, Vicki agreed to pass on any information she learned. Through a family member, Vicki heard that Derek had left Minnesota and was hiding out with his mother in Sedona, Arizona—where, lo and behold, he had an outstanding warrant for an old DUI. Urged on by Missi, Vicki alerted the local police, who picked him up in early September 2016 and held him in the county jail for a few days. It wasn't much, but the women took satisfaction in seeing him face at least some consequences.

Still, Derek had a remarkable ability to keep perpetrating the same scam. After his release for the DUI, he began dating a new woman, posing as Navy SEAL Richard Peterson. She soon discovered that he had stolen and pawned some of her jewelry. He was arrested, pleaded no contest, and was taken back to jail, but was bailed out and never showed up for his sentencing. By January 2017, he'd popped up in Las Vegas, where he met another woman and joined a country club, racking up charges before skipping town in April.

When new victims reached out to Cindi Pardini, she'd add them to the group text so they could share their stories with the other women. It was frustrating to find out about

Derek's latest escapades only after the damage had been done. His victims watched and waited, hoping he'd soon make a mistake that would take him out of action for good.

CONSUME ENOUGH MEDIA ABOUT SCAM ARTISTS AND, strangely enough, you, too, might find yourself wanting to date one. In *The Big Con*, perhaps the seminal book on American con men, David Maurer calls them "the aristocrats of crime." The writer and critic Luc Sante once wrote that "the best possess a combination of superior intelligence, broad general knowledge, acting ability, resourcefulness, physical vigor, and improvisational skills that would have propelled them to the top of any profession." On film, they're played with a spring in their step and a glint in their eye: Think Paul Newman in *The Sting*, Leonardo DiCaprio in *Catch Me If You Can*. The con man looks good in a suit and is in on the joke. ("Humor is never very far from the heart of the con," wrote Sante.) And who doesn't want to be in on the joke? Our appetite for stories about cons is, in part, a way of reassuring ourselves that we'd never be so foolish as to be taken. It's in our own self-interest to dismiss the victim of a con as greedy (you can't cheat an honest man, as the adage goes) or just plain dumb: if being scammed is somehow their fault, that means it couldn't happen to us.

One excellent way to dispel yourself of any con man fantasies, however, is to spend some time with the people they've hurt. Derek's victims are negotiating ruined credit scores and calls from collection agencies. Several were so flattened by the experience, they've had old medical problems flare up or have struggled to go back to work.

"You just lose days," Linda told me. She'd plastered her wall with sticky notes mapping out Derek's crimes: "That's what I was doing instead of looking for a job; instead of taking care of the motorcycle, the bank accounts, the bad checks. Instead of moving on with my life; instead of living." Saddled with the rent for a house she couldn't afford, she'd scraped together enough to pay for all but the very last month; now she has an eviction on her record. She and her son crashed on friends' couches while she found a place to live, and, she told me, her ex-husband began campaigning for full custody of their son.

Even more damaging than the financial ramifications was the damage to their fundamental faith in the world, that bedrock sense that things are what they seem. "My mind was all over the place—Am I being taken or am I being overly suspicious?" Derek's Las Vegas victim, Kelly, recalls. "It's so far-fetched—you're just like, there's no way. He gets into your life, your family's life, your finances. I didn't know that people like him existed." The damage rippled outward, affecting the women's families and friends as well: "It just about killed my mother," Linda said. "He would sit and talk with her for hours. She's like, 'Was all of it a lie?'"

Many of the women I spoke with felt compelled to make the same point: that this wasn't just a dating scam story. They reminded me that Derek had scammed hospitals and insurance companies long before he began meeting women on dating sites, and that he'd conned many people beyond just fortysomething divorcées. He won over their parents, friends, and coworkers; he convinced hotel clerks and Mercedes salesmen and bankers and real estate agents and doctors. He was able to finagle country club memberships and hospital admissions. He met actual navy veterans, who took him at his word.

Derek's victims kept underlining this point, I think, because they understood that crimes against women, particularly ones that happen in a domestic context, are often discounted. "It's a he-said, she-said domestic fight" to the police, Linda said. "They lump it right in with divorce and family law." She said an officer told her, "Well, it's not like anyone got hurt; we have higher priorities." They knew that some people hear *dating scam* and translate that to *pathetic/desperate woman*.

The implication is that these women should've known better, or perhaps that they're complicit in their own victimization. If a woman reports her ex for stealing from her, who's to say she's not just brokenhearted and vindictive? Derek himself was happy to exploit such stereotypes; when his victims uncovered his real identity, he'd sometimes threaten to expose them as bad mothers or alcoholics, crazy women who couldn't be trusted.

Even Derek's victims, who understand better than anyone else how these things work, repeatedly questioned one another's choices when speaking with me: How did she let it go on that long? Why did she let him move in when she barely knew him? How did she not see through this or that obvious lie? It's a testament to the persistent belief that cons always happen to someone else that women who had fallen for Derek Alldred's schemes heard other victims' very similar stories and thought, *I never would have fallen for that.*

For Missi and Linda, their crossed paths have resulted in the peculiar sort of friendship that can arise from shared trauma. Derek entwined their lives without their consent, taking Missi out on the boat he'd bought with Linda's money; showing Missi photos of Linda's son, his "nephew." Initially, there was some slight underlying tension between the two women due to the fact that Derek hadn't stolen any money from Missi, while he'd drained more than $200,000 from Linda's retirement account. Joy had floated the theory that Missi was the one Derek "really" cared for, an idea that Linda dismissed out of hand: "That man is not capable of love."

On a warm day last spring, I followed Linda over to Missi's house, in the suburbs of St. Paul. We talked about Derek for four hours, dissecting his actions and puzzling over his motivations. Late in the evening, Linda told another wild part of the saga, involving a half-million-dollar house Derek was going to buy for them before the escrow money mysteriously went missing.

"You listen to Linda, and you're like, 'How did you take that at face value?'" Missi said.

"I had my other stuff going on," Linda said, a bit testily. "He could've told me the sky was purple, and I would've been like, 'Hmm, okay.' I had irons in every fire at that point."

"And I didn't, so I would call him out on things," Missi said. She suddenly sounded very sad. "But I kept letting him come back."

ON MAY 17, 2017, RICHIE TAILOR LEFT THE TOWN HOUSE he shared with his new girlfriend, Dorie, to have dinner with his brother and sister-in-law. Dorie was idly scanning through pictures on the iPad Richie had left behind when she saw one that brought her up short. It was a screenshot of an Instagram post showing a man in a hospital bed. "A BIG THANK-YOU for everyone's prayers and support . . . Should be out of the hospital Monday," the caption read. The name on the account was "Derek M. Allred." "I was like, 'Heck, that's Richie,'" Dorie told me. When she googled "Derek Allred" (an alternative spelling he sometimes used), she found the trove of news stories and mug shots. Suddenly, all those fraudulent charges that kept cropping up on her credit cards made sense.

Dorie printed out the articles and brought them to the police department in The Colony, the small town outside Dallas where she lived. "I thank God to this day that it was a female officer that took my statement," she said. "She took it seriously." While Dorie waited to hear if the police came up with any leads, she scoured the internet for information about Derek. Like so many of the other victims, she stumbled on Cindi Pardini. The two women talked on the phone. "I heard about all the havoc he left behind," Dorie told me. "I vowed that there was no way there'd be another victim after me."

Dorie made sure to show the Colony detectives pictures of Derek in his navy uniform, and the detectives contacted the Naval Criminal Investigative Service. Under the Stolen Valor Act of 2013, seeking profit by using phony military honors is a federal crime—which meant that NCIS could launch a multistate investigation.

After Dorie caught on to him, Derek began staying with his other girlfriend, Tracie Cunningham. But it didn't take long for Tracie, who works at a post-acute rehab facility, to get sick of having him around all day. He was, she'd decided, entirely too whiny, constantly insisting that she drive him to the hospital for some emergency or another. "There are a lot of men out there who will get a little headache, and they think they have a massive tumor, that they're dying," she told me. "It's a man thing. He had some of that. Real dramatic."

Just after Memorial Day, Tracie finally dumped him. A few hours later, while she was at work, she got a call from the NCIS agent, who told her that she'd been dating a con man. Derek hadn't stolen anything from Tracie as far as she could tell ("except time and a little dignity"), but when she heard about the other victims, she immediately agreed to help NCIS capture him.

At the agent's urging, Tracie sent Derek a text, taking back the breakup—"I'm sorry, baby, I was hormonal!"—and made plans to give him a ride home after his next medical appointment. When Derek was ready to be picked up, Tracie alerted the NCIS officer and his team. "They hightail it over there, and I'm on my way, too, because I'm not missing this,"

Tracie told me. She pulled up to the patient loading area. Through the hospital's sliding glass doors, she spied Derek in handcuffs, flanked by two agents. "I turn on my hazards, pop out with my cellphone, start snapping pictures," Tracie said. "The NCIS agent is like, 'No!' but I'm like, 'Oh yeah, I need pictures of this. This is for justice for other people.'"

WITH DEREK FINALLY IN CUSTODY, HIS VICTIMS CELE-brated, texting one another grim fantasies about the future that awaited him in prison. NCIS agents interviewed victims around the country, whose stories bolstered the case that Derek was a habitual offender.

A few days before Christmas, Derek pleaded guilty to two counts of identity theft and one count of mail fraud, charges with a combined maximum penalty of 24 years in prison. As of press time, his sentencing hearing hadn't yet been scheduled. His victims are hoping he'll serve long enough that he'll come out an old man, less able to flirt his way into women's bank accounts.

In the meantime, they continue the slow work of putting their lives back together. Missi has finally gotten to the point where she can make jokes about Derek with her daughters. Linda has started tentatively dating again, after more than a year. The other day, when she was out to dinner with a guy, she peeked in his wallet, just to make sure the name he told her matched the name on his ID.

Dorie, Derek's last victim—for now, at least—recently submitted the police report and a file of articles about Alldred to her bank and credit card companies to clean up the financial mess he'd made. Citibank promptly reversed the $7,000 in fraudulent charges that he'd racked up on one of her cards, but Chase has refused to credit her for the $10,000 he spent on another. "They refused to refund me," she told me, "because they said I knew the guy." (When asked for comment, Chase said that Dorie had authorized Derek's use of the card, and that she'd told a fraud supervisor that many of the transactions were valid.)

THIS PAST SUMMER, I MADE AN APPOINTMENT FOR A video visit with Derek at the Denton County Jail, in Texas. I had so many lingering questions: Who was on the other side of the line when Derek had those hourlong conversations with his "daughter" or his "admiral"? How had he finagled his university email address and ID card? Did he have a secret stash of money somewhere? And then there was the question I imagined was unanswerable, but that I needed to ask anyway: What did it feel like to be so skilled at faking love?

I sat in the visitation room, doodling in my notebook as the appointed time came and went. I'd resigned myself to the idea that nothing was going to happen when the screen suddenly illuminated, and I saw Derek Alldred's angular face and blunt chin, familiar from all those mug shots. He was in an orange jumpsuit, and the camera caught him at an awkward overhead angle, like an unflattering selfie. I told him I was a journalist, and he seemed unfazed. "I was going to decline the visit, but the guard said, 'Are you sure? It's a pretty girl,'" he said, flashing me a smile. By the end of our conversation, Derek said he wanted to tell his side of the story to me and only me, and promised we would talk again soon. I hung up the phone feeling a particular kind of journalistic high, an I-got-my-story cockiness.

Over the next few months, I spoke with Derek several times. He was never quite ready to reveal anything of substance in the half-hour blocks of time that the prison videophone system allotted us. He wanted to wait until a certain court date had passed, or he needed to consult his lawyer. "Two sides to every story," he kept telling me. "Two sides." He professed to want to be fully forthcoming with me, but our calls always seemed to get cut off at crucial moments; sometimes, he just never answered. At first, I chalked our communication difficulties up to the institutional roadblocks of prison communication, but they kept piling up.

It took me much longer than I'd like to admit to realize what I had felt that first day after I left the Denton County Jail and drove too fast past the hayfields of North Texas, singing along to Merle Haggard: that my future was sunny and full of promise, because I had met a man who was going to give me everything I wanted.

Originally published in the *Atlantic*, April 2018; Derek Alldred was given a 24-year prison sentence in August 2018.

# PART II

# WHERE CRIME MEETS CULTURE

# Out Came the Girls

BY ALEX MAR

Here is an image, picked from the notebooks of an eleven-year-old girl in a suburb of Milwaukee, Wisconsin: a head portrait, in pencil, of a man in a dark suit and tie. His long neck is white, and so is his face—bald and whited out, with hollows where his eyes should be.

Here is another: an androgynous kid (a girl, like the artist?) in a sweatshirt and flared jeans leaping across the page. She has huge, glassy black eyes and dark, stringy hair; she reaches out with one hand and brandishes a dagger in the other. Filling the page around her, tiny rainbows and clouds and stars and hearts—all the signatures of the little girl the artist recently was—burst in a fireworks display.

There are cryptic messages, too: a page covered in "Xs"; another inscribed HE STILL SEES YOU. These notebooks are charged with the childlike paranoia of sleepovers after binge-ing on horror movies, of Ouija boards and *light as a feather, stiff as a board* . . .

What is occult is synonymous with what is hidden, or-phic, veiled—but girls are familiar with that realm. We have the instinct. Girls create their own occult language; it may be one of the first signs of adolescence. This is a language of fantasy, of the desire for things we can't yet have (we're too young), of forces we can't control (loneliness, an unrequited crush, the actions of our family). This invention of a private language, both visual and verbal, shared with only a chosen few, gives shape to our first allegiances; it grants entry into a universe with its own rationale—the warped rationale of fairy tales. Its rules do not bleed over into the realm of the mundane, of parents and teachers and adult consequences.

But in May 2014, the occult universe of two young girls did spill over into the real. And within days of her twelfth birthday, all of Morgan Geyser's drawings and scribblings—evidence of the world she had built with her new best friend—were confiscated. More than three years later, they are counted among the state's exhibits in a case of first-degree intentional homicide.

ON A FRIDAY NIGHT IN LATE SPRING 2014, IN THE SMALL, drab city of Waukesha, Wisconsin, a trio of sixth-grade girls gets together to celebrate Morgan's birthday. They skate for hours under the disco lights at the roller rink: tame, mousy-haired Bella Leutner; Anissa Weier, with her shaggy brown

mop top; and Morgan, the "best friend" they have in common, with her moon of a face, big glasses, and long blond
hair. They are three not-so-popular girls at Horning Middle
School, a little more childish than the others, a little more
obsessed with fantasy and video games and making up scary
stories. Morgan casts herself as a creative weirdo, and she
relates to her new friend Anissa on this level, through science fiction—Anissa, who has almost no other friends and
who moved down the block after her parents' recent divorce.
When they get back to the birthday girl's house, they greet
the cats, play games on their tablets, then head to Morgan's
bedroom, where they finally fall asleep, all three together in
a puppy pile in the twin-size loft bed.

In the morning, the girls make a game out of hurling clumps
of Silly Putty up at the ceiling. They role-play for a while—as
the android from *Star Trek* and a troll and a princess—then
eat a breakfast of donuts and strawberries. Morgan gets her
mother's permission to walk to the small park nearby.

As they head to the playground, Bella in the lead, Morgan lifts her plaid jacket to show Anissa what she has tucked
into her waistband: a steak knife from the kitchen. Anissa
is not surprised; they have talked about this moment for
months.

After some time on the swings, Anissa suggests they play
hide-and-seek in the suburban woods at the park's edge.
There, just a few feet beyond the tree line, Morgan, on Anissa's cue, stabs Bella in the chest.

Then she stabs her again and again and again—in her

arms, in her leg, near her heart. By the time Morgan stops, she has stabbed her 19 times.

Bella, screaming, rises up—but she can't walk straight. Anissa braces her by the arm (both of them are small), and she and Morgan lead her deeper into the trees, farther away from the trail. They order Bella to lie down on the ground; they claim they will go get help. Lying on the dirt and leaves, the back of her shirt growing damp with blood, slowly bleeding out in the woods, Bella is left to die.

About five hours later and a few miles away, while resting in the grass alongside Interstate 94, Morgan and Anissa are picked up by a pair of sheriff's deputies. The deputies approach them carefully, aware that they are possible suspects in a stabbing but confused by their age. One of the men notices blood on Morgan's clothes as he handcuffs her. When he asks if she's been injured, she says no.

"Then where did the blood come from?"

"I was forced to stab my best friend."

Morgan and Anissa do not yet know that Bella, against all odds, has survived. After their arrests, over the course of nearly nine combined hours of interviews, they claim that they were compelled to kill her by a monster they had encountered online. When discovered, the girls were making their way to him, heading to Wisconsin's Nicolet National Forest on foot, nearly 200 miles north. They were convinced that, once there, if they pushed farther and farther into the nearly 700,000-acre forest, they would find the mansion in which their monster dwells and he would welcome them.

Morgan and Anissa packed for the trip—granola bars, water bottles, photos by which to remember their families. (As Anissa tells a detective, "We were probably going to be spending the rest of our lives there.") Though they were both a very young, Midwestern 12, they had been chosen for a dark and unique destiny that none of their junior high classmates could possibly understand, drawn into the forest in the service of a force much greater and more mysterious than anything in their suburban American lives. What drew them out there has a name: Slender Man, faceless and pale and impossibly tall. His symbol is the letter "X."

GIRLS LURED OUT INTO THE DARK WOODS—THIS IS THE stuff of folktales from so many countries, a New World fear of the Puritans, an image at the heart of witchcraft and the occult, timeless. Some of our best-known folktales were passed down by teenagers—specifically teenage girls.

When Wilhelm and Jacob Grimm published their first collection in 1812, they'd collected many of the stories from young women—from a handful of lower-class villages, but also from the far more sophisticated German cities of Kassel and Münster. At least one of the girls—Dortchen, a pharmacist's daughter Wilhelm would later marry—was as young as 12. In their earliest published form, 125 years before the first Disney adaptation, these stories are closer to the voices of the original storytellers, less polished, blunt.

The common belief is that many of these tales, when told to children, serve as warnings for bad behavior, harsh lessons, morality plays. But on the flip side, they're remark-able for their easy violence and malleable moral logic, like that of a child. Even mothers are potential villains (con-verted to stepmothers in later editions); even the youngest protagonists may kill or maim—as in Dortchen's story of Hansel and Gretel, who burn that evil old woman alive in her own oven. Punishments are meted out, but unevenly; one offending parent meets her death, while the other is for-given for his sadistic deed—the smoothest path to a happy ending.

The sense that these stories, however peculiar or perverse, rose up from the heart of the culture, seemingly authorless, gives them a unique authority. It is part of why they endure. The same can be said of religious allegories and rituals, or, today, of the new legends that emerge from the internet with the barest of contexts and the illusion of timelessness; time-less elements, those that seem to transcend our moment, are essential to the spinning of myths. The characters are arche-types, blank, faceless—"the girl," "the boy," "the old woman"; the settings are those of epics—a faraway castle, a mountain few can summit, a dark forest.

Nearly a third of the original 86 tales of the Grimms' collection feature young people, many of them girls, making their way into the woods—lured out by a trickster, or the need to pass a life-or-death test. In these stories, to enter the forest is to exit everyday life, leaving its rules behind; to en-counter magic, and sometimes evil; and finally, deep within the tangle of trees, to be initiated, transformed—maybe even to conquer death—in order to cross into the next phase of life. To enter the forest is to cross over into adolescence.

The woods are also (according to common knowledge) the natural domain of witchcraft, the site at which wayward women gather in the dead of night, naked, to conspire against their neighbors, to blight the crops, to make blood pacts with the devil. They travel out to the edge of town—out into the darkness, between the tops of trees, carried through the night air by demons. At least, this was the Puritan nightmare. In the first American settlements, simple houses stood close together, without streetlights to guide the way at night, and a dark wilderness stretched out just beyond the town limits. The settlers clung for comfort and stability to their vision of a harsh and unforgiving god—but the woods beyond were free from authority.

There are also the woods as they belong to the Pagans of today—those we usually mean when talking about present-day witchcraft in this country. For the Pagan movement, nature is the seat of the sacred, and the black trees the architecture of a natural temple. There the witches—Pagan priests, many of them women, some of them naked—gather for ritual. In that renegade space, they circle out under the moon, chanting, invoking their gods and goddesses.

Then there are the generations of adolescent girls who have experimented with witchcraft—whether some form of Paganism, or folk spells, or totally improvised rites and incantations. For them, the woods have been an occult "room of one's own," a site at which to assert that they are separate and unique, a place to be unseen and unselfconscious. This is an impulse, untrained: as Emily Dickinson writes, "Witchcraft has not a pedigree, / 'Tis early as our breath." Girls are drawn out from their homes, even in the cleanest of suburbs with their bright glass malls, drawn to seek out some kind of magic; to be surrounded by trees, wrapped in the dark, hidden; to become perfect, if only for an hour.

To be an adolescent girl is, for many, to view yourself as desperately set apart, powerfully misunderstood. A special alien, terrible and extraordinary. The flood of new hormones, shot from the glands into the bloodstream; the first charged touches, with a boy or a girl; the first years of bleeding in secret; the startling feeling that your body is suddenly hard to contain and, by extension, so are you. It's an age defined by a raw desire for experience; by the chaotic beginning of a girl's sexual self; by obsessive friendships, fast emotions, the birth and rebirth of hard grudges, an inner life that stands outside of logic. You have an undiluted desire for private knowledge, for a genius shared with a select few. You bend reality on the regular.

Add to this heightened state a singular intimacy with another girl who feels the same isolation—you've encountered the only other resident of your private planet—and the charge is exponentially increased.

THERE MAY ONLY BE ONE OTHER CRIME, COMMITTED BY girls, that closely evokes that of Morgan and Anissa. It took place 60 years earlier, in 1954, in New Zealand.

Pauline Parker and Juliet Hulme met at their conservative all-girls' school in the Victorian city of Christchurch and became the closest of friends. Pauline was sixteen and Juliet only a few months younger. It was an unexpected friendship, as their families had little in common: Pauline's parents were working-class (her father ran a fish-and-chip shop), while Juliet's were wealthier and well traveled, from England, her father the rector of the local university. But the girls had something that drew them together: They'd both been sickly children—Pauline with osteomyelitis (which left her with a limp) and Juliet with pneumonia (which would lead to tuberculosis)—and that brought with it a peculiar kind of isolation. Excused from gym class, the pair spent that period walking through the yard holding hands; they spoke almost exclusively to each other. The headmistress took Juliet's mother aside to express her concern that the girls might be growing too close—but Hilda Hulme did not want to interfere.

From this closeness the two built a wholly immersive imaginative life. They bonded through regular sleepovers at Juliet's house, and the swapping of chapters of the baroque novels they were writing, packed with tales of doomed romance and adventure. Pauline was stocky and boyish, with short black hair and a scar running down one leg; Juliet's hair had blond highlights, and she was taller and slimmer and wore well-tailored clothes. Pauline shuffled when she walked and was often ready to lash out; Juliet carried herself with the elegance and easy confidence of an aristocrat. They called each other by secret pet names based on their fiction (Pauline was "Gina" and Juliet "Deborah"). They dreamed of running away together to America, where their work would be published to great acclaim and adapted for film. They rode their bikes far into the countryside, took off their jackets and shoes and socks, and danced until they were exhausted. Some late nights, Pauline would sneak away and ride her bike to Juliet's house, where Juliet would slip out through a balcony. They would steal a bottle of her parents' wine and drink it somewhere out on the grounds, or ride Juliet's horse through the dark woods.

On a bright June afternoon in 1954, Pauline and Juliet took a walk through a local park with Pauline's mother— the place was vast, with a few hiking paths cleared between the young pines and outcroppings of volcanic rock. When they'd gotten far enough away from any other visitors, Juliet provided a distraction—a pretty pink stone she planted on the ground—and as Honorah Parker bent down to take a look, Pauline removed a piece of brick she'd hidden in her bag, wrapped in a school stocking, and brought it down on her mother's head. The woman collapsed to the ground, and the girls took turns bludgeoning her—about forty-five blows to the head, her glasses knocked from her face, her dentures expelled from her mouth—until she was dead.

According to Pauline's journals, in the year leading up to the murder Pauline and Juliet had created their own religion, unimpressed by Christianity and inspired by elements in their lives both secular and sacred. They'd drawn on the

Hollywood movies at their local theater for their coterie of "saints" (Mario Lanza, Orson Welles, Mel Ferrer), erected a "temple" (dedicated to the Archangel Raphael and to Pan) in a secluded corner of Juliet's backyard, and marked their personal holidays with elaborate, choreographed rituals. They believed they could have visions at will—visions of a "4th World" (also called "Paradise" or "Paradisa"), a holier realm inhabited by only the most transcendent of artists, a plane of existence far above that of Pauline's father, with his fish-and-chip shop, or her undereducated mother. With enough practice, each would soon be able to read the other's mind. Each made the other singular and perfect.

What eventually drove Pauline and Juliet to kill Pauline's mother was the fear of being torn apart: Juliet's parents, who were separating, wanted Juliet to stay with her father's sister in Johannesburg while they prepared to return to England; Honorah had refused to allow Pauline to go along. If this were to happen, the world they'd built together—over so many daydreamy afternoons and secret nights out among the trees—would collapse. The girls could not permit that.

In April of 1954, Pauline wrote: "Anger against mother boiled up inside me. It is she who is one of the main obstacles in my path. Suddenly a means of ridding myself of the obstacle occurred to me." And then in June, a series of entries:

> We practically finished our books today and our main
> like for the day was to moider mother. This notion is
> not a new one, but this time it is a definite plan which

we intend to carry out. We have worked it all out and are both thrilled with the idea. Naturally we feel a trifle nervous but the anticipation is great.

We discussed our plans for moidering mother and made them a little clearer. Peculiarly enough I have no qualms of conscience (or is it peculiar we are so mad?).

I feel very keyed up as though I were planning a surprise party. So next time I write in this diary Mother will be dead. How odd yet how pleasing.

And early on the morning of June 22, on a page of her journal labeled, in curling letters, "The Day of the Happy Event": "I am writing a little of this up on the morning before the death. I felt very excited and 'The night before Christmas-ish' last night . . . I am about to rise!"

FOR FIVE MONTHS BEFORE THE STABBING, MORGAN AND Anissa discussed how they would kill their friend. They learned to speak in their own private code: "cracker" meant "knife"; "the itch" was the need to kill Bella; their final destination, the Nicolet National Forest, was "up north" or "the camping trip."

Like those girls in Christchurch, they were drawn to each other out of loneliness. Each saw the other as an affirmation of her uniqueness; they shared a hidden, ritualized world. Morgan and Anissa's private universe was spun not from the matinee idols and historical novels of the early 20th century but from the online fictions of our own time. They had devoted themselves to an internet bogeyman.

Like a fairy-tale monster, Slender Man emerged through a series of obscure clues, never fully visible. He first appeared online, in the summer of 2009, in two vague images that were quickly passed around horror and fantasy fan forums. In the first, dated 1983, a horde of young teenagers streams out of a wooded area toward the camera, while behind them looms a tall and pale spectral figure with its hand outstretched. The image is coupled with a message: "We didn't want to go, we didn't want to kill them, but its persistent silence and outstretched arms horrified and comforted us at the same time . . ." In the second photo, dated 1986, we see a playground full of little girls, all about six or seven years old. In the foreground, one pauses to face the camera, smiling, as she climbs a slide; in the background, in the shade of a cluster of trees, others gather around a tall figure in a dark suit. If you look closely, you can make out wavy arms or tentacles emanating from its back. A label states that the photo is notable for being taken on the day on which "fourteen children vanished," and as a record of "what is referred to as 'The Slender Man.'" Making this all the more meta-real, these photos were presented as "documents": the 1986 image bears a watermark from "City of Stirling Libraries"; the photographers, respectively, are listed as "presumed dead" and "missing."

These images were created by a 30-year-old elementary school teacher (Eric Knudsen, who goes by the name "Victor

Surge") in one of the collections of forums on the website Something Awful. Surge decided to take part in a new thread called "Create Paranormal Images." The game was to alter existing photographs using Photoshop and then post them on other paranormal forums in an attempt to pass them off as the real thing. The monster was deliberately vague, his story almost completely open-ended—and so the internet rushed in to make of him what it wanted. Bloggers and vloggers and forum members wrote intricate false confessionals of encounters with Slender Man and posted altered photographs and elaborate video series, all predicated on the assumption that "Slender" was a real entity and a real threat.

Over the next several years, the monster spread at an exponential rate, mainly through alternative-reality games—online texts and videos created by fans feeding off the narratives of other users in real time, creating a "networked narrative" that blurs the lines between reality and fiction. And as the story spread, it quickly lost its point of origin, becoming instead the creative nexus, for hundreds of thousands of users, of a dark, sprawling, real-time fairy tale. A sort of 4th World.

All that users knew at first was that Slender has the appearance of a lean man in a black suit, and there his humanoid features end. He is unnaturally tall—sometimes as tall as twelve feet—and where his face would be is only blanched, featureless skin, stretched taut as a sausage casing, with shallow indentations in place of eyes and mouth. Occasionally, when he shows himself, a ring of long, grasping black tentacles, like supple branches, emerges from his back. Slender Man's motives are unclear, but he is associated with sudden disappearance and death. And he has a pronounced appetite for children. Like a gothic Pied Piper, he calls the children out and leads them away from their world, never to be seen again. And when he allows them to stay in their suburban homes, he infects them with the desire to kill, and the longing to be initiated into his darkest, innermost circle.

Slender Man, his fans have decided, has a peculiar attachment to the woods. Any woods, anywhere. Elaborate Photoshopped images populate the internet—of Slender lurking in the trees at the edges of suburban backyards, or appearing in the background of snapshots taken by unsuspecting hikers. Scores of YouTube clips show twentysomethings running through the woods, chased by Slender Man (who sometimes even makes an appearance, in a bad suit, on stilts, with a white stocking over his head). And then there are the "archival" photos, of historical Slender Man sightings around the world. One of the most arresting images shows Slender standing among the massive pines of a half-felled forest behind children in what might be 19th-century dress: it could be an early photo of Appalachia, or perhaps the Black Forest (some believe the monster first emerged long ago in Germany, the birthplace of some of our darkest folktales).

For Slender's hundreds of thousands of online devotees, he was a trip, a monster they were crowdsourcing in real time. His many, many fans and cocreators were mostly college-age guys, or guys in their early 20s—people with a lot of time to devote to the unreal. But because the internet is so wide open, and because there were so many avenues leading to Slender—from video games like *Minecraft* (where Anissa Weier first discovered him) to alternate-reality games, entire YouTube channels, and fan-fiction forums—there was no way to control who was exposed to this new monster and what they made of him. Morgan and Anissa, among the youngest members of the Slenderverse, were quickly consumed by the swirling, open-ended storyline. They latched onto him as a source of private ritual, the linchpin in the occult universe they were building together.

From the beginning, their friendship was forged by a kind of urgency. Anissa, in particular, suffered from bullying after recently transferring to their school (a fact she kept from her parents) and needed this months-old bond with Morgan to last. (Morgan would later claim that she'd gone ahead with the stabbing to keep Anissa "happy": "It's, um, hard enough to make friends, I don't want to lose them over something like this.") Their bond was only heightened by the alternate reality they inhabited together.

The Slender Man phenomenon actually feeds on the divide between young people's reality and that of adults: he exists, he grows, in the gap between adolescents' intuitive sense of the truth—their willingness to embrace the mysteries—and the cool logic of their parents and teachers. "It should also be noted that children have been able to see [Slender] when no other adults in the vicinity could," reads one fan site. "Confiding these stories to their parents [is] met with the usual parental admonition: overactive imaginations."

The girls told each other they could see and hear Slender, and in her notebooks Morgan drew the image of the faceless man again and again.

IN SALEM, MASSACHUSETTS, IN 1692, A DARK STORY SPUN BY a cadre of teenage girls had radical real-world consequences. Their false accusations were as fantastic as any folktale—a form that had become popular in Europe earlier that century—and as starkly good-versus-evil as the biblical drama that their harsh Puritan community thrived upon.

The "afflicted girls" of Salem—Abigail Williams and ten others—charged their neighbors with consorting with the devil, and of tempting them to do the same. Abigail, then fourteen, openly rebelled against her stepmother and claimed to wander the woods at night. She told everyone who would listen that she had no fear and nothing could harm her—she'd made a pact with Satan! Most outrageous of all, she said that she'd taken part in a gathering of nine witches during which they'd consumed an unholy sacrament. "I will speak the truth," she told the crowd when called into court. "I have been very wicked."

As the Slender Man legend evolved, the shadowy figure operated more like the Satan of Puritan times. Posters claimed that anyone who learned about Slender was in danger of becoming obsessed with him through a kind of mind control; increasingly, he killed through others—humans known as his "proxies," his "husks," his "agents." He took possession of them, and they did his bidding.

The fairy-tale concept of evil lurking in the woods may be as old as the idea of Satan himself. And all of them—children's monsters, Slender Man, the Devil—are kept alive by the stories we tell one another. Abigail Williams claimed to have had a vision of elderly Rebecca Nurse offering her "the Devil's book"; in church, she cried out that she saw another of the village women perched high in the rafters, suckling a canary; she spotted malicious little men walking the streets of town recruiting new witches. Pauline Parker and Juliet Hulme's visions were more mystical and ethereal. Two months before the murder, over Easter vacation, Pauline stayed with Juliet and her family at the beach, and the pair had their first shared revelation. On Good Friday, out for a walk before sunrise, they saw what Pauline described as a "queer formation of clouds," "a gateway" into the 4th World. They suddenly realized that they had "an extra part of our brain which can appreciate the 4th World . . . [W]e may use the key and look into that beautiful world which we have been lucky enough to be allowed to know of."

As for Morgan and Anissa, in Waukesha, they, too, shared visions they claimed were tangible, hyperrealistic. Like the adults posting on Slender Man forums, the girls told each other that they were able to see "Slendy"—but with a vivid reality that set them apart from any healthy adult fan. According to Anissa, after she first told Morgan about the monster, Morgan claimed she'd spotted him when she was five, in a wooded area near her family's house. Anissa told Morgan that she'd seen him twice, in trees outside the window of the bus they shared to school.

When a detective questions Anissa shortly after her arrest, she asks, "So back in December or January, Morgan told you, 'Hey, we should be proxies,' basically?"

ANISSA: Yeah.

DETECTIVE: And you said what?

ANISSA: I said, "Okay, how do we do that?" And she said, "We have to kill Bella."

DETECTIVE: Okay. [Pause.] And do you know why she said that?

ANISSA: Because we had to supposedly prove ourselves worthy to Slender.

DETECTIVE: And what did you think of this?

ANISSA: I was surprised—but also kind of excited, 'cause I wanted proof that he existed. Because there are a bunch of skeptics out there saying that he didn't exist, and then there are a bunch of photos online and sources online saying that they did see him . . . So I decided to go along, to tag along, to prove skeptics wrong.

DETECTIVE: So did you think that you actually had to kill someone to do it?

ANISSA: Yeah.

DETECTIVE: Like, for real?

ANISSA: Mm-hmm.

About an hour into the interrogation, the detective asks Anissa, "When Morgan said to you, 'If we don't do this for Slender, our families and loved ones will be killed,' do you honestly believe that?" Anissa, crying, answers in an astonished-kid voice: "Well, yeah." More specifically, she believes that Slender Man "can easily kill my whole family in three seconds." Just hours earlier, during their long trek to the Nicolet National Forest, the girls had announced each time they'd caught a glimpse of him along the way—in the suburban woods, among the trees by the highway. They could hear the rustling of him following close by.

MORGAN GEYSER'S DRAWINGS OF SLENDER MAN VEER from stark, repetitive images evoking a phantom—a page covered in his symbol ("X"), a blank face with "Xs" for eyes—to the increasingly particular. In one pencil sketch, a girl with kitty-cat ears and tail lies on the ground, eyes closed, a skull floating above her head; looming over her is another humanoid kitty girl, who looks straight at the viewer, a scythe in one hand. The speech bubble above her head reads: I LOVE KILLING PEOPLE! And in the most elaborate image, a slim, bald, and faceless figure towers over a row of children; enormous, octopoid tentacles emerge from his back, like long black fingers. Above this Slender creature's head is written a message, as if to the artist herself: YOU ARE STRANGE CHILD . . . IT WILL BE OF MY USE.

In that inscription, an adolescent girl, channeling the voice of a monster, exiles herself—she is "strange" and warped—

only to accept herself again. The monster tells her, *Here in the Slenderverse, your strangeness is unique; your loneliness has a purpose; I am calling you to your destiny.* Just as in the 4th World, Pauline and Juliet's weirdness, their "madness," gives them psychic powers and untouchable brilliance. By some Brothers Grimm logic, a dark trial, a call to murder, becomes the girls' only prospect. On ten separate occasions in her interrogation, Morgan calls the stabbing "necessary."

In another sketch, a long-haired kid in a bloody sweatshirt looks as if she has thrown her arms around the neck of Slender Man, who embraces her in return. She is crying; his reddened cheeks are either bloodied or blushing. The two appear to be close, intimate; they are, perhaps, comforting each other. Here the meaning of that earlier inscription—HE STILL SEES YOU—seems to change. As if following the plotline of a teen romance, perhaps Slender's message has become, instead, I SEE WHO YOU REALLY ARE. Slender Man has inspired reams of online fan fiction, some of it romantic or even erotic, about teenage girls involved with the monster. Titles include "My Dear Slenderman," "Into the Darkness," "Love Is All I Want," "To Love a Monster," "I Slept with Slender Man," and "Slenderman's Loving Arms." A few of these stories have some 150,000 reads.

The occult is orphic, a word meant to evoke Orpheus and his dark romance. An ancient Greek myth tells of how, after the death of the musician's wife, he followed her into the underworld—only to fail at his one chance to bring her back to life. To build a private, occult world with someone is to travel with them into the dark—and the danger inherent in that is, inevitably, erotic.

Months before her mother's murder, Pauline Parker was sent to see a doctor at the suggestion of Juliet Hulme's father: he was concerned that his daughter's friend might be a lesbian. At their trial, there was much speculation about a possible sexual relationship between the two—a romance perhaps born out of their shared writings and nighttime escapades in the garden. Even putting aside the possibility of a lesbian romance, any sexuality for an unmarried woman, never mind a girl, was liability enough in the 1950s. When the case went to trial, the Crown prosecutor asked his witnesses leading questions about "orgies" and "sexual passion."

And what of the girls of Salem, and what they claimed to have seen of the dark? Abigail Williams was made notorious by Arthur Miller's 1953 play *The Crucible* (which premiered, incidentally, the same year Pauline and Juliet met); she became the lead harpy, the great finger pointer, a 17-year-old girl capable of sending men and women to their deaths, embittered by her affair with local farmer John Proctor. But, in reality, Abigail was only 11 in 1692, and Proctor was 60. Miller made large assumptions about what shaped her; he spun her story into one of young female sexuality as a corrupting force. In Miller's play, she has suddenly come into the sexuality of an adult, but with an adolescent's inability to control her impulses. A new darkness—a dark eroticism and sexual envy—infuses his character's thoughts, has lured her out into the woods, out past the borders of good society, in search of a hex. And when she levels her accusations, her conviction is as compelling, as unassailable, as that of a child.

At the same time, in both Christchurch and Waukesha, the attacks were striking in their childishness. In spite of the girls' months of secret talks and journaling and to-do lists, when carried out, the attacks were stupid and clumsy; they had no idea what they were doing. Some of the details they had thought through were fairy-tale-specific: Juliet's idea to distract Honorah Parker with a pink gemstone she placed on the park path; Anissa's idea to lead Bella into the woods through the offer of a game of hide-and-seek. Think of the fact that Morgan and Anissa could still lure their friend into the woods through such a simple game; the bursts of energy with which that game is played; and Bella "hiding" from people she should truly have hidden from. Picture her attackers out there in the suburban woods, playing in high spirits—and then turning to another game, a dare, passing the knife back and forth between themselves until Anissa gives an order clear enough to bring their play to an end. That morning, Morgan brought the knife with her in the way that she might have brought a wand to a Harry Potter movie screening. And perhaps she believed that she could perform magic with a toy—but that idea brought with it no real-world consequences. Playing with a knife, of course, did.

Their childish incomprehension of the gravity of violence, and the callousness that comes with that, is painfully evident in the girls' interviews while in custody. When Anissa describes her nervousness as they approached the playground that morning, the detective asks what she was most nervous about. She answers, "Seeing a dead person. 'Cause the last time I saw a dead person it was at a funeral and it was my uncle." When asked what Morgan was upset about in the park, Anissa says, "Killing. She had never done that before. She'd stabbed apples before—with, like, chopsticks—but she'd never actually cut a flesh wound into somebody."

Pauline and Juliet continued to behave like immature girls, unaware of what was at stake, even after their arrest. When Pauline was taken into custody alone—at first, police believed Juliet was not directly involved—she didn't want to break her habit of journaling, and so she wrote a new entry, stating that she'd managed to pull off the "moider" and was "taking the blame for everything." (A detective on the case quickly seized it as evidence.) Once both girls were at the station, sharing a cell, they were placed on suicide watch—but they spent their first night (a police officer would later report) gossiping in their bunk beds, unconcerned about their new environment. During the trial, about a dozen foreign publications were represented in the courtroom, with most British newspapers printing a half column daily, often on their front page—rare attention for a New Zealand case. In a courtroom packed with spectators, Pauline and Juliet were out of sync with the tone of the proceedings. Seated together in the dock, they appeared relaxed and indifferent, often whispering excitedly to each other and smiling. One journalist described their attitude throughout as one of "contemptuous amusement."

Then there is the physical fact of just how young all four of these girls were at the time of their crimes, Morgan and Anissa in particular—something driven home by their regular images in the press. Morgan's and Anissa's faces are recognizable. Their booking photos, published as a single split-screen image, are iconic: these suspects have the round cheeks and unfashionable eyeglasses of children. Photos from their first hearings three and a half years ago show the two in dark blue jail uniforms, their handcuffed wrists locked to shackles around their waists; at the same time, they are petite (the size of 12-year-olds) and flat-chested. By their 2016 hearings, both girls, photographed in an array of cotton day dresses, have clearly entered puberty, with developed breasts; their bodies are transforming into those of young women right in front of us, their adolescence taking place in captivity. Anissa's hair, once cut just below her chin, now falls a few inches below her shoulders. Here it is made visible: the uneasy border between "child" and "adult," between the softness of girlhood, still visible in their baby fat, and the latent sexual threat of early womanhood. Did the changes in their bodies increase the chance of them paying a greater price for their crime?

WISCONSIN LAW ALLOWS FOR ANYONE AGE TEN OR ABOVE to be tried as an adult for a violent crime. This ratchets the stakes up much, much higher: Both Morgan and Anissa were initially charged with first-degree intentional homicide, facing up to 45 years in prison (they each pled not guilty for reason of mental illness or defect). If the judge had allowed both their cases to be moved to juvenile court, they would have remained in a juvenile facility, set for release at 18.

In the earliest days of this country, American jurisprudence followed the doctrine of *malitia supplet aetatem*—or, as translated, "malice supplies the age." Following the example of English common law, a child of seven or older who understood the difference between right and wrong—as if these were simple, stable concepts—could be held fully accountable. He could even be eligible for the death penalty. As Blackstone's *Commentaries* summed it up in the 1760s, "one lad of eleven years old may have as much cunning as another of fourteen." It was not until more than a century after the founding of the United States, in 1899, that a juvenile court system was established. Industrialization had made clearer the need to protect children as a separate class—or, in Jane Addams's words, to create a court that would ideally play the role of the "kind and just parent."

But the biggest shift in juvenile justice has been our evolving understanding of the adolescent brain. Neuroscience research has shown that the prefrontal cortex is not fully developed until 25 years old, impairing a person's impulse control. There is also the lack of emotional development: the Supreme Court has described adolescence as "a time of immaturity, irresponsibility, impetuousness, and recklessness." As recently as 2005, the court outlawed the execution of minors as "cruel and unusual punishment," in a case in which the American Medical Association and the American Psy-

chological Association filed briefs on new research into adolescent brain development. The same ruling leaned heavily
on a 2002 case that prohibited the execution of individuals
with intellectual disabilities: Because juveniles are immature,
"their irresponsible conduct is not as morally reprehensible as
that of an adult." The Supreme Court was not arguing that
adolescence is a kind of mental disability, but perhaps that
both share symptoms in common—vulnerability, instability,
a skewed or heightened worldview—that render their actions
harder to judge.

One of the earliest entries into the Grimms' original
collection—one that would never make it into the later, popular edition—is a story called "How Some Children Played
at Slaughtering." Like all the Grimms' folktales, it is short
and terse, and it goes something like this: In a small city in
the Netherlands, a group of children are playing, and they
decide that one should be the "butcher," one the "assistant,"
two the "cooks," and another, finally, the "pig." Armed with
a knife, the little butcher pushes the pig to the ground and
slits his throat, while the assistant kneels down with a bowl
to catch the blood, to use in "making sausages."

The kids are discovered by an adult, and the butcher boy
is taken before the city council. But the council doesn't know
what to do, "for they realized it had all been part of a children's game." And so the chief judge decides to perform a
test: he takes an apple in one hand and a gold coin in the
other and holds them out to the boy; he tells him to pick one.

The boy chooses the apple—laughing as he does, because

in his mind, he's gotten the better deal. Still operating by a child's logic, he cannot be convicted of the crime. The judge sets him free.

IN THE MONTHS BEFORE BELLA'S STABBING IN 2014, MOR-gan Geyser, nearly 12, was both entering into adolescence (she had just gotten her period) and descending into mental illness.

After her initial five-hour interview came to an end, Morgan, still without her parents, in clothes and slippers provided by the Waukesha Police, was placed in the Washington County Jail for juveniles. Anissa was there, too, but they were not allowed to interact. Morgan could have no visitors other than her parents, who were required to sit on the other side of a glass divider; only after a few months into her stay was she permitted to touch or hold them, and even then only twice a month. Over the summer, she became, as her mother, Angie, described her, "floridly psychotic." She continued to have conversations with Slender Man, as well as characters from the Harry Potter series (at one point, she claimed that Severus Snape kept her up until three a.m.); she saw unicorns; she treated the ants in her cell like pets.

In the fall of that year, Morgan was moved to the Winnebago Mental Health Institute for a few months of 24-hour observation, to determine if she had a chance of being competent enough to stand trial. There, she was given a psychological evaluation that concluded that she suffers from early-onset schizophrenia—very rare for someone so young.

Her state-appointed doctor learned that Morgan, since the age of three, had been experiencing "vivid dreams which she wished she could change"; and in the third grade, she began "seeing images pop up on the wall in different colors." She believed she could see ghosts and feel their embrace. At a hearing in December 2014, the judge found Morgan capable of standing trial and ordered her back to Winnebago for treatment—but the facility could no longer take her, now that she had been deemed "competent." Her parents asked for her $500,000 bail to be reduced to a signature bond so that she could be moved to a group home for girls with mental and emotional issues, but the request was denied because the home was not considered secure enough.

By late 2015, Morgan Geyser, diagnosed with schizophrenia, was still not being treated for her disease. She'd become attached to her visions and feared losing them, her only companions in her isolation. Alongside her "friends," she wandered through the forest of her thoughts.

CARL JUNG TOOK LONG WALKS THROUGH THE SPRAWL-ing Black Forest as a teenager, during which he improvised his own strain of Pagan mysticism, communing with the trees. He spoke of that same wilderness in a lecture in 1935, as the opening setting of the 15th-century romance *Hypnero-tomachia Poliphili*. The novella begins, "At length my ignorant sleepes, brought me into a thick wood," and then descends, as Jung describes it, "into the underworld of the psyche." Jung said that forests, as dream imagery, were "symbols for secret depths where unknown beings live." (His mentor, Sigmund Freud, wrote of his own method of analysis as a walk through "a dark forest.") In Jung's *Liber Novus* (also known as *The Red Book*), completed around 1930, he wrote of the nature of the human imagination: "Thoughts are natural events that you do not possess, and whose meaning you only imperfectly recognize . . . [T]houghts grow in me like a forest, populated by different animals."

Morgan's hallucinations—magical characters speaking to her, imaginary friends, lifted from the pages of books or the internet—are grounded in something more specific: her genetic inheritance. Her father, Matt, began his lifelong struggle with schizophrenia at 14 years old (he receives government assistance due to his illness). In a recent documentary, *Beware the Slenderman*, he talks about his coping mechanisms for living with schizophrenia: He runs numbers in his head and tries to "put up static" to block out his visual and auditory hallucinations. Matt and his wife, Angie, decided early on to delay sharing the fact of Matt's illness with their daughter until she grew older—why make her fearful of a genetically inherited disease that she might never have to face? She'd shown no clear warning signs.

In the film, Matt Geyser describes a life in which the boundaries between the real and the unreal are painfully blurred and an intellectual understanding of the difference is not enough to protect you. If, earlier on, he had decided to share his burden with Morgan, this is the picture he might have drawn for her: "Right now there's, like, patterns of, like, light and, like, geometric shapes that's like, always racing—like always, like right now. Everything seems normal to me 'cause this is my everything; this is how I've always seen things." But the more threatening hallucinations—including, he says, a "glaring demon-devil"—are more complicated. "You can, like, see it, and, like, you know it's not real. But it totally doesn't matter because you're, like, terrified of it," he says, becoming emotional. "I know the devil's not in the backseat, but—the devil is in the backseat. You know?"

In January 2016, after 19 months without treatment, Morgan was finally committed to a state mental hospital and put on antipsychotics. By spring, her attorney claimed that her hallucinations were receding and her condition was improving rapidly. But in May of that year, after two years of incarceration, Morgan attempted to cut her arm with a broken pencil and was placed on suicide watch.

Late this September, Morgan accepted a plea bargain, agreeing to be placed in a mental institution indefinitely and thus avoiding the possibility of prison. Just weeks earlier, Anissa had also accepted a deal, pleading guilty to the lesser charge of attempted second-degree homicide. A jury recommended she be sent to a mental hospital for at least three years.

THE JOINT TRIAL OF PAULINE PARKER AND JULIET HULME also hinged on the question of their mental health. Were the girls delusional? Clinically paranoid? Or had they been completely aware of the consequences of their actions and chosen to go ahead with their plan regardless? The defense argued that the girls had been swept up in a folie à deux, or "madness between two"—a rarely cited, now-questionable diagnosis of a psychosis developed by two individuals socially isolated together. The crime was too sensational and the defense too exotic for the jury to be persuaded. They deliberated for a little over two hours before finding the girls guilty.

Juliet got the worst of it. She was sent to Mount Eden Prison in Auckland, notorious for its infestation of rats and its damp, cold cells (particularly bad for an inmate who'd recently suffered from TB). There Juliet slept on a straw mattress and had one small window she could not see out of; the bathrooms had no doors, and sanitary napkins were made from strips of cloth. She split her time between prison work (scrubbing floors, making uniforms in the sewing room) and writing material the superintendent called "sexy stuff." She gorged herself on poetry: Byron, Shelley, Tennyson, Omar Khayyam. She taught herself Italian—she dreamed of making a living as either a writer or a diva of the Italian opera—and she bragged in a letter that she and Pauline were exquisite singers. She also bragged about her studies, even her talent in knitting—she bragged incessantly. In a letter to a friend, Juliet's father worried that she was "still up in the clouds . . . completely removed and occupied with herself and her grandiose ideas about poetry and writing." Five months after the crime, Juliet was "still much the same as she was immediately after the event. She feels that she is right and others are wrong." She remained unbowed, still immersed in literature and a vision of the great artist she could become. These were "delusions" she was not willing to let go of.

In spite of the harsh conditions of Juliet's incarceration, the girls' sentences were ultimately lenient. After five and a half years, both were released by order of the executive council, and each was able to start her life over under an alias.

Juliet Hulme, now Anne Perry, moved to England; using the shorthand she learned in prison, she got a job as a secretary. But she hadn't lost sight of her and Pauline's plan to one day move to California. When she was turned down for a visa (her criminal history was hard to overlook), she began working as a stewardess for an airline that often flew to the United States. One day, upon arriving in Los Angeles, she disembarked and never got back on the plane. She rented a lousy apartment, took on odd jobs, and wrote regularly. By her 30s, back in England, she'd launched a career as a crime novelist. She has since published more than 50 novels, selling over 25 million books worldwide.

In one of her earlier novels, the lead murder suspects seem inspired by Pauline and Juliet: a slightly androgynous suffragette and the taller, radiant, protective woman with whom she lives. They are brilliant and fearless; the suffragette's partner is exalted as having "a dreamer's face, the face of one who would follow her vision and die for it." In a later book, the detective-protagonist seems to speak for the unconventional mores of the author herself when he states that "to care for any person or issue enough to sacrifice greatly for it was the surest sign of being wholly alive. What a waste of the essence of a man that he should never give enough of himself to any cause, that he should always hear the passive, cowardly voice uppermost which counts the cost and puts caution first. One would grow old with the power of one's soul untested . . ."

The next chapter of Pauline's life was not marked by such bravado. She became Hilary Nathan and eventually moved to a small village in South East England. There she purchased a farmworker's cottage and stables, and taught mentally disabled children at a nearby school; she attended daily mass at the local Catholic church. After retiring, she gave riding lessons at her home. When her identity and location were revealed in the press in 1997, Pauline, then 59, quickly sold her property and disappeared.

She left behind an elaborate mural, on the wall of her bedroom, that the buyers believed she had painted herself—a collection of scenes that are part fairy-tale illustration, part religious allegory. Near the bottom, there is an image of a girl with dark, wavy hair (like her own) diving underwater to grasp an icon of the Virgin Mary; in another, the same girl—as a winged angel, naked and ragged—is locked in a birdcage. At the mural's peak, a beautiful blonde (a girl who resembles Juliet) sits astride a Pegasus—glowing, exuberant, arms outstretched. And the blonde appears again, on horseback, seemingly about to take flight, as the Pauline figure tries to bridle the animal.

On display in these images is both the narcissism of adolescence and the remorse of adulthood, the penance of a woman who has resolved to receive the sacrament every single day. And what bridges these two elements is an image at the mural's center: the Pauline girl seated, head bowed, under a dying tree against a dying landscape. The occult language of nature—those late nights in the garden, those dark plans in the woods—had nothing left to give her. It had lost its Pagan power.

A POWERFUL NARCISSISM IS IN FULL VIEW DURING THE interrogation of Anissa Weier. After being arrested for the stabbing of Bella Leutner, the first question Anissa asks the detective is not about her friend's condition (that would not happen until two and a half hours later) but about how far she and Morgan had walked that day—"'Cause I'm not usually very athletic and I just wanna know." She seems very impressed by the challenges they faced on their long walk after leaving Bella, harping on the distance, the threat of heat exhaustion and mosquitoes, going without an allergy pill all day ("Is it bad?"), and the limited snacks (the granola bar she'd packed was "disgusting"; the Kudos bar was much better). She recounts with incredible precision everything she and Morgan ate that day, including free treats at a furniture store (a glass of lemonade and two cookies each). Near the end of her interview, she seems about to share a revelation with the detective:

ANISSA: I just realized something.
DETECTIVE: What's that?
ANISSA: If I don't go to school on Monday, that'll be the first day that I miss of school.

Anissa was later diagnosed with a "shared delusional belief"—a condition that faded the longer she was separated from Morgan. Her parents had gotten divorced just the year before and, along with the bullying at her new school, she'd been upset, unmoored—but otherwise mentally stable. While it is fairly easy, based on the video footage, to believe that something is wrong with Morgan—she is detached, spaced-out—it seems quite clear that Anissa is not ill. She appears more frightened than Morgan, more in touch with the reality of the situation, crying occasionally throughout. She doesn't read as flighty; she doesn't speak in a distant, spooky voice; she seems upset, but grounded. She answers questions with the eagerness and precision of a girl who wants to be the best student in class. And this is precisely why it's so upsetting to watch footage of the following exchange, about the immediate aftermath of the stabbing:

DETECTIVE: So [Bella] was screaming?

ANISSA: Mm-hmm. And then, um, afterwards, to try to keep her quiet, I said, "Sit down, lay down, stop screaming—you'll lose blood slower." And she tried complaining that she couldn't breathe and that she couldn't see.

DETECTIVE: So she started screaming, "I hate you, I trusted you"?

ANISSA: Mm-hmm.

DETECTIVE: She got up?

ANISSA: Yeah. She got up and tried to walk towards the street . . . It led to the other side of Big Ben Road.

DETECTIVE: So she tried to walk towards the street and what happened?

ANISSA: And then she collapsed and said that she couldn't see and she couldn't breathe and also that she couldn't walk. And so then Morgan and I kind of directed her away from the road and said that home was this way—and we were going deeper into the forest area.

DETECTIVE: So she said—she fell down and said she couldn't breathe or see.

ANISSA: Mm-hmm. Or walk.

DETECTIVE: Or walk. And you had told her to—

ANISSA: To "lay down and be quiet—you'll lose blood slower." And that we're going to get help.

DETECTIVE: But you really weren't going to get her help, right?

ANISSA: Mm, no.

At this point in the interview, Anissa is wrapped in a large wool blanket. The detective handed it to her because the space is chilly. Perhaps she was trying to gain Anissa's confidence, or perhaps it was simply instinctive, offering comfort to a young girl being held in a concrete room. Anissa has been crying—but whether this is from genuine remorse or a kid's fear of getting into trouble is anyone's guess. The look on her face does not tell us enough. And now the detective reads it back to her, the story of two girls who led their friend into the woods.

Originally published by the *Virginia Quarterly Review*, fall 2017

# The End of Evil

### BY SARAH MARSHALL

The crowd was growing. Hundreds had gathered across the road from the prison, bundled against the midwinter chill and warming themselves with a clever vendor's coffee and doughnuts. Though dawn had not yet broken, the ground was littered with beer cans. Celebrants lit sparklers, strangers joined in song, and children did their best to stay awake. One family, the Cochrans, told reporters they had left their home in Orlando, Florida, at two o'clock in the morning so they could be sure not to miss the festivities. They had brought their six-year-old twins, Jennifer and May Nicole, because, Mrs. Cochran said, "I thought it would be educational for them, kind of like a field trip."

The throng had appeared as if from nowhere: the day before, there was only one man waiting outside Florida State Prison. His name was George Johnson, and when the camera crews found him, he was standing beside the trunk of his car, selling T-shirts for ten dollars apiece. "Do you think it's appropriate," a reporter asked him, "to be making money off some man's execution?"

"I don't see why not," George said. "He—"

The broadcast cut him off. Everyone already knew what he did.

Within hours, George was doing a brisk business. Printed in the bright red of cartoon blood, his T-shirts showed a sweating, wide-eyed man strapped into an electric chair, staring out at the viewer with an expression that managed to seem both helpless and imperious. The words splashed above him read BURN BUNDY BURN. The shirts were selling particularly well, George said, among women.

Ted Bundy had been on Florida's death row for nearly a decade, after receiving three death sentences in two separate trials, for the 1978 murders of three victims who could be called young women but could also just as fairly be called girls: 20-year-old Lisa Levy, 21-year-old Margaret Bowman, and 12-year-old Kimberly Leach. Now, in the early hours of January 24, 1989, it seemed Bundy's time was finally about to run out.

When Ted Bundy was apprehended in Pensacola in the early hours of February 15, 1978, six weeks after he escaped from a Colorado jail, the FBI had already publicly linked him to thirty-six murders across five states. In the ensuing decade, both the random speculations of onlookers and the educated guesses of law enforcement often pushed the number far higher. Many said it had to be a hundred or more, and cited Bundy's own enigmatic statement to the Pensacola detectives who had questioned him about the FBI's claim. "He said the figure probably would be more correct in the three digits," Deputy Sheriff Jack Poitinger said.

Ron Holmes, a criminal justice professor who interviewed Bundy on two occasions, claimed that the total was 365, and that Bundy had raped and killed his first victim at the age of eleven. "Ted Bundy is not insane," Holmes told the press. "Ted Bundy knows the difference between right and wrong. But Ted Bundy does what he wants to do when he wants to do it." Holmes hadn't taped either of his interviews with Bundy, but he didn't need that kind of proof to convince people of what they already wanted to believe.

Ted Bundy was everywhere and nowhere, guilty of everything because he had admitted to nothing—nothing, that is, until the last few days before his scheduled execution. Then, as Florida restaurants put up signs advertising Bundy fries and Bundy barbecues and vendors stocked up on electric chair–shaped lapel pins, Bundy said he was ready to confess—for a price. He would describe every murder he had committed, but only in exchange for a stay of execution. He needed a few more months to tell the whole story, he said, but he was willing to meet with investigators from around the country to show that he was serious. He would answer their questions if they would advocate for his life.

Florida governor Bob Martinez remained unmoved. "Justice has been on hold for a decade," he announced, "and it's about time that Ted Bundy paid for his crimes." To the viewers across the country who tuned in to watch the countdown to Bundy's execution, it was hard to imagine that the man whose name had become synonymous with the term "psychopath" deserved to draw another breath.

"'Ted Bundy' is to serial killers," Bundy's postconviction lawyer Polly Nelson once wrote, "as 'Kleenex' is to disposable handkerchiefs: The brand name that stands for all others." In America, in the decades since Ted Bundy's crimes, captures, trials, and resulting infamy, the term "serial killer" has itself become a kind of brand name for evil, one promising an ever-familiar fable about inhuman darkness disguised in human form, appearing out of nowhere, and terrorizing humanity until humanity can destroy it.

"If it should ever occur to you to relate this to anybody," Ted Bundy told one of the detectives he confessed to in the hours before his death, "you can tell them that I get no secret joy or pleasure out of it. That my own special kind of hell and madness that I lived in ten, twenty years ago was as wrong and as terrible as it could be. And I'm sorry."

Is it possible to see this apology as genuine? Is there any sense in trying? Ted Bundy is the textbook psychopath who shows us how to recognize the evil in our midst. His story is the story we all know. And yet the longer you listen to it—and listen not just to the legend, but to the people who knew Ted Bundy, and even to the man himself—the more you will find yourself hearing the story of a man who was not a mastermind, was not a genius, and who seems to have understood as little about what motivated him as the people around him did. As you draw closer to its center—and closer and closer to the demon core—you may begin to feel that the longer you spend inside this story, the less sense you can find.

IN THE FALL OF 1974, TED BUNDY MOVED AWAY FROM Seattle to start his first year of law school in Utah, and left behind not just an adoring girlfriend, a proud family, and a vast circle of friends, but a region in panic. Between February and July of 1974, eight young women had gone missing—seven in Washington and one in Oregon—and local detectives had few leads. Almost all they had to go on was the fact that on the day both Janice Ott and Denise Naslund vanished in broad daylight from Lake Sammamish State Park, a man in a cast had been seen introducing himself to various women and asking them to help him move his boat. One woman accompanied the man as far as the parking lot and noticed that he drove a light brown Volkswagen Beetle. No one saw him approach 18-year-old Denise, who disappeared after she left her friends to go to the bathroom, but a witness did overhear the man introducing himself to Janice, a 23-year-old social worker who was sunbathing when a stranger knelt beside her and asked for help.

"Sit down and let's talk about it," Janice said. To the witness who later described their interaction to the police, the conversation seemed warm and friendly. The man promised he would give Janice a ride in his boat, and in the meantime, he introduced himself. His name was Ted.

Later, media accounts of what were then known as "the Ted Murders" suggested that Washington police immediately realized they had a repeat offender on their hands, and that the killer had held Seattle in his thrall since the disappearance of his first known victim, Lynda Healy, in the early hours of February 1. In fact, it wasn't until "Ted" turned up at Lake Sammamish, nearly six months later, that the now eight missing persons cases were linked.

It was also the first time some of the cases had received significant investigation. Despite the eerie circumstances surrounding the disappearances—Donna Manson had left a pot of soup on a burner turned to warm in her Evergreen State College dorm room; Kathy Parks had left her desk lamp on in her room at Oregon State University; Susan Rancourt had just put a load of clothes in the dormitory washing machine when she vanished from Central Washington State College—police officers were still inclined to dismiss the girls as runaways until they were overwhelmed by evidence to the contrary. Sometimes even that wasn't enough. After Lynda Healy, a 21-year-old University of Washington student, disappeared from her own bedroom in the middle of the night, her housemates pulled back her covers to find that both Lynda's pillow and the mattress beneath it were soaked with blood. The police were unimpressed. Probably, they said, Lynda woke up with a bad nosebleed and took herself to the hospital. She was sure to turn up soon. Detectives believed their alternate explanation for the bloodstains also ruled out the possibility of foul play: "Because they assumed Lynda

Healy was possibly having her period at the time of her disappearance," wrote Bob Keppel, the King County detective who would help head the area's "Ted Squad" task force, "[the police] couldn't figure out why anyone would kidnap her—they assumed no kidnapper would want to have sex with her."

The "Ted" killer's "method of operation seemed flawless, almost scholarly, leaving his hapless pursuers on the police task force very little in the way of clues," Keppel wrote of the investigation in his book about the case, *The Riverman*. Yet for nearly six months—quite possibly for longer—the killer had evaded the police in part because of their own blindness. Because they assumed Lynda had simply walked off into the night, the officers who investigated her disappearance didn't see the need to dust her room for fingerprints or to test a semen stain they found on her sheets. What evidence they did remove from the scene was destroyed six months later, as routine then dictated in a missing persons case—well before the police were able to conclusively link Lynda's disappearance to the seven that followed: Donna Manson the following month, then Susan Rancourt, then Kathy Parks, Brenda Ball, Georgann Hawkins, Janice Ott, and Denise Naslund, and then . . .

There was nothing to worry about, until suddenly there was. After Janice and Denise both disappeared from Lake Sammamish in a single afternoon, the police started paying attention. So did the press. "Our investigation collapsed under the volume of unsolicited tips and Ted sightings," Keppel wrote, "because we had no way to manage the information that was suddenly pouring in . . . the backlog of calls was so huge that Denise Naslund herself could have called in and told us she was fine and we wouldn't have found the message for a week."

The missing persons case turned into a homicide investigation on September 7, 1974, when two grouse hunters found a human skull, spinal column, and rib cage on a wooded mountainside overlooking Interstate 90, east of Seattle. Searchers found a second spine and jawbone the following day. And in the underbrush there was one final clue: three grease spots—remnants of the oil that soaked into the earth as three bodies lay side by side, disintegrating until they were nothing but bones. By the following day, investigators had identified two of the three sets of remains: they belonged to Janice Ott and Denise Naslund.

"The worst we feared is true," King County detective Nick Mackie told the press.

The news terrified the region. This was not the kind of destruction locals were used to, and it suggested that something was changing, that something might already be gone. In the past, a local woman told Tacoma's *News Tribune*, "murder was something you read about happening in California or somewhere. Now it's right in our backyards." Captain Herb Swindler of the Seattle Police Department consulted a psychic about the case and argued that a "demon cult" might be to blame, while others theorized that "Ted" was the Zodiac Killer, or a disciple of the Manson Family. Yet even as investigators dealt with the public's mounting terror, they still found time to undermine one another's work. When the Seattle Police Department and the King County Sheriff's Office created a combined task force, King County officers withheld information from the Seattle PD, worried that the competing jurisdiction might solve the case first and steal the glory. The joint task force folded within weeks. If nothing else, Bob Keppel would later recall, the people they investigated were always cooperative. "Everyone that we talked to as a suspect was helpful," Keppel told Bundy biographers Stephen G. Michaud and Hugh Aynesworth. "Even the best suspects, the murderers we talked to. 'Hey, man, I kill people,' they'd say. 'But I don't kill like that.'"

Throughout the blistering summer of 1974, as the rest of the country followed President Nixon's impeachment and the removal of US troops from Vietnam, Seattle residents waited for a break in the "Ted" case. It was a time when women feared for their safety, and men professed fear for the women they loved—men including Ted Bundy. Later his mother would remember a night when Ted, while visiting his family in Tacoma, watched his younger half sister, Sandra, get ready for a date. "Ted said to me, 'You know, Mom, she looks like all those other girls,'" Louise Bundy told *Seattle Times* reporter Richard Larsen. "'I hope you know where she's going and who she's with.'"

Ted was equally protective of his girlfriend, Liz, and her young daughter. Liz was a 24-year-old single mother when she moved to Seattle in 1969, and she had been in town only a few weeks when she met Ted in a University District tavern. Liz, shy about her secretarial job, said she worked making heart valves in the university's medical instruments department. Ted, 23 and still years away from finishing his bachelor's degree, said he was a law student writing a book about Vietnam. Both were pretending to be other people and seemed to find a sense of safety in each other. "It's as if we knew each other before in some former life," Liz remembered Ted telling her, after they had been dating for a few weeks. He became not just a boyfriend but a member of the family—and he adored Liz's daughter, reading to her, baking a chocolate cake for her fifth birthday, and watching Saturday-morning cartoons with her while Liz slept in. "Their favorite was *Dudley Do-Right of the Mounties*," Liz wrote in *The Phantom Prince*, her memoir of their relationship. "Ted could mimic Dudley perfectly."

The relationship that started with mutual lies soon seemed one in which they kept no secrets from each other. "My story about making heart valves had become a joke," Liz wrote. "Every Sunday night Ted would say, 'Well, you'd better get to sleep early so you'll be rested up for making those heart valves tomorrow.'" And Ted allowed Liz into his life, joking about the sulfurous "Tacoma aroma" that shrouded his working-class hometown, introducing her to his mother and stepfather, and weeping when he told Liz he was illegitimate: he had never known his father, and his mother had given birth to him when she was a teenager, something he said he did not learn until he was a teenager himself.

But Ted had big dreams. He was going to law school. He was going to make a name for himself. Liz supported Ted financially, since, she said, "neither of us doubted wealth was in Ted's future. He was marked for success." She was also sure they would get married and start a family. At first, Ted seemed to agree. They got engaged in early 1970, but Ted quickly broke it off. They were too poor, he said. They weren't ready. Liz got pregnant, and had an abortion at Ted's urging. Ted applied to law schools, and was devastated when he was accepted only at his last choice, the University of Utah. Their relationship stagnated. Ted saw other women. Liz got jealous. Liz saw other men. Ted got jealous. And gradually Liz saw a new pattern of behavior emerging: Ted would be cold and absent one day, then reappear the next, warm and present, showering her with declarations of his love.

Around the same time, Liz noticed another pattern: young women were disappearing across the Pacific Northwest. One woman, Georgann Hawkins, vanished en route to her sorority house, which was only three blocks from Liz's apartment. "Like most women living in the University District," Liz wrote, "I was deeply disturbed by these disappearances. Walking at night from my garage to my front door scared me." She might have felt safer if Ted had been around to protect her, but he seemed more distant than ever. "I was hurt that he hardly ever wanted to make love," she wrote. "There had to be someone else. I wished I knew what she was like so I could be more like her."

Sometimes Liz even wondered whether her Ted was the "Ted" the police were searching for—worries she usually dismissed as quickly as she allowed herself to entertain them. He had a VW, but so did she. She had found plaster of Paris in his dresser—the same kind a person would use to put together a makeshift cast like the one witnesses had described—but he told her he had it in case he actually did break something. And the composite sketch didn't look like her Ted, but the description sounded like him: the tennis whites; the unusual, almost East Coast–sounding accent; and the story about the sailboat. Ted didn't have a boat, but he always talked about getting one someday.

When Liz could find no other way to ignore her suspicions, she thought of how they might damage Ted's future. "I visualized Ted and me married," she wrote. "He would be campaigning for governor when it was revealed that his devoted wife had gone to the police in 1974, claiming that he was a murderer." But in October, about a month after Ted left for Utah, Liz finally found she couldn't ignore her fears any longer. One of her friends went home to Salt Lake City to visit family and learned about the recent murder of a local teenager named Melissa Smith. "I don't want to scare you," she told Liz, "but it's happening in Utah."

That month, Liz called the King County Police Department's tip line. Soon afterward, her suspicions again gave way to guilt. She didn't have to worry: her tip immediately vanished beneath a drift of paperwork about likelier suspects. The Ted Squad wouldn't begin investigating her Ted until August 1975. By then, he had already been arrested in Utah.

Ted Bundy was arrested for the first time not for murder, rape, or kidnapping, but because he'd gotten lost. One warm night, he was driving around a Salt Lake City suburb when he got disoriented and pulled over to find his bearings. When he got back on the road, he noticed a car tailing him. He would later deny he knew it was a patrol car until he ran a red light and saw police lights behind him. Then, he said, he did what any law-abiding citizen would do: he pulled over and did his best to cooperate. He allowed the police to search his car, where they found an ice pick, a pantyhose mask, a ski mask, several pieces of rope, a pair of handcuffs, and a crowbar.

The tools looked suspicious—like a burglary kit, maybe— but at a meeting three days after the arrest, Detective Daryle Ondrak still hesitated before mentioning the search. "I don't know if this means anything," Ondrak said, "but I was involved with a stop this weekend and the guy had a pair of handcuffs in his car." As Ondrak described the man— well-spoken, apparently educated, and driving a tan VW— Detective Jerry Thompson wondered if this was the same man who had tried to abduct 18-year-old Carol DaRonch from a mall in Murray, Utah, the previous November. The suspect had lured Carol her into his tan VW by posing as a police officer, then tried to handcuff her and bludgeon her with a crowbar before she escaped.

In October 1975, DaRonch identified Ted Bundy in a

police lineup. Of the people who were surprised by his sub-sequent arrest, Bundy seemed the most shocked of all. He said he'd expected to be back on campus in time for a 2L class later that day.

EVEN AFTER TED BUNDY WAS CONVICTED OF ATTEMPTED kidnapping, even after authorities connected him not just to the "Ted" murders of the Pacific Northwest but to at least seven more murders and missing persons cases in Utah and Colorado, and even after he was extradited to Colorado and charged with the murder of a nurse named Caryn Campbell, who had vanished from a Snowmass ski resort, it was still possible for people to look at Ted Bundy and feel not hor-ror at what he was accused of, but shock that anyone so po-lite and clean-cut—so middle-class—could be suspected of such things. "If you can't trust someone like Ted Bundy, you can't trust anyone—your parents, your wife, anyone," said his former boss Ross Davis, whose two young daughters Ted Bundy had regularly babysat.

"I wouldn't hesitate to line him up with my sister," one of Bundy's friends in Utah told the press at the time of his ar-rest. With remarkable frequency, men described Ted Bundy's essential goodness in terms of how much they trusted him with the women in their lives—and as Captain Swindler of the Seattle Police tried to connect Ted Bundy to the "Ted" murders, he found that the department's new prime suspect had already been close to his daughter Cathy. She had dated Ted years before, and she had trusted him, too. "He was someone," she said, "who had a great deal of compassion in dealing with other people."

At the time of his arrest, it was difficult even to describe the crimes Ted Bundy was accused of: the term "serial killer," coined during this period by profiler Robert Ressler, still existed only in FBI circles. Ressler's criteria included at least three murders of victims unknown to the perpetrator, with cooling-off periods in between. In the past, killers who fit this mold—the Texarkana Moonlight Murderer, the Austin Servant Girl Annihilator, the Axeman of New Orleans— were colorfully named phantoms who terrorized a region for a few months or years, then disappeared. The public rarely needed to match a human face to a series of seemingly inhuman crimes, and in the rare case where a perpetrator was revealed, he was one of society's rejects: no one wanted the Boston Strangler to take his daughter on a date. Ted Bundy was different. What did it mean for a man who had succeeded in American society to be capable of committing—or even imagining—such violence? Did it say something about the country that made him? Or did the police just have the wrong man?

The general public had no words for Ted Bundy, and perhaps this was why, when he escaped police custody in June 1977—a feat he accomplished by leaping out the second-story window of the Pitkin County Courthouse law library when the guard stepped outside for a smoke—he became more folk hero than bogeyman. Aspen radio station KSNO announced a "Ted Bundy hour," and played listener requests including

Helen Reddy's "Ain't No Way to Treat a Lady." A local woman named her quarter horse foal Ted Bundy, because, she said, "It'll know how to run." Aspen residents fund-raised for a courthouse plaque reading TED BUNDY LEAPT HERE, and a folk singer commemorated the event in ballad form:

> *So let's salute the mighty Bundy*
> *Here on Friday, gone on Monday*
> *All his roads led out of town*
> *It's hard to keep a good man down*

When Ted Bundy was captured after six days on the run—exhausted, starving, freezing, injured, hallucinating, and reportedly twenty pounds lighter than he had been when he'd escaped—he still managed to grin roguishly for the cameras and make sure the headline writers knew he was in on the joke. "He said it was just too nice a day to stay inside," the police officer charged with questioning him told the press.

In December 1977, Ted Bundy's former coworker Carole Ann Boone came to visit him in jail. As Ted and Liz drifted apart, his letters to Carole had shifted from friendly to intimate, but Carole still wasn't prepared to see the man she called her "Sweet Theodore" in custody. "I was shocked to see him in a cell," she told authors Michaud and Aynesworth. She was positive that Ted was innocent—a position she would maintain, publicly, for the rest of her life.

When Carole described her jailhouse visit with Ted, she spoke of a man who seemed not just physically apart from the wider world, but no longer of it. "It is hard to describe," she said, "except that in some strange way he was as far away, as far removed, as a person can be. Exiled in the midst." During Carole's visit, she noticed a spot on the floor where the gray paint had been worn away, exposing the pink material beneath. It was the place where Ted turned when he paced around his cell. Not long before, Ted had asked his former attorney John Henry Browne which states he thought were most likely to carry out the death penalty following the end of its national moratorium in 1976. "Texas and Florida," Browne replied.

Carole saw something else that day, something she didn't mention to the guards: a hole in the cell's ceiling. Not long after Carole's visit, on December 30, Ted Bundy climbed up through the hole and into the crawl space above, and escaped through the warden's apartment. He had pulled his sheets over a pile of clothes, crumpled papers, and law books, so the guards would think he was still in bed. It was the kind of ruse that should have worked only in a cartoon, but it worked for Ted Bundy. It wasn't until noon the following day that anyone noticed he was missing. By the time the police alerted the public and set up roadblocks, he was already more than a thousand miles away.

Back in Seattle, Keppel informed Liz of Ted's escape, and told her to contact him immediately if Ted tried to reach her. "As I lay awake that night, listening to every creak in the house," Liz wrote, "I admitted to myself that I might be afraid of Ted."

Liz didn't hear from Ted in the days following his escape, but some part of her knew how to find him. "One morning in mid-January," she wrote, "I picked up the newspaper and saw a picture of a frightened woman peering out of a gap in the drawn drapes of her sorority house. The story said an intruder had raped and murdered two young women and beaten two others as they slept in their beds at Florida State University . . . Now I had the ominous feeling that [Ted] was in Tallahassee."

Liz didn't have to wait long for her fears to be confirmed. A month later, on February 16, 1978, she got a call from Ted. "It's OK," he told her. She could tell that he was crying. "It's OK," he said again. "I'm in custody. It's all over." Unwilling to ignore her fears any longer, Liz asked him if he was a suspect in the murders she had read about.

"I wish we could sit down alone," Ted said haltingly, "and talk about things, with nobody listening. About the way I am."

AFTER HE WAS CAPTURED IN FLORIDA, TED BUNDY changed, in the public eye, from an outlaw to a monster. It was no longer possible to separate the man from his alleged crimes, just as it was no longer possible to tell a story about a girl who simply vanished, then reappeared months later as a skull, a jawbone, a broken tooth, or a strand of hair—a changeling offering mute testimony that something terrible had happened not here in our world but in that strange realm called "thin air." Now there was no such separation. What had happened at Florida State University had happened in our world. It had happened here.

At the Chi Omega sorority house, a man had stolen upstairs in the earliest hours of January 15, 1978, and gone from bedroom to bedroom, bludgeoning his sleeping victims with an oak log. Twenty-year-old Kathy Kleiner and 22-year-old Karen Chandler survived that night, though they were beaten so severely that drops of their blood were later found on the ceiling. Both Lisa Levy and Margaret Bowman were strangled and bludgeoned to death, and Bowman was beaten with such violence that her temple was crushed and fragments of her skull were driven into her brain. Levy was raped vaginally and anally with a bottle of Clairol hair mist, and her autopsy would reveal that she had been sexually assaulted with enough force to damage her internal organs. Her killer had bitten deeply into one of her buttocks and nearly torn her nipple from her breast. Contrary to what Liz read in the newspaper, Levy was the only victim to be sexually assaulted, but the manner in which Bowman, Kleiner, and Chandler were attacked suggested a form of domination akin to rape. Someone had wanted not just to hurt or even kill these women, but to obliterate them.

It had all happened in a matter of minutes. The attacker had moved from room to room, beating each woman in a violent frenzy, then pulling the covers up to her chin and moving on. After he left the sorority house, he went to a duplex eight blocks away and assaulted Cheryl Thomas, a

21-year-old dance student who lived there, in the same way that he had attacked Kathy Kleiner and Karen Chandler—and then he was gone again. Thomas, Kleiner, and Chandler had no memory of their assaults, let alone of their assailant. The only description the police had came from Nita Neary, a Chi Omega sister who caught a momentary glimpse of the killer as she returned from a date. She described him as a white male in his early 20s, between five eight and five ten, weighing around 150 pounds, with brown hair. In other words, he could have been any one of countless students on FSU's own campus.

When the *Florida Flambeau* printed a front-page story on the attack, it had no more information to report, nothing that could make the community feel safer. "So far," FSU's student paper told readers, "he has managed to elude a dragnet that has every detective in Leon County working around the clock." The rest of the issue was shot with ads for self-defense devices ("Every 10 minutes, an American Woman is attacked . . . DON'T THINK IT COULDN'T HAPPEN TO YOU!"). On sorority row, university officials visited each house to warn the girls about the danger that might still lurk on campus. "We're here because we want to tell you the facts," they told the sisters at Pi Beta Phi, "and we want to put the fear of the Lord in you."

Students withdrew from the university. Some never returned. "It was a very dark time," remembered Ron Eng, the Chi Omega house's handyman. "I can remember walking across campus a few days [later], trying to make a class or something like that, and no girl would look a man in the eyes."

Three weeks after the murders at Florida State, 12-year-old Kimberly Leach disappeared from her school in Lake City, a small town east of Tallahassee. She had forgotten her purse after homeroom that morning, and she and her friend Priscilla left their PE class so she could retrieve it. On the way back to the gym, Priscilla was momentarily distracted, and looked up just in time to see Kim walking toward a stranger's car. Two months later, her friend's remains were found in an abandoned hog shed.

Six days after Leach disappeared from her junior high school, Ted Bundy was captured in Pensacola. For the second time, he was arrested because he'd gotten lost. At 1:30 in the morning on February 15, 1978, patrolman David Lee noticed an orange Volkswagen Beetle driving down an alley behind a restaurant he knew to be closed. Deeming this behavior suspicious, Officer Lee, like the Salt Lake City Police had before him, acted on a gut instinct and followed the driver. When he radioed the license plate and found that the car was stolen, he gave chase. The driver tried to speed away. Lee followed. Finally, the driver pulled over and cooperated as Lee began cuffing him. Then he escaped Lee's grasp and tried to run away. Lee fired a warning shot, then fired at the man. He missed, but the man fell to the ground as if he had been injured. After Lee handcuffed him and pushed him into the back of his patrol car, the man remained silent, save for one phrase.

"I wish you'd killed me," he said.

The Pensacola police initially had no idea who the man was, though by then he was on the FBI's Most Wanted list. At first, he refused to give his name. Then he told police he was willing to confess—but he had conditions. If they wanted to know what happened, he said, then "it would all come out. I mean not—and again I know what you want—but I'm interested in the whole thing. I'm interested in everything. OK? . . . And it's—it's got to be dealt with." He was transferred to Tallahassee before the Pensacola police could bring him any closer to a full confession.

As it turned out, they didn't need one. From this point forward, there would be few surprises: not when Ted Bundy was indicted for murder, not when he insisted on representing himself at trial, not when he decided to accept counsel after all, not when his trial attracted a crush of media attention that put him in living rooms across the country, and least of all when he was sentenced to death not once but three times: first for the murders of Lisa Levy and Margaret Bowman, and then for the murder of Kimberly Leach.

"That he most probably looked normal and walked among us seemed the greatest of horrors," a Florida State student wrote in the *Florida Flambeau*. The murders, he wrote, "stripped away a little of the humanity from most of us. Right now, Tallahassee is a town of open wounds. We are like sharks, excited by the smell of our own blood . . . Quite correctly, many have said these murders are one of the strongest arguments ever for capital punishment."

TED BUNDY LOOKS AT SHERIFF KEN KATSARIS, WHO stands behind him, reading aloud the list of atrocities for which he will soon stand trial. Bundy's smile vanishes. For a moment, he seems near tears. Then he looks back at the cameras.

This is the picture you have seen: the man looking out from under a lowered brow, his mouth quirked in a half smile, his eyes deep-set, shadowy, but still focused directly on the camera lens, looking through the flash, through the decades, and into you. This is the Ted Bundy we know today: the man who was pure evil, and proud of his evil, and wanted the world to witness just how evil he was. This is the man who, in the words of one of the countless TV specials dedicated to his life and crimes, "had the capability of being virtually anything he wanted, but . . . instead chose to become a monster obsessed with murder."

This picture was taken on July 28, 1978, when Bundy was indicted for the murders of Lisa Levy and Margaret Bowman. Katsaris made the unusual decision of inviting the press to watch as he read the indictment to the defendant. Katsaris was dressed for the occasion in a sharp black suit. Bundy wore a jail-issued jumpsuit and sandals.

"What do we have here, Ken?" Bundy asks as he is led out to stand beside Katsaris. "Let's see. Oh, it's an indictment! All right. Why don't you read it to me?"

"Mr. Bundy—" Katsaris says.

"You're up for election, aren't you?" he interrupts.

"Mr. Bundy—"

"You finally got it, didn't you?"

"Mr. Bundy—"

"You told me that—you told them you were going to get me," he says, gesturing to the reporters and camera crews arrayed before them. Suddenly, he seems a little calmer: he has an audience to play to. "He said he was gonna get me," Bundy says, and turns back to Katsaris. "OK, you've got the indictment. It's all you're gonna get. Let's read it. Let's go."

As Katsaris reads the charges, the defendant walks out in front of him, as if to replace the entity described in the indictment with the real Ted Bundy, who could never have done these things. "My chance to talk to the press," he says, and smiles for the cameras, or tries to. It looks painful to sustain.

"I'll plead not guilty right now," he says, and raises his hand, smiling again. The shutters click.

ONE SUMMER, WHILE RESEARCHING A STORY ABOUT Florida, I found myself at the prison where Ted Bundy died. I had already done everything else I could think to do in the state. I had watched trained dolphins perform to "Foot-loose," then taken a boat tour of the Everglades and watched wild dolphins perform for no one, and tried not to eavesdrop too much on the other passengers' conversations. ("It's like catching snowflakes," a lawyer from Miami said about his work.) I had lined up with all the other tourists at Key West and taken a picture of the end of America. I had sustained mosquito bites above my hairline and on the soles of my feet. I had gone to the Florida Citrus Center and contemplated alligator claw key rings and back scratchers, alligator tooth necklaces, and dried alligator heads, and I had finally seen the LIVE BABY GATORS promised on all the billboards, where they appeared in cartoon version, wearing diapers and pink bows and looking as rosy-cheeked as reptiles can be imagined. I had done everything on my list, but I still felt that something was missing—and so, instead of going to Disney World, I went to the unremarkable patch of grass that had once been, for a few hundred citizens, the happiest place on earth.

Florida State Prison is often called Starke, taking its name from the closest nearby town, and maybe it was because of this name that I always thought it would look stark in its own way: dry and heat-tortured, glimmering with mirage but incapable of sustaining real life. I didn't know I was imagining such a place until I saw it contradicted by reality. I had been reading about Ted Bundy since I was a high school student in Oregon, when I became fascinated by the endless true-crime books and TV specials and tabloid spreads about all the terrible things it seemed were always happening to girls not so different from myself. But the more I learned, the more I found myself trying to move beyond dread and into something harder to find in the pages of a paperback: comprehension. Ted Bundy had been a person, too, I realized.

I wasn't so different from the girls he murdered, but I also wasn't so different from him. We were members of the same species. Was it truly impossible to understand his actions beyond simply attributing them to evil? Was it dangerous even to try? I didn't understand how it could be, but it seemed to me that most people thought it was. Gaze long enough into the abyss, everyone knows, and the abyss gazes into you—and its gaze is apparently enough to destroy you. I didn't understand how that worked, but it seemed like everyone around me did.

I had pictured Ted Bundy spending the last years of his life in a place that was the opposite of the Washington forests where he had grown up, but Starke is in central Florida, and, for sheer verdancy, central Florida puts the Pacific Northwest to shame. It is a land that dares things not to grow. Kudzu snakes across power lines and dangles from the trees, kissing the flat surfaces of carefully mown lawns. As you travel north toward the prison, the vines do not just choke the trees but swallow them whole. The 357 prisoners on Florida's death row as of this writing make it the second most populous in the nation, and in the area surrounding the prison, seemingly every roadside sign advertises gas, boiled peanuts, or God. FROGS ARE COMING, reads one. THERE'S ALWAYS FREE CHEESE IN THE DEVIL'S MOUSETRAP, reads another. WHEN SATAN COMES KNOCKING AT YOUR DOOR, a third sign instructs, SIMPLY SAY, "JESUS, WOULD YOU PLEASE GET THAT FOR ME?" In the end, they all say the same thing: you could be good, if only you wanted to be.

Ted Bundy's postconviction lawyer Polly Nelson traveled this same highway in April 1986, when she met her client for the first time. She had been practicing law for only a few months, and neither she nor Jim Coleman, Ted Bundy's principal postconviction lawyer, had any idea who Bundy was when they agreed to take his case. "Which one was he, the guy who killed the nurses in Chicago?" Nelson recalls wondering when a coworker asked if she wanted to help a Florida inmate apply for a stay of execution. After she and Coleman looked over the petition the inmate had prepared, they decided to represent him. Ted Bundy—who had been painted in the press as a legal mastermind even after his spectacular defeat in both of the capital murder trials at which he had served as a member of his own counsel—was representing himself just as ineffectively as he had since his indictment in Tallahassee.

The comparison between Ted Bundy's legal reputation and his behavior in court paralleled his reputation as a criminal mastermind: both were directly contradicted by his actions. While living in Utah, he had saved receipts for the small quantities of gas he purchased close to the Wildwood Inn in Colorado, where Caryn Campbell disappeared, around the time she disappeared. The receipts were discovered neatly collected in his desk—not far from a ski resort brochure with an "X" beside the Wildwood Inn—after Bundy consented to a search. The police asked him if he had ever been to Colorado. Bundy swore he hadn't, not long before they found the receipts and brochure.

During the penalty phase of his trial for the murder of Kimberly Leach, Ted had called in Carole Ann Boone as the defense's sole witness. Acting as his own counsel, Ted questioned her about his good character. Then, while she was still on the stand, he married her. The newlyweds even found a way around the prison's lack of conjugal visits, and in October of 1981, Carole gave birth to a healthy baby girl.

"The effect of [his daughter] in Ted's life," Polly Nelson wrote, "was to give him his first glimmer of heartfelt love. Until then I think he had believed that no such emotion truly existed, that the rest of us had been faking it too. [His daughter's] unconditional, unguarded, uncomplicated, real love for him touched him very deeply and elicited a strange new feeling that opened his mind to the possibility of the existence of love." When I spoke to Nelson nearly three decades later, Ted's transformation in these moments was still fresh in her mind. "He just lit up," she said.

Nelson's descriptions of meeting Ted Bundy for the first time—and of all the hours they spent together as she worked on his appeal—are remarkably different from other writers' depictions of the same experience. She believed he was guilty just as fervently as she believed in her duty to save him from the death penalty, and the difference between her view of him and the impressions that others described to the public was based not on what Ted Bundy had done, but what he might be. "He fascinated me," Michaud wrote, "like a viper motionless in a crevice: a black, palpable malignancy . . . Often he made me literally sick to my stomach, and sometimes it was all I could do to get out of the prison and back to the car before I vomited."

During their first meeting, Nelson wrote, Ted did his best "to impress me, please me, block out for the moment what he knew I knew about him. He wanted me to see him as he liked to think of himself: sophisticated, urbane, polite, respectful." Yet she always saw him not as the man he wanted her to see him as, but as a person trying to pretend he was someone else. "I always had the impression," she wrote, "that he was consciously creating himself, his persona. His natural instincts, I think, gave him no clue how a normal person would act."

By the time Nelson and Jim Coleman took Ted Bundy's case, their client had become a character in the American imagination—a transformation helped in no small part by a crime desk reporter–turned–thriller author named Thomas Harris. Harris's time observing Bundy's trial influenced his creation of Hannibal Lecter, the cold, calculating, erudite villain of the bestselling series that included *The Silence of the Lambs*. "Nothing happened to me . . ." Lecter explains. "I happened." Hannibal Lecter, born bad, believes he is superior to the people around him, having transcended their pointless attachments to each other—and, remarkably, Harris's other characters agree with him. They are frightened, it seems, that if they listen too closely to Hannibal Lecter, they will be swayed by his logic and become evil themselves. As Ted Bundy sat on death row, and as the legend of the genius serial killer grew up around him, the public came to view him with the same fear.

Yet when Nelson met Ted Bundy, she felt not terror or re-
vulsion, but pity. In appealing their client's death sentences,
Coleman and Nelson chose to focus on his mental health,
and on whether he had been competent not just to act as his
own counsel in his Florida trials but even to make the decisions required of a defendant. Bundy's new lawyers argued
that their client's mental illness had destroyed his right to
a fair trial, and that both trials' prosecutors and judges had
been either unable to comprehend his mental illness or unwilling to address the issue.

Perhaps the most glaring evidence supporting this theory came in the form of a plea deal Bundy rejected before
he went to trial for the murders of Lisa Levy and Margaret
Bowman. Had he accepted it, he would have pled guilty to
both murders and to the murder of Kimberly Leach in exchange for three life sentences. Instead, he decided at the last
minute to reject the plea, then complained bitterly about the
inadequacy of his counsel. The case went to trial, and Bundy
served on his own defense team, alongside a group of lawyers
who were forced to work without a coherent defense strategy,
since their client—and cocounsel—refused to address any of
the evidence against him.

"When Bundy sabotaged the plea agreement," Coleman
told me, "it was pretty clear at that point that there was
something going on that was related to mental illness, and
that this was not a rational thing that he had done: trying to
fire his lawyers on the grounds that they didn't believe in his
innocence, when he was about to plead guilty." In the course

of rejecting the plea deal so that he could stand trial, Coleman and Nelson argued, Bundy had already proven that he was not competent to do so.

This logic either makes sense to you or it doesn't. It makes sense if you are willing to believe that Ted Bundy really was mentally ill, and that his mental illness affected his ability not just to defend himself at trial but to make rational decisions about any aspect of his life. It makes sense if you are willing to consider applying a new diagnosis to Ted Bundy, and moving away from one that has been applied to him to the exclusion of all others: psychopath.

"Psychopathic killers," Dr. Robert D. Hare writes in his 1993 bestseller *Without Conscience: The Disturbing World of the Psychopaths Among Us*—published two years after the film adaptation of *The Silence of the Lambs*, starring Anthony Hopkins as Hannibal Lecter, swept the Academy Awards— "are not mad, according to accepted legal and psychiatric standards. Their acts result not from a deranged mind but from a cold, calculating rationality combined with a chilling inability to treat others as thinking, feeling human beings." Psychopaths, according to Hare, are incapable of experiencing even the faintest tremors of love or empathy, and can never be taught to feel any differently. If you encounter a psychopath, Hare says, you can do only one thing: flee. "If we can't spot them," he writes, "we are doomed to be their victims."

In addition to solidifying the public's understanding of psychopaths, Hare invented the most widely used tool for diagnosing them: the Psychopathy Checklist, first published in 1980, and known as the PCL-R since its only revision, in 2003. The checklist comprises twenty questions whose answers trained examiners rate on a scale of zero to two, typically after talking with the patient for about two hours. In the context of a prison diagnosis, some scored criteria—like "shallow affect" and "lack of empathy"—may be bolstered by an examiner's assessment of state-provided information such as a trial transcript or police record, while others—like "juvenile delinquency" and "revocation of conditional release"—are based entirely on a patient's past interactions with law enforcement. Because of its frequent use in criminal sentencing, the PCL-R necessarily conflates the concepts of "criminal" and "psychopathic": a PCL-R score of thirty out of forty makes you a psychopath, and at least five of the list's items can be scored solely on a subject's history of trouble with the law. Today, since black Americans are incarcerated at five times the rate of white Americans, a black American is also five times likelier to have a ten-point head start on the Psychopathy Checklist.

Despite this, the PCL-R—which Hare sells on his website for $460, in a bundle that includes an interview guide, a rating booklet, and a set of QuikScore™ forms (with webinar training available for an additional $499)—is regarded by laypeople and legal insiders alike not as a highly subjective questionnaire but as an infallible means of separating good from bad. Today, the diagnosis of "psychopath" is meted out as freely in the courtroom as it is during prime time, and its effect is always the same: instant dehumanization.

When it comes to assigning blame, no designation could be more comforting. The psychopath is born bad. Nothing can fix him. Society cannot be at fault, and there is no point in wondering whether timely treatment could have averted the inevitable. He does what he wants to do. He knows it is wrong. He can control himself; he simply chooses not to. The idea that the psychopath is somehow more deserving of blame because he was born bad—that his lack of empathy serves as proof of his evil, despite a diagnosis that says he cannot feel it, no matter how he tries—is a paradox few have attempted to address.

THE EVIDENTIARY HEARINGS CONCERNING THE ISSUE OF Ted Bundy's mental competence began on October 22, 1987. Jim Coleman started by questioning Mike Minerva, the public defender who had been appointed to represent Ted Bundy after his indictment in Tallahassee, regarding a note he made in the case file soon after he began preparing for the Chi Omega trial. "I believe," Minerva wrote, "[Bundy] has a basic defect in his reasoning process which prevents him from reviewing the case in a realistic manner." Throughout both their preparation for the trial and the trial itself, Minerva testified, Ted was "keeping everybody off balance," and demanded that his entire defense team come to see him for several hours each night, in visits that served no purpose but to keep him from being alone.

"Did you believe that insanity might be an issue in the case?" Coleman asked.

"Yes, I did," Minerva said.

"Were you able to pursue the insanity defense?"

"We were not able to pursue it. No, sir."

"Why was that?"

"Mr. Bundy did not want us to do that."

Despite his client's refusal to address the issue, Minerva hired Wayne State University psychiatry professor Dr. Emanuel Tanay to evaluate Ted, and to advise the defense team on whether their client would be capable of accepting the plea deal they were negotiating. After Tanay interviewed Ted, Minerva testified at the evidentiary hearings, he "expressed great reservations [about whether] Mr. Bundy would actually be able to go through with the agreement because of his mental illness." At the time, Tanay wrote: "I would anticipate that in the unlikely event that the prosecution's case against [Bundy] would weaken, he would through his behavior bolster the prosecution's case."

Yet for a brief period, Minerva testified, it seemed as if Ted Bundy really would take the plea. "We went through the whole thing with him, and his mother talked to him, and Carole Boone talked to him," Minerva told me. "They all were trying to convince him that it was OK with them . . . because they were going to still believe that he was innocent, that he was entering a plea so he could stay alive. He agreed to it. And then he comes in the very next morning and takes it all back in open court."

I asked Minerva why he thought Bundy had rejected the plea deal.

"I don't know," he said. "That's over my head. I don't know." Bundy's abilities as a lawyer were, Minerva recalled, "scattershot." Mostly, he said, Ted "knew the performance": when to stand, which phrases to use. After his trial began, Ted continued to dictate his lawyers' actions and require their nightly visits, leaving them not just unprepared but increasingly sleep-deprived. He was not only unwilling but also apparently unable to comprehend the evidence against him, and refused to discuss it with his lawyers, instead talking to the press and performing for the media at every opportunity. He also impulsively cross-examined a prosecution witness before his lawyers could stop him, leading the witness to describe the horrific aftermath of the Chi Omega murders, including the pains paramedics had taken to ensure that Kathy Kleiner and Karen Chandler didn't choke to death on their own blood. To the public—and to the jury—it was hard to imagine that Bundy had a motive for such questioning beyond the desire to revel in his own destructive power. What other rational motive could there be?

As the trial progressed, Bundy's attorney Ed Harvey requested another competency hearing, because, he later testified, "it was obvious to me that . . . what he was doing during his trial was hurting himself." The court denied Harvey's motion, and Ted Bundy, always the staunchest believer in his own competence, was happy with the ruling. "At that point," Harvey testified at the evidentiary hearings, "I felt that the relationship between Mr. Bundy and everybody on the staff was such [that] we could not ethically go on and represent him. There was no lawyer-client relationship left. So I made a motion to withdraw as counsel . . . [and] the court appointed him as chief counsel and relegated us to the official position of being just standby counsel." Once again, Ted Bundy was on his own.

At Coleman and Nelson's evidentiary hearings, Dr. Dorothy Lewis, a Yale professor and psychiatrist, testified that she had, after evaluating Ted Bundy, outlined a history of alternating periods of mania and depression dating back to 1967. She diagnosed Ted with bipolar disorder, to which she also attributed his behavior at trial. According to Lewis, the question of whether Bundy was competent to act as his own counsel was not even at issue. "I don't even think Mr. Bundy was competent to accept or reject a plea," she said.

Immediately after the state finished calling its witnesses— concluding with a psychiatrist who stated that Ted's concern for "his dental care, his body cream, his skin condition . . . shows that Mr. Bundy definitely is not depressed"—Judge G. Kendall Sharp announced that he would not need to listen to any final arguments, and required no time to deliberate. "After hearing all of the testimony," he said, "the Court now concludes that [Ted Bundy] probably is the most competent serial killer in the country at this time . . . he is a most intelligent, articulate, and complex individual. This Court views him as a diabolical genius."

Judge Sharp made no secret of the fact that he had made up his mind in advance. Before the hearings began, Polly Nelson wrote, "a television reporter [asked] if he thought a

hearing on Bundy's competency would be a waste of time."
The judge answered, "Absolutely."

ON JANUARY 23, 1989, HOURS BEFORE HIS SCHEDULED
execution, Polly Nelson visited Ted along with Dr. Lewis.
"Have you felt good at all to have gotten it off your chest?"
Dr. Lewis asked Ted, who had already made extensive con-
fessions to the investigators who had flooded the prison over
the past several days.

"It doesn't feel any better," Ted told her. "Not yet, 'cause
I haven't really told anybody, I don't think, the whole story."

Now, with Lewis recording the proceedings and Nelson
standing by, Ted did his best to tell it. He said "something
happened" the summer before he started high school—
something that left him feeling "really out of touch with my
peers—really out of touch. I mean, my old neighborhood
friends went on to groups, and high school, being [part of]
a bigger community—and I was sort of just stuck. I spent
a lot of time with myself." Ted would run naked through
the forest behind his house and "fantasize about coming up
to some girl sunbathing in the woods," he said, "or something innocuous like that." As he grew older, his fantasies
grew darker. He scoured the library for descriptions of violence, and developed a taste for true detective magazines
and their photographs of dead bodies. At 21, after his first
girlfriend—a beautiful, wealthy young woman he idolized—
ended their relationship, his dependence on pornography
and his own fantasy life began to deepen. "It was like I just

ran for cover emotionally," he said. "And, of course, that was the only thing that ever made sense."

Ted's fantasies came to include "some faceless character" assaulting his ex-girlfriend. "I think he raped her," Ted told Lewis and Nelson. "But he didn't—he didn't—I didn't, I didn't take it—he didn't kill her or anything like that."

But the line between "he" and "I" had begun to disintegrate. In the first months of 1969, Ted said, he felt "the entity begin to reach the point where it's necessary to act out. No longer just to read books, or to masturbate, or fantasize, but to actually begin to stalk, to look." The fantasy, he said, "became more graphic each time it was aroused." That spring, Ted recounted, "I really, for the first time, approached a victim, spoke to her, tried to abduct her, and she escaped. That was frightening in its own way. But that was the first—the kind of step that you just—that you don't—that I couldn't ever return from."

"Did you ever think about talking to a psychiatrist or someone about this?" Lewis asked.

"No," Ted said. After that first approach he had stopped himself, and believed that he could manage without help. He met Liz that summer. He went back to school. "Things seemed to be good," he said. "I felt like I had myself back together. I was disturbed about what I was doing in 1969 . . . and, yet, I figured that it was in control, really.

"It wasn't," he said. "I wasn't."

"Did you ever think you were crazy?" Lewis asked later in the conversation.

"Oh, yes," he said. "There are times I've, the rage and the madness was just so strong, I was just so . . . I'd be screeching, screeching, cursing, you know. That's when I was, deep down inside I was watching this, I said, 'You're absolutely mad. This is just madness.'"

But after each murder, he could still tell himself that it was over. "I convinced myself, OK, this is it, I've satisfied myself. No more. I'm OK now. I feel good. I feel like I don't need that, I know I don't need that anymore.

"I can remember that very feeling," he told them. "It's very strong in 1974, leaving the state of Washington, going to law school in Utah, feeling all of this is behind me. I got this over now," Ted said. "This is going to be OK."

"IT WAS A PERFECT WINTER DAWN," MARGARET VANDIVER later wrote. She had provided pro bono paralegal services to Ted Bundy, and after visiting him before his execution, she stood across the road from the prison, walking back and forth between the mass of revelers and the few death penalty protesters who stood apart from the celebration. Believing the prison lights would dim at the moment of the execution, some onlookers began a raucous countdown—"Ten, nine, eight, seven"—as if they were anticipating not a man's death but a space shuttle launch.

Earlier, prison officials laid out a breakfast of coffee, grits, ham, bacon, and eggs for the execution's audience. It was a generous spread: Ted Bundy was allowed to choose two witnesses, the state supplied another ten, and the rest of the chairs were filled with as many spectators as the space could hold. "There wasn't any room for anybody to move, it was so jam-packed," said Fred Lawrence, the Methodist minister who prayed with Ted Bundy in his final hours.

Ted addressed his last words to Lawrence, and to Coleman. "Jim and Fred," he said, "I'd like you to give my love to my family and friends."

"He seemed disoriented," Coleman remembered. "He seemed helpless. And he seemed very small."

"Is that all there is?" Ray Parrish, a college student from Kimberly Leach's hometown, asked the reporters outside the prison. "I don't feel any different," he said.

For the six-year-old Cochran twins, Jennifer and May Nicole, whose family had left Orlando at two o'clock in the morning so they could join the festivities, the "field trip" their parents planned had been an educational one. Jennifer told reporters from the *Gainesville Sun* that "she understood why Ted Bundy was going to die. 'He killed a lot,' she said."

May Nicole had a harder time focusing on the lesson at hand. "We saw a deer this morning," she announced.

The party was over. The crowd dispersed. The TV stations packed up their equipment. The vendors counted their takes. The sky was the pink of an Easter egg, until the sunrise faded and it was just another day.

IT IS IMPOSSIBLE TO BELIEVE IN EVIL WITHOUT BELIEVing in choice. When we talk about the psychopath, we describe a person born without a conscience, yet we often talk about this lack as if it is not a disability but an advantage: proof that someone has evolved beyond the pesky morals that hobble the rest of us and is now free to enjoy a consequence-free life of sex, theft, and violence. Whether psychopaths actually do enjoy this life is, according to Dr. Hare, not a question even worth asking. Therapy—especially "attempts to teach psychopaths how to 'really feel' remorse or empathy"—is "doomed to failure," Hare writes in *Without Conscience*, primarily because psychopaths don't want to change. "They see nothing wrong with themselves," Hare explains, "experience little personal distress, and find their behavior rational, rewarding, and satisfying; they never look back with regret or forward with concern. They perceive themselves as superior beings." To Hare, and to the psychiatrists and legal professionals who continue his work, a diagnosis of "psychopathy" is wholly separate from mental illness, and cannot serve to mitigate a defendant's guilt. The only guilt it can mitigate is a jury's: if it is wrong to kill a human being, it can still be acceptable to recommend the death penalty for someone who is not really human.

When I asked Ted Bundy's attorneys whether they would describe him as a psychopath, their responses were not just unanimous but unambiguous. "No," Minerva said, without hesitation. "I think he was severely, deeply mentally ill," he said. "Psychotic. I always believed that."

"I think we understood why he did what he did," Coleman said. "We knew it was a product of a mental illness."

"He was mentally ill," said Joe Nursey, a lawyer who worked

with the defense team during Ted Bundy's abandoned plea bargain and subsequent trial, and is now a supervising attorney at New York's Office of the Appellate Defender. "Anybody who looks at it with any degree of honesty knows that he was mentally ill," Nursey said. "Just being with him long enough, you saw it . . . His mind [didn't] function rationally: on any level, on anything."

Nelson was silent for a long time as she considered my question. "You know," she said, "'psychopath' to me implies some kind of evil motivation, like an evil corporation knowingly polluting. And I don't see that in Ted. He was much more like an addict."

More often than not, the lawyers I spoke with found the term "psychopath" so poorly defined that they didn't feel comfortable applying it to anyone. The word, Coleman said, "becomes a cop-out. Judges latch onto it to avoid having to deal with what's actually going on. It's presented to juries as a way for them to not struggle with understanding the defendant's behavior, and to attribute to it this label that basically explains everything."

"It's a cheap word," Nursey said. "It's a word that is used to avoid trying to understand something in a larger context. Medicine has not developed to the point where we understand the mental illness that leads people to commit what appear to everybody to be random, cold-blooded acts of violence . . . These are out-of-control people, but we won't acknowledge that they have a mental illness. We just want to say they're pure mean."

For decades, Ted Bundy has served as the textbook example of psychopathy not just for tabloid readers and true-crime enthusiasts, but for revered psychologists like Hare. But after hearing the same thing about Ted Bundy from so many of the people who both knew him as a person and accepted his guilt, I had one question left: If Ted Bundy wasn't a psychopath, who is?

"The better question," Nursey told me, is, "'Does the term have any real meaning?' And it doesn't."

One of the most troubling aspects of Hare's description of the psychopath, particularly in *Without Conscience*, is its sheer simplicity. There is only one diagnosis, "the psychopath," into which every patient must fit. Personal history, age, gender, past trauma or abuse, evidence of brain injury, and diagnoses of other personality disorders or even mental illnesses don't enter into the equation. And while it is comforting to believe that the only reason a person can commit or be complicit in the most horrific of crimes is because they were simply born bad, we have to wonder whether this sense of comfort leads us to accept certain conclusions not because they are logical, but because we want them to be true.

We can say that Ted Bundy was a psychopath, but we can also attribute his behaviors to the mental illness his lawyers observed in him, and doing so reveals a very different picture from the one we know. It shows us a man who appears to have been unable to control his actions or make the decisions that would have saved his life, who put on shows of competence and superiority because he needed to force the world to see a version of himself that he was no longer sure existed, and who loudly proclaimed his own innocence because, to him, it had become a kind of truth.

"I think he always viewed himself as being two personalities, in effect," Coleman told me. "One good and one bad. He viewed the good Bundy's role as protector of the bad Bundy, because that was the only way to protect the good Bundy . . . So denying that he was guilty—I don't think, in his mind, he was doing anything contradictory. He really did believe it."

"The person standing before you couldn't kill anyone," Ted told the jury at one of his trials. It was a tactic he used repeatedly, despite the fact that it never convinced anyone of anything. "The bottom line," he told another jury, at his Orlando trial, "is that the person who murdered Kimberly Leach is not in the courtroom today." The jury deliberated for less than an hour before recommending the death penalty.

Dr. Al Carlisle, the psychiatrist who evaluated Ted prior to his sentencing in Utah, concluded after six weeks of interviews that "the constant theme running throughout the testing was a view of women being more competent than men. There were also indications of a fairly strong dependency on women, and yet he also has a strong need to be independent. I feel this creates a fairly strong conflict in that he would like a close relationship with females but is fearful of being hurt by them. There were indications of general anger and, more particularly, a well-masked anger toward women."

Polly Nelson researched Ted's childhood in preparation

for the evidentiary hearings, and learned, she wrote, "that, contrary to Ted's description of an idyllic family background, his grandfather had been a violent and bizarre man who beat his wife and talked aloud to unseen presences. Ted's grandmother had been hospitalized for depression several times and treated with electroshock therapy." Eventually, "the family had conspired to get Ted and his mother out of his grandfather's house—and out to Seattle to start a new life." But, Nelson wrote, "Ted's mother denied there had been any problems."

Ted told a similar story. He was fiercely protective of his mother, especially when it came to guarding her from any suggestion that she might have influenced his behavior. During Carlisle's evaluation, Ted insisted he felt no resentment toward his mother, because "she had sacrificed a great deal to have and raise an illegitimate child."

"My mom loved me enough to give birth to me, to care for me and love me," he wrote to authors Michaud and Aynesworth. "This seemed to be more than enough."

Louise Cowell was 17 when she gave birth to Ted in a home for unwed mothers. She decided to give her baby up for adoption, and left him there. When she returned three months later, it was not because she had changed her mind about being a mother, but because her parents had changed her mind for her. When Louise brought Ted home, her parents alternated between passing him off as her brother and simply hiding him away.

"She tried to do the right thing," Nelson said. "She knew

her limitations and her feelings about him. And then she was pressured to do otherwise. She was young."

Carlisle also noted Ted's intense attachment to Liz. During his evaluation, Ted wept as he recounted a time when Liz had been unfaithful. "My world was so destroyed," he said.

"In this life we are fortunate to find one person to love and love completely," Ted wrote to Liz shortly after his first arrest. "I am lucky because I love you in this way . . . In this hour when my whole life is threatened, the only thing I regret is losing you and [your daughter]. So I give you one more thing. It is the one part of me that cannot be taken away. I give you my love as deep and as powerful as any human being can have for any other. I give it to you as the woman who has captured my soul . . . Without you there would be no life."

At the sentencing hearing for his Utah trial, Ted was particularly outraged by Carlisle's claim that he was dependent on women. "Good grief!" he said. "I don't know that there's a man in the courtroom who isn't. And if he isn't, maybe there's something wrong with him. Our mother is a woman."

"I think when you are as desperately dependent on something as he was . . . you resent it," Nelson told me. "I think a lot of men feel that way."

"He received no pleasure from harming or causing pain to the person he attacked," Ted said, in one of the many interviews he conducted with Michaud and Aynesworth under the premise that he was theorizing about what the real killer might have done. "He received absolutely no gratification,"

Ted insisted. "He did everything possible within reason— considering the unreasonableness of the situation—not to torture these individuals, at least not physically."

Lisa Levy was unconscious when Ted Bundy assaulted her, raping her with a hair spray can and nearly biting her nipple from her breast. How many of these other girls and women were unconscious, or already dead, when he carried out his assaults? In many cases, we cannot know, just as we cannot know what need he served by staying with some of his victims' bodies until dawn, and by returning to their corpses sometimes weeks after he killed them, perhaps until there was nothing left to return to.

"If there was anything he was ashamed of," Nelson said, "it was that. Any kind of contact he had with the body after death. He couldn't wrap any story around that."

We have found a way to wrap a story around most of Ted Bundy's actions. In all too many depictions of him, there is, lurking in the background, the idea that every man wants to rape women, but Ted Bundy just got carried away and took things too far. The necrophilia, the mutilation, and the destruction and visitation that seemed to feed his compulsion more than any recognizably sexual motive are harder to cram into a ready-made narrative. They reveal a man who perhaps felt the need not to revel in his victims' pain but to destroy the body that should have given him the love he needed but never gave him enough, never enough so that he could truly feel it, never enough so that he could finally become whole—or else to steal inside it, to disappear, and to no longer be alone.

When I talked with Nelson, I asked her if Ted Bundy's gradual progression to serial murder seemed as inevitable to her as it did to him. "I wouldn't say it seemed inevitable to him," she countered. "He was always hoping it wasn't. We all think we're strong enough to resist our temptations, and like all of us, he just thought, OK, I'm stronger than this. Now I know, so now I really can be strong.

"And whether anything could have happened at any time," she continued, "so that this could not have happened, I think definitely . . . I think he's on a spectrum, and other people are on parts of that spectrum, and very few of them end up like he did. But he had all the right ingredients."

THE JUNGLE GROWTH OF CENTRAL FLORIDA STOPS abruptly about a mile from Florida State Prison. The trees disappear. The sky is suddenly endless. The first real clue that you are approaching the complex is a sign that reads, FLORIDA STATE PRISON NOW HIRING. If you're not going in for a job interview, or to meet with an inmate, it is easy to drive straight past it. There is no place to pull off the highway, let alone a marker setting one drab stretch of shoulder apart from the rest, and this seems right to me. I came here because I wanted to see the spot where so many people shared so much joy at the death of a man, and because maybe by standing in this place I would understand not just their joy but the man whose death inspired it. But there is no place to look at, and I am looking for something no one has. I am looking for an answer.

Of all the aspects of the psychopath diagnosis that Ted Bundy challenges, perhaps the most striking is the one that does not apply to him at all: satisfaction. Psychopaths, Dr. Hare assures us, celebrate the way they are, and see the rest of us as weaker beings. One never encounters descriptions of the psychopath that include not just the way their inability to feel love harms the people around them, but what it is like to survive without love, and to endure what must, at times, seem like an empty hell.

Nor does one encounter the suggestion that the psychopath can, with age, feel moments of relief, flickers of love, as Nelson says Ted Bundy felt for his daughter. The same daughter left Ted's life forever in 1986, when Carole Ann Boone quietly moved back to Washington, taking their child with her. "I think he agreed to it," Nelson said of their departure. Before they left, Ted drew so close to an execution date that he had said goodbye to his family—his head already shaved for the electric chair's sponge—before he received a stay. Ted seemed to recognize, Nelson said, that his wife and daughter would have a better life without him. And, she added, "as things were heating up so much, [his daughter] was going to see the news or the newspaper. He didn't want her to have that impression of him."

Then, too, there was the question of whether Ted Bundy truly wanted to stop. After his first escape, in Aspen, he told Michaud and Aynesworth, he didn't feel the urges that had dominated him before his arrest. He believed that he had cured himself, and was free. The second time he broke out of custody, he was high on the thrill of escape until he got as far south as Atlanta. Then, suddenly, something happened.

"I was waiting for the bus," Ted said, "and I was watching all these people—these people who had real lives, backgrounds, histories, girlfriends, husbands and families. Who were smiling and laughing and talking to each other. Who seemed to have so much of what I wanted. All of a sudden, I just felt smaller and smaller and smaller. And more insecure, too. And more alone . . . Bit by bit by bit, I felt something drain out of me." Within two weeks, he would murder Lisa Levy and Margaret Bowman.

A lifetime is not long enough to comprehend the pain Ted Bundy caused. I limit myself to one woman's life and I know I cannot fathom such a loss, let alone such losses. I don't believe anyone can. I am powerless to understand, to begin to imagine, just who his victims were. I can tell you only what I have learned from true crime: that Lynda Healy was studying child psychology; that Georgann Hawkins's mother called her "the Pied Piper" because of how many friends she always had at her side; that Donna Manson made a list titled "Things to give to people," and it went:

A string of beads
A taste
A rose
An ear
A hand to help

I will never grasp the totality of these women: of both their own lives and the lives that touched theirs; of their loves and fears and anger, of the possible worlds they walked beside, and the world as it was, as it was when it was theirs, and in moments that were theirs alone, and that could never be translated for the public into another humanizing fact, another reason that this was a girl who deserved to live.

"You can go as high as you want," Bundy told Aynesworth when the writer wondered how many victims the "person" they were discussing might have killed, at a time when both men understood they were talking about Ted Bundy himself. "The higher the number," Bundy said, "the better. The more horrified people will be, the more they will read, and the more interested they'll be in finding out what makes a person like this tick . . . Make it up. I'm not going to do it. I can't . . . but you can."

Ted Bundy was adamant about the few insights he did have about himself. If he could not explain why his compulsions had emerged, he could at least cling to the knowledge that there was a time when they had not controlled him. In response to Beverly Burr, a Tacoma resident who begged him to confess to the murder of her eight-year-old daughter, Ann Marie, Ted wrote: "You said she disappeared August 31, 1961. At the time I was a normal 14-year-old boy." In a few years, things would change forever. But not then. Not yet.

"We're right down to it," Bundy said near the end of his final meeting with Nelson and Dr. Lewis, hours before his death. "I've pieced together an explanation of sorts which makes sense, yet I don't know. I wish I did know . . . that's what I'd like to understand, why. I think for me sometimes it's sadly, just because.

"Forgive me for digressing a little," he said. "Maybe this will help. You asked me why I never sought help. At first I didn't think I needed it. Then I suffered from delusions that I could handle it myself. Then it was too late because I knew if I sought help, that was—I didn't trust anybody."

Dr. Lewis asked Ted to relax as deeply as he could, to reach back into his childhood, and to tell her what he saw. "Ted had laid his head down on his hands," Nelson wrote, "but his handcuffs cut him and he was unable to concentrate. I cupped his head in my hands. I had never been this way with Ted before, touching him, comforting him. But today was different . . . Today I was a human being and he was a human being."

"Well," Bundy said at last, "looking back now I couldn't, I couldn't, certainly didn't, see it or understand it. I can only say that . . . what I lacked and didn't understand and express was love.

"By love," he said, "I mean the ability to sense someone else's feelings and when to comfort them and to protect them and do good things for them. And in turn have that same kind of feeling, be the focus of that same kind of feeling.

"I feel that it wasn't there in me," Ted said. "I mean, how else?"

———

WHEN I FIRST LEARNED ABOUT TED BUNDY, I WAS 16 AND working through myth after myth, trying to understand why the dark forces inside a man needed, so badly, to destroy me. Sometimes victimhood seemed inevitable. And sometimes it seemed like the best thing that could happen to a girl. Once you were dead, you could be loved forever. Once you were dead, no one asked if you had fought back hard enough, if you hadn't really wanted it after all.

I learned, from all these stories, that there were good men who wanted to save me, but only after I was dead, and I learned that there were bad men who wanted—needed—to kill me. But I didn't understand where this need came from, and the answers people gave me never made sense. He wanted to be evil. He had become superior to other men—the less capable of love he was, the more superior he became—and he realized there was nothing to stop him from possessing all the women he wanted, because isn't that what all men wish they could do? And that, as far as I could tell, was why you weren't supposed to put the good men in a room with the bad man for too long: they were afraid they would start seeing things his way.

So I went to the bad men. Listen, I said, to the shape I conjured, who usually looked like Ted, usually was Ted, though our life spans had overlapped by just a few months. Listen, I said, when I imagined him driving me up the mountain some dark night, up a narrow logging road, the way long, the radio gone to static. *Listen*, I'd say. *Just tell me what you need from me. Why is my body the one you have to tear apart? What do you think you'll find?*

"It's funny how he's still the poster boy for serial killers after all these years," Nelson said, near the end of our conversation. It was hard for me, I told her, to imagine knowing the real person first, and then watching the myth be built around him. I had only ever known the myth.

"Not that he'd be unhappy with that," she said. "He would much rather go down as a brilliant, manipulative serial killer than a disturbed individual, out of control and sad. You're going to be ruining it. That was worth a lot to him."

Why am I trying to ruin this for you, Ted? Why am I here? It's not just because I was a girl, and you were the worst of all the bad men I ever learned about, and I thought figuring out why you needed me to die would mean figuring out why the whole world did. It's not just because calling you "a force of evil" isn't good enough for me—not just because, more and more, I am coming to believe that "evil" refers to nothing, means nothing, attaches itself to acts of violence or cruelty, but is never, by itself, an identifiable force. And it's not just because I learned to understand my value to society by imagining how much I would be missed if I were taken away by someone like you, and it's not just because I studied these stories to learn how to survive (don't take the shortcut through the alley, don't talk to strangers, don't go into "thin air"), and it's not just because you are human and I am human. It's because I see myself in you.

AS A TEENAGER, THE STORY I FOUND WHEN I LOOKED
and looked for the evil people seemed to see when they
looked at Ted Bundy was always, to me, the story of a lost
boy: one who couldn't understand relationships and con-
nections around him, and who was always on the outside,
looking in. "I didn't know what made things tick," Bundy
told Michaud. "I didn't know what made people want to be
friends. I didn't know what made people attractive to one
another. I didn't know what underlay social interactions."

The first time I read these words—still a teenager, still
meant to identify with the murdered girl and no one else—I
recognized them as my own. I had to think through nearly
every interaction in advance. I felt I had no basic understanding of the people around me, and this made me feel like I was
completely alone in the world, and sometimes meant that
when I looked at the people around me, I could feel only
fear, and sometimes hostility. Something had broken—who
knew what, or when, or how?—in my early life, in my ability
to trust people, to reach out, to feel that I could be seen and
known as I was, and loved unconditionally. Some early relationship had faltered enough, some early trauma had broken
me enough, to make me feel so lost—this, at least, is what I
think now: something happened. And then something else
happened. Something lost hold of me; something gave. I
learned, slowly, to trust other people. I reached for them. I
knew them. I loved them, and I felt their love.

And why was it that I was allowed to move on, and you

weren't? I never felt the urge to hurt the people around me, but that wasn't a choice; it was a lack of compulsion. And if I had wanted to hurt people, would I have tried to get help? Where would I have gone? Where would I go tomorrow, if the need suddenly appeared and took control of me?

The insects' singing vibrates the grass. I am sweating so much I think I might be melting. I have come as close to looking at you as I possibly can, Ted, and like Polly Nelson before me, I feel only pity. I thought I wasn't allowed to feel just that: I thought I had to feel fear when I looked at you, fear of the demon core you held, because looking at it too closely would mean witnessing your evil, and knowing that it burned in me, too. Isn't that what all these terrified men see when they look at you, Ted? But we can be scared this way only by beliefs we feel we could share. I do not believe that the harm you caused made you somehow powerful, but for all the time I have been looking at you, I have felt the people around me looking at you that way. Why are we so determined to estimate a victim total? Why are the numbers we guess always so high? How many people do we want you to have killed?

What made you the way you were? Which chemicals did your brain misproduce, which cells didn't divide, how many crucial grains of love and nurture were blown out of your life and allowed to stay in mine at the moment when they most mattered? I am tired of being told that there is something in the abyss that will glower back at me, and make me want to stop looking. I have grasped for your demon core, Ted, and I have found nothing, again and again. The good men lied. I have found only humanity, only a need to love and feel loved as well as we can, and the fact that some of us can do this easily, and some of us hardly at all, and I cannot imagine a reality where someone would choose violence over love, emptiness over love, feeling lost the way you did, lost the way I did, over love, when love is there. I don't think love was there for you, and I don't know why it wasn't, and I'm tired of being told there's no point in searching for answers that might lead to solutions, tired of living in a world where some people are just born bad, and all we can do is wait to catch and destroy them, and where catching and destroying a monster means waiting until they start killing women and girls. I am tired of living in a world where this is the only story we can tell. I am tired of this story. I want a new one.

IT IS DIFFICULT TO SEE TED BUNDY AS HUMAN. IT IS DIFficult even to entertain the belief that he did not need to destroy as many lives as he did, or that his own life could have been different. Believing this means believing that Ted Bundy and others who commit crimes like his are not born irreparably wrong, are not unavoidably evil, do not belong to a separate species from the rest of us. This is a frightening conclusion to draw: that the actions and crimes and atrocities we so often call "inhuman" do, in fact, belong to humanity, because they are committed by human beings. Rejecting the label of "psychopath," not just for Ted Bundy but for anyone, means accepting that it is not a hard, scientific fact that we could never do what they have done—and that we could, under different circumstances, go down the same path they did.

But there is hope in this conclusion, too. It means their paths were not inevitable. It means there was a time when they might have come back, away from violence, away from emptiness, and toward attachment, toward empathy, toward the bright and benevolent side of human behavior we have grandiosely labeled "humanity." It means that those we call lost do not need to stay lost forever. It means that we, too, can be found.

Originally published by *The Believer*, February 2018

# The Ethical Dilemma of Highbrow True Crime

The "true-crime boom" of the mid- to late 2010s is a strange pop-culture phenomenon, given that it is not so much a new type of programming as an acknowledgment of a centuries-long obsession: people love true stories about murder and other brands of brutality and grift, and they have gorged on them particularly since the beginning of modern journalism. The serial fiction of Charles Dickens and Wilkie Collins was influenced by the British public's obsessive tracking of sensational true-crime cases in daily papers, and since then, we have hoarded gory details in tabloids and pulp paperbacks and nightly news shows and Wikipedia articles and Reddit threads.

I don't deny these stories have proliferated in the past five years. Since the secret is out—"Oh, you love murder? Me too!"—entire TV networks, podcast genres, and countless limited-run docuseries have arisen to satisfy this rumbling hunger. It is tempting to call this true-crime boom new because of the prestige sheen of many of its artifacts—*Serial* and *Dirty John* and *The Jinx* and *Wild Wild Country* are all conspicuously well made, with lovely visuals and strong reporting. They have subtle senses of theme and character, and they often feel professional, pensive, quiet—so far from vulgar or sensational.

But well-told stories about crime are not really new, and neither is their popularity. *In Cold Blood* is a classic of American literature, and *The Executioner's Song* won the Pulitzer; Errol Morris has used crime again and again in his documentaries to probe ideas like fame, desire, corruption, and justice. The new true-crime boom is more simply a matter of volume and shamelessness: the wide array of crime stories we can now openly indulge in, with conventions of the true-crime genre more emphatically repeated and codified, more creatively expanded and trespassed against. In 2016, after two critically acclaimed series about the O.J. Simpson trial, there was talk that the 1996 murder of Colorado six-year-old JonBenét Ramsey would be the next case to get the same treatment. It was odd, hearing *O.J.: Made in America*, the epic and depressing account of race and celebrity that won the Academy Award for Best Documentary, discussed in the same breath with the half dozen unnecessary TV specials dredging up the Ramsey case. Despite my avowed love of *Dateline*, I would not have watched these JonBenét specials had a magazine not paid me to, and suffice it to say they did

very little to either solve the 20-year-old crime (ha!) or examine our collective obsession with it.

Clearly, the insight, production values, or cultural capital
of its shiniest products are not what drives this new wave of
crime stories. *O.J.: Made in America* happened to be great and
the JonBenét specials happened to be terrible, but producers
saw them as part of the same trend because they knew they
would appeal to at least part of the same audience. I've been
thinking a lot about these gaps between high and low, since
there are people who consume all murder content indis-
criminately, and another subset who only allow themselves
to enjoy the "smart" kind. The difference between highbrow
and lowbrow in the new true crime is often purely aesthetic.
It is easier than ever for producers to create stories that look
good and seem serious, especially because there are tem-
plates now for a style and voice that make horrifying stories
go down easy and leave the viewer wanting more. But for
these so-called prestige true-crime offerings, the question of
ethics—of the potential to interfere in real criminal cases
and real people's lives—is even more important, precisely because they are taken seriously.

Like the sensational tone, disturbing, clinical detail, and
authoritarian subtext that have long defined schlocky true
crime as "trash," the prestige true-crime subgenre has developed its own shorthand, a language to tell its audience
they're consuming something thoughtful, college-educated,
public-radio influenced. In addition to slick and creative production, highbrow true crime focuses on character sketches

instead of police procedure. "We're public radio producers who are curious about why people do what they do," Phoebe Judge, the host of the podcast *Criminal*, said. Judge has interviewed criminals (a bank robber, a marijuana brownie dealer), victims, and investigators, using crime as a very simple window into some of the most interesting and complicated lives on the planet.

Highbrow true crime is often explicitly about the piece's creator, a meta-commentary about the process of researching and reporting such consequential stories. *Serial*'s Sarah Koenig and *The Jinx*'s Andrew Jarecki wrestle with their boundaries with the subjects (Adnan Syed and Robert Durst, respectively, both of whom have been tried for murder) and whether they believe them. They sift through evidence and reconstruct timelines as they try to create a coherent narrative from fragments.

I remember saying years ago that people who liked *Serial* should try watching *Dateline*, and my friend joked in reply, "Yeah, but *Dateline* isn't hosted by my friend Sarah." One reason for the first season of *Serial*'s insane success—it is still the most downloaded podcast of all time—is the intimacy audiences felt with Koenig as she documented her investigation of a Baltimore teenager's murder in real time, keeping us up to date on every vagary of evidence, every interview, every experiment. Like the figure of the detective in many mystery novels, the reporter stands in for the audience, mirroring and orchestrating our shifts in perspective, our cynicism and credulity, our theories, prejudices, frustrations, and break-throughs.

This is what makes this style of true crime addictive, which is the adjective its makers most crave. The stance of the voyeur, the dispassionate observer, is thrilling without being emotionally taxing for the viewer, who watches from a safe remove. (This fact is subtly skewered in Gay Talese's creepy 2017 Netflix documentary, *Voyeur*.) I'm not sure how much of my eye-rolling at the popularity of highbrow true crime has to do with my general distrust of prestige TV and Oscar-bait movies, which are usually designed to be enjoyed in the exact same way and for the exact same reasons as any other entertainment, but also to make the viewer feel good about themselves for watching. When I wrote earlier that there are viewers who consume all true crime, and those who only consume "smart" true crime, I thought, *And there must be some people who only like dumb true crime.* Then I realized that I am sort of one of them.

There are specimens of highbrow true crime that I love, *Criminal* and *O.J.: Made in America* among them, but I truly enjoy *Dateline* much more than I do *Serial*, which in my mind is tedious to the edge of pointlessness. I find myself perversely complaining that good true crime is no fun—as self-conscious as it may be, it will never be as entertaining as the Investigation Discovery network's output, most of which is painfully serious. (The list of ID shows is one of the most amusing artifacts on the internet, including shows called *Bride*

*Killa*, *Momsters: When Moms Go Bad*, and *Sex Sent Me to the Slammer.*) Susan Sontag famously defined "camp" as "seriousness that fails," and camp is obviously part of the appeal of a show called *Sinister Ministers* or *Southern Fried Homicide*. Network news magazine shows like *Dateline* and *48 Hours* are somber and melodramatic, often literally starting voiceovers on their true-crime episodes with variations of "it was a dark and stormy night." They trade in archetypes—the perfect father, the sweet girl with big dreams, the divorcée looking for a second chance—and stick to a predetermined narrative of the case they're focusing on, unconcerned about accusations of bias. They are sentimental and yet utterly graphic, clinical in their depiction of brutal crimes.

It's always talked around in discussions of why people like true crime: it is . . . funny? The comedy in horror movies seems like a given, but it is hardly permitted to say that you are amused by true disturbing stories, out of respect for victims. But in reducing victims and their families to stock characters, in exaggerating murderers to superhuman monsters, in valorizing police and forensic scientists as heroic everymen, there is dark humor in how cheesy and misguided these pulpy shows are, how bad we are at talking about crime and drawing conclusions from it, how many ways we find to distance ourselves from the pain of victims and survivors, even when we think we are honoring them. (The jokey titles and tongue-in-cheek tone of some ID shows seem to indicate more awareness of the inherent humor, but in general, the channel's programming is almost all derivative of network TV specials.) I'm not saying I'm proud of it, but in its obvious failures, I enjoy this brand of true crime more straightforwardly than its voyeuristic, documentary counterpart, which, in its dignified guise, has maybe only perfected a method of making us feel less gross about consuming real people's pain for fun.

Crime stories also might be less risky when they are more stilted, more clinical. To be blunt, what makes a crime story less satisfying are often the ethical guidelines that help reporters avoid ruining people's lives. With the popularity of the podcasts *S-Town* and *Missing Richard Simmons*, there were conversations about the ethics of appropriating another person's story, particularly when they won't (or can't) participate in your version of it. The questions of ethics and appropriation are even heavier when stories intersect with their subjects' criminal cases, because journalism has always had a reciprocal relationship with the justice system. Part of the exhilarating intimacy of the first season of *Serial* was Koenig's speculation about people who never agreed to be part of the show, the theories and rabbit holes she went through, the risks she took to get answers. But there is a reason most reporters do all their research, *then* write their story. It is inappropriate, and potentially libelous, to let your readers in on every unverified theory about your subject that occurs to you, particularly when wondering about a private citizen's innocence or guilt in a horrific crime.

Koenig's off-the-cuff tone had other consequences, too, in the form of amateur sleuths on Reddit who tracked down people involved with the case, pored over court transcripts, and reviewed cellular tower evidence, forming a shadow army of investigators taking up what they saw as the gauntlet thrown down by the show. The journalist often takes on the stance of the professional amateur, a citizen providing information in the public interest and using the resources at hand to get answers. At times during the first season of *Serial*, Koenig's methods are laughably amateurish, like when she drives from the victim's high school to the scene of the crime, a Best Buy, to see if it was possible to do it in the stated timeline. She is able to do it, which means very little, since the crime occurred 15 years earlier. Because so many of her investigative tools were also ones available to listeners at home, some took that as an invitation to play along.

This blurred line between professional and amateur, reporter and private investigator, has plagued journalists since the dawn of modern crime reporting. In 1897, amid a frenzied rivalry between newspaper barons William Randolph Hearst and Joseph Pulitzer, true-crime coverage was so popular that Hearst formed a group of reporters to investigate criminal cases called the "Murder Squad." They wore badges and carried guns, forming essentially an extralegal police force who both assisted and muddled official investigations. In search of a better story and to sell more papers, it was common for reporters to trample crime scenes, plant evidence, and produce dubious witnesses whose accounts fit their preferred version of the case. And they were trying to get audiences hooked in very similar ways, by crowdsourcing information and encouraging readers to send in tips.

Of course, the producers of *Serial* never did anything so questionable as the Murder Squad, though there are interesting parallels between the true-crime podcast and crime coverage in early daily newspapers. They were both innovations in the ways information was delivered to the public that sparked unexpectedly personal, participatory, and impassioned responses from their audiences. It's tempting to say that we've come full circle, with a new true-crime boom that is victim to some of the same ethical pitfalls of the first one: Is crime journalism another industry deregulated by the anarchy of the internet? But as Michelle Dean wrote in the *Guardian* of *Serial*, "This is exactly the problem with doing journalism at all . . . You might think you are doing a simple crime podcast . . . and then you become a sensation, as *Serial* has, and the story falls to the mercy of the thousands, even millions, of bored and curious people on the internet."

Simply by merit of their popularity, highbrow crime stories are often riskier than their lowbrow counterparts. Kathryn Schulz wrote in *The New Yorker* about the ways the makers of the Netflix series *Making a Murderer*, in their attempt to advocate for the convicted murderer Steven Avery, omit evidence that incriminates him and put forth an incoherent argument for his innocence. Advocacy and intervention are complicated actions for journalists to undertake, though they are not novel. Schulz points to a scene in *Making a Murderer* where a *Dateline* producer who is covering Avery is shown saying, "Right now murder is hot." In this moment the creators of *Making a Murderer* are drawing a distinction between themselves and *Dateline*, as Schulz writes, implying that, "unlike traditional true-crime shows . . . their work is too intellectually serious to be thoughtless, too morally worthy to be cruel." But they were not only trying to invalidate Avery's conviction; they (like *Dateline*, but more effectively) were also creating an addictive product, a compelling story.

That is maybe what irks me the most about true crime with highbrow pretensions. It appeals to the same vices as traditional true crime, and often trades in the same melodrama and selective storytelling, but its consequences can be more extreme. Adnan Syed was granted a new trial after *Serial* brought attention to his case; Avery was denied his appeal, but people involved in his case have nevertheless been doxxed and threatened. I've come to believe that addictiveness and advocacy are rarely compatible. If they were, why would the creators of *Making a Murderer* have advocated for one white man, when the story of being victimized by a corrupt police force is common to so many people across the US, particularly people of color?

It does feel like a shame that so many resources are going to create slick, smart true crime that asks the wrong questions, focusing our energy on individual stories instead of the systemic problems they represent. But in truth, this is probably a feature, not a bug. I suspect the new true-crime obsession has something to do with the massive, terrifying problems we face as a society: government corruption, mass violence, corporate greed, income inequality, police brutality, environmental degradation, human-rights violations. These are large-scale crimes whose resolutions, though not mysterious, are also not forthcoming. Focusing on one case, bearing down on its minutiae and discovering who is to blame, serves as both an escape and a means of feeling in control, giving us an arena where justice is possible.

Skepticism about whether journalists appropriate their subjects' stories, about high and low, and about why we enjoy the crime stories we do, all swirl through what I think of as the post–true crime moment. Post–true crime is explicitly or implicitly about the popularity of the new true-crime wave, questioning its place in our culture, and resisting or responding to its conventions. One interesting document of post–true crime is *My Favorite Murder* and other "comedy murder podcasts," which, in retelling stories murder buffs have heard on one million Investigation Discovery shows, unpack the ham-fisted clichés of the true-crime genre. They show how these stories appeal to the most gruesome sides of our personalities and address the obvious but unspoken fact that true crime is entertainment, and often the kind that is as mindless as a sitcom. Even more cutting is the Netflix parody *American Vandal*, which both codifies and spoofs the conventions of the new highbrow true crime, roasting the genre's earnest tone in its depiction of a *Serial*-like investigation of some lewd graffiti.

There is also the trend in the post–true crime era of dramatizing famous crime stories, like in *The Bling Ring*; *I, Tonya*;

and Ryan Murphy's anthology series *American Crime Story*, all of which dwell not only on the stories of infamous crimes but also why they captured the public imagination. There is a camp element in these retellings, particularly when famous actors like John Travolta and Sarah Paulson are hamming it up in ridiculous wigs. But this self-consciousness often works to these projects' advantage, allowing them to show heightened versions of the cultural moments that led to the most outsize tabloid crime stories. Many of these fictionalized versions take journalistic accounts as their source material, like Nancy Jo Sales's reporting in *Vanity Fair* for *The Bling Ring* and ESPN's documentary on Tonya Harding, *The Price of Gold*, for *I, Tonya*. This seems like a best-case scenario for prestige true crime to me: parsing famous cases from multiple angles and in multiple genres, trying to understand them both on the level of individual choices and cultural forces.

Perhaps the most significant contributions to post–true crime, though, are the recent wave of personal accounts about murder and crime: literary memoirs like *Down City* by Leah Carroll, *Mean* by Myriam Gurba, *The Hot One* by Carolyn Murnick, *After the Eclipse* by Sarah Perry, and *We Are All Shipwrecks* by Kelly Grey Carlisle all tell the stories of murder seen from close-up. (It is significant that all of these books are by women. Carroll, Perry, and Carlisle all write about their mothers' murders, placing them in the tradition of James Ellroy's great memoir *My Dark Places*, but without the tortured, fetish-y tone.) This is not a voyeuristic first person, and the reader can't detach and find joy in procedure;

we are finally confronted with the truth of lives upended by violence and grief. There's also *Ear Hustle*, the brilliant podcast produced by the inmates of San Quentin State Prison. The makers of *Ear Hustle* sometimes contemplate the bad luck and bad decisions that led them to be incarcerated, but more often they discuss the concerns of daily life in prison, like food, sex, and how to make mascara from an inky page from a magazine. This is a crime podcast that is the opposite of sensational, addressing the systemic truth of crime and the justice system, in stories that are mundane, profound, and, yes, addictive.

Originally published by *Vulture*, August 2018

# The Lost Children of "Runaway Train"

BY ELON GREEN

On a Friday morning in April 1990, Christopher Matthew Kerze, 17, told his mother, Alona, he had a headache. And so, having no reason to suspect otherwise, she agreed he could stay home from school, and went to work.

When she returned at 3 that afternoon, Alona found a note on the kitchen table, written in Christopher's scrawl:

Mom,
Something important came up + feeling somewhat better.
Back by six. (Unless I get lost.)
Love,
Chris

The words "get lost" were underlined twice.
Alona found that the family van was gone, and their dog,

B.W. Bowser, who tended to be leashed during the day, had gotten loose, which she thought was odd.

By 10 p.m., there was still no sign of her son. Alona called her sister, who lived in the area. Then she called her husband, Jim, who had left the Kerzes' house in Eagan, Minnesota, early that morning. A credit analyst, he'd gone to Wisconsin on business. Jim immediately drove home, and he pulled into the driveway around midnight.

Still no sign of Christopher.

It was at this time that Patrick, Christopher's younger brother, told his parents that Jim's Mossberg bolt-action 20-gauge shotgun, which was kept in a closet—separate from the ammunition—was gone.

"We just went crazy at that moment," said Jim.

CHRISTOPHER'S DISAPPEARANCE DID NOT, AT FIRST, RE-ceive much media attention. Eagan, a city of about 64,000, has a fair number of such cases. "It wouldn't be unusual for us to have two or three runaway missing person cases in a weekend," said Stefanie Bolks, a detective in the Eagan Police Department who calls herself "a longtime copper." Since Christopher went missing, she said, hundreds of minors in her jurisdiction have run away. But only one other person—a young woman who has been gone for two and a half years—remains unaccounted for.

Occasionally, said Bolks, the kids are fleeing abusive homes. But mostly, she said, they simply don't want to abide

by house rules, and their disappearance is relatively brief—
no more than a day or two. "I mean, we have regulars that
take off every Thursday or Friday, and then they're gone for
the long weekend," she said. "A lot of times, it's just that the
kids are incorrigible."

Not so with Christopher, however. "What you need to
know is, he's always been a very great kid," Jim told me. He
was a National Merit Scholar semifinalist; he was invited
to join the National Honor Society; and, even as a gangly
teen, he'd made the high school swim team. Though never a
top-tier competitor, he twice made the regionals. Watching
Christopher swim the medley—breaststroke, crawl, back-
stroke, and fly—is one of Jim's fondest memories. "He gets
an ovation when he's done," he said. "His time stunk, but
who cares? He actually did it."

Christopher loved to camp. Loved to ski. He was adept
at playing with the software of a computer—an original
Macintosh—back when such an activity was still relatively
esoteric. A friend's dad owned a warehouse, and they'd play
laser tag. He played cello in grade school, clarinet in junior
high and high school. "He was a smart kid, a good sense of
humor," Jim said.

When Bolks inherited the case, in 1994, Christopher had
been gone four years. The local investigation had reached
a dead end. Nothing was found of the boy's clothing, his
glasses or the gun, and the police department had received
only "a handful" of tips. But there was reason to hope that all

this might change, as Christopher's case had recently gotten a great deal of publicity.

THE ATTENTION CAME IN THE FORM OF A MUSIC VIDEO for a song called "Runaway Train" by the alternative rock band Soul Asylum, who, in 1993, were at the height of their success. The group had just released their sixth—and most popular—album, *Grave Dancers Union*, which ended up going triple platinum. "Runaway Train"—which would remain on the Billboard charts for more than 40 weeks, and which the band would play at Bill Clinton's inaugural ball—was one of its singles.

The idea for the song's video had begun with a milk carton—and, by extension, another missing kid.

Etan Patz, abducted in SoHo in May 1979, may be the most famous missing American child of the last half century, and the case's fame rests, in part, on Patz's face being displayed on the side of a milk carton. Depending on whom you ask, his was either the first or among the first. And that lit the spark for the video, its director, Tony Kaye, has said: "I was being driven home one night and I saw a poster—I think it was a milk poster . . . where it was missing kids on the carton."

"Runaway Train" is a power ballad about depression. But Kaye decided the music video ought to be about something else: missing children. Over the course of four and a half minutes, the video toggles between footage of the band singing—the stuff of traditional music videos—and kids making a break for it; at the end, it depicts an abduction. Dotted throughout are photos and names of real missing children along with the date on which each disappeared.

Securing photos of those children required the help of the National Center for Missing & Exploited Children and its founder, Ernie Allen. In a recent conversation with me, Allen recalled the power and efficacy of the milk carton campaign. "Photos of missing children work," he said, with the fervor of a man who has been making that argument for a long time. If enough people are armed with the best possible images and information, he reasoned, there's a much better chance of locating and recovering a missing child. (The milk carton campaign, the origins of which are murky, fell by the wayside after Dr. Benjamin Spock and others suggested it needlessly scared children.)

When Kaye approached him, Allen was enthusiastic. He felt, and Kaye agreed, it was best to focus on "endangered runaways," which the US Department of Justice would eventually define as children who had been "physically or sexually abused at home" or were "substance dependent" or "in the company of someone known to be abusing drugs."

Further requisites: The children had to have been missing for at least a couple of years; their absence must have been reported to the police and entered into the Federal Bureau of Investigation's national crime database; and, finally, it was imperative that parents grant permission to disseminate their child's photo.

At the time, according to Allen, there were 1.6 million

runaways a year. While many return home after a short time, Allen knew it was the kids who had been gone awhile that were at greater risk for harm. The reality, to which "Runaway Train" alludes in its closing minute, is that sometimes what looks like a runaway is actually an abduction. "You don't ever really know, in most missing persons cases, what the circumstances are," Allen noted.

In any case, he said, the video was "an opportunity to provide massive exposure to a huge segment of the population that may not routinely see missing child photos, and making whoever sees these photos think, I might be able to do something. I might have actually seen this person." So Allen agreed to help Kaye and the band. But first, he extracted a promise from Kaye: If any child were recovered, his or her photo must be immediately removed from circulation and replaced with the photo of another missing child. What this meant, in practice, was that if things went according to plan, Kaye would have to repeatedly recut the video.

When the video debuted in May 1993, 13 children were featured. Sixteen-year-old Elizabeth Wiles was the first to come home.

"I LIKED A GUY WHO WAS OLDER THAN ME AND MY PARents told me no," said Liz Vatovec, née Wiles. She's now 39, and lives with her husband outside of Nashville, where she is a real estate broker and a licensed contractor. It was oddly jarring to realize that the blond kid from the decades-old photo of her reunion with her mother was my senior.

I contacted a few of the children—that is, the lucky ones who lived to no longer be children—from "Runaway Train." Of the ones I reached out to, only Vatover agreed to be interviewed.

Wiles, then 13, left her family's home in Lamar, Arkansas. She and her boyfriend, Ron, hitchhiked to California, where she and her family had lived before moving to Arkansas. He worked odd jobs until they could afford a place of their own. They told anyone who inquired that she was 17. "People didn't seem to be overly concerned about a 17-year-old having a dysfunctional family and leaving home, and people kind of sympathized with me a little bit and just looked the other way," she said.

They stayed for two and a half years.

In May 1993, Elizabeth and Ron were at a friend's house in San Diego. The television was on, and they weren't paying much attention to it. But then Wiles saw her own face on MTV. Her biological father, Duane, had—without consulting Elizabeth's mother, Debra, from whom he was divorced— given her photo to the National Center for Missing & Exploited Children. The video had begun airing that month.

"I just kind of freaked out," she said.

A week later—she'd hesitated, at first—Elizabeth called her mother, who had not heard from the girl, not even a postcard, since she'd left home. As they wept, Elizabeth apologized and said she wanted to come home. There were no recriminations; Debra was just happy to have her back.

Her mother, Elizabeth tells me, always suspected she was

alive, though she didn't know for sure. "She said that she knew I was okay, that if there was something wrong, she would know," Elizabeth said. "She tried not to worry about me." "Did you really not contact her?" I asked. "I can be a stubborn person," she said. "It's not a good quality of mine."

When she came home, there was a return to relative normalcy. There were house rules she had to abide by. After a few months, Elizabeth got a GED. She attended college but never finished.

Her lack of traditional schooling is one of her regrets. "I still go back and wonder if I could've become a scientist or went into quantum physics or something," she said. "I'm okay with it, though. Again, I have a really nice life. [Running away] made me who I am."

Elizabeth met Soul Asylum once, backstage at a concert in Little Rock, and in August 1993 she appeared on NBC with her mother, the band's frontman Dave Pirner, and Ernie Allen. She's had no contact with the band since then, but the song that brought her home has remained a part of her life. "I probably hear it a handful of times a year," she said. "Sometimes we're at a store or whatever, and they've got the music playing in the background. That song comes on, and of course my husband now knows everything about it. We're shopping, and we just both pause like, *Okay, nobody else knows the meaning of that to us.*"

BECAUSE OF SOUL ASYLUM'S AGREEMENT THAT THE video would be recut whenever one of its runaways returned home, multiple versions exist. One of the versions on You-Tube has far more views than the others: nearly 60 million. It's in that version—if you stop it at precisely 3 minutes and 30 seconds—that you can see a photo of Martha Wes Dunn. In the photo, she is holding a black dog. The 15-year-old, who had a scar on her cheek from a childhood injury, vanished from Daingerfield, Texas, on September 5, 1990. Her father reported her missing around five the next morning, and Deputy Martha Cox took the case.

I spoke about Dunn's case with Morris County Sheriff's Office Chief Deputy Robbie Gray, who has been on it since 1999. Dunn had been in Oklahoma with some relatives. Her parents had brought her home to Texas to start the school year on September 4. She'd been unhappy about it and they'd argued. The last time they saw her was at home on September 5 around 2:20 p.m. It's known that that night, around 10, Dunn spoke with her boyfriend, 17-year-old Eric Owens, by phone. The next day, she and Owens were gone.

One theory held that they ran away together to live in Hayworth, Oklahoma, where Owens's aunt lived. The couple was reportedly seen there "several times." (The aunt denied this.) Another theory: They'd hitchhiked to Kansas, where Owens's mother lived. Wichita, perhaps. Neither story panned out, said Gray.

On September 30, a few weeks after the disappearance, Dunn's father, John, called the police to report that he'd received a call from a friend in Durant, Oklahoma. The friend had said he'd seen Dunn and Owens, and they were "dirty and hungry." He got them cleaned up and fed. "That's what the father told the deputy," said Gray. "Of course, they called up there and never found them or anything like that."

There was another, considerably darker possibility, suggested by Dunn's father: that Owens, who had been involved with drugs in Oklahoma, was targeted by a dealer who kidnapped them both. But there was no ransom demand. Indeed, said Gray, "There was no signs of anything like that happening."

Neither Dunn nor Owens has been seen again.

Is there any reason, I asked Gray, to believe they were anything but runaways? "No, not really," he said. "The reason why is, if you knew her parents, they were kind of strange. They were different, I'll put it that way. When this happened, you would have actually thought, *Okay, yeah, she's trying to get out from underneath them.*"

By the time "Runaway Train" aired, said Gray, "things went cold." Even the popularity of the video couldn't move the needle much. There was a tip that Dunn was working as a waitress near New Boston. ("Of course, I called over there, and that wasn't true.") About a year ago, Gray heard about a woman in Mississippi who reportedly resembled Dunn's age progression photo. That, too, came to nothing. And that, he said, was the last time anyone called about Martha Wes Dunn.

"I don't know if I would go so far as saying that she's alive," said Gray. But there's no evidence to the contrary. That makes

Dunn one of only two long-term missing persons cases in Morris County in the last 25 years. (As of 2013, Daingerfield had a population of only 2,526.)

Dunn's sister, Tina Holstine, posted a video about her to YouTube and wrote, in part:

*I just hope your out there this video is for my sister she went missing in 1990 never to be seen again. We have been to oklahoma and other places she might would be was told she was ok and to just leave it alone. But we can't just back down and forget about her we just want to see her again. The police put her down as a run away couse of her age. Eric Owens come to our house and took her they were into drugs pretty bad and our only conclusion is that she can't get back to us couse she couldn't find us so I done this video for her. If your watching siss we love you and just want you back.*

Attempts to reach Holstine were unsuccessful.

"RUNAWAY TRAIN," SAID DAVE PIRNER, WAS A MIRACLE: "We were able to turn a blatant promotion item into a public service announcement and got away with it." Since *Grave Dancers Union*, Soul Asylum has gone on to release five more albums. In fact, Pirner and his band—of whom he is the only remaining original member—released a new album in March called *Change of Fortune*.

It's been more than 20 years since the song's release, but to Pirner's astonishment and maybe consternation, it continues to resonate. (The video immediately spawned imitators.

There were, at the very least, versions in the UK and Canada with entirely different children.) When we talked in September, he'd just been contacted by a Syrian man who wanted to use the song with a photo collage of children who had been maimed by war.

Pirner knows, though, that "Runaway Train" is an inescapable association. Not that long ago, he told me, "I went to an Irish bar and there was a guy playing Irish songs in the corner on his guitar. He had a sign on the wall next to him and it said DANNY BOY, TEN BUCKS. I just laughed because I understood exactly. It's like the only Irish song that people know, so they always request it. I should have a placard like that around my neck that says RUNAWAY TRAIN, TEN BUCKS."

I asked Pirner, who splits his time between Minnesota and Louisiana, if he had any children. Yes, he said, a 13-year-old. Had the song changed his parenting at all? Yes, he said, "Runaway Train" had likely made him more protective than he would have otherwise been. "I was probably more aware of the possibilities of creeps and predators," he said. "It seems hard for me to even explain something like that to a kid without scaring him, but I guess that's the whole idea."

FOR ME, THE STORY BEGINS AND ENDS WITH CHRISTOpher Kerze, who disappeared that Minnesota spring 26 years ago. The arc of his life is devastatingly incomplete.

The day after he left, Jim and Alona received an envelope in the mail, postmarked Duluth. In it was another handwritten note, addressed to "Mom, Dad, And Readers." Kerze explained that he'd lied about being sick in order to take the family's 1988 light blue Dodge Caravan "to not even I know where."

Furthermore, wrote Kerze, he intended to commit suicide. He declined to give a reason. But he understood how deeply it would hurt those he loved, and for that he expressed regret.

"Take heart," he continued, "because if just one person is better off for having known me, my life will not have been wasted."

The next day, two days after Kerze was last seen, police found the family's van abandoned by the side of the road in Itasca County in northern Minnesota, about 20 miles north of Grand Rapids.

And yet: all these years later, no one can say with certainty what happened. When Kerze left the house, he took the shotgun but not the ammunition. No traces of him have ever been found—not the shotgun, not his glasses, not his clothes, and not his body. And, as Ernie Allen said, "He could've changed his mind. The reality is he is missing until he's found."

The uncertainty is, for Jim Kerze, both hope and torment. But he hasn't given up. "My pipe dream is that Christopher works for a little company in Cleveland, is married and has three kids. He's a very quiet employee. He's not a person who would lead the charge. He's one of those guys in the back to hold the place together.

"Smart, could do the job, hold the place together, be very

relied on. But you wouldn't want to ask him to try to sell stuff to the public because that's not his personality. His personality is the other way."

He paused. "I know that the reality, intellectually, is probably a lot different. But you have to have some way to hope."

Originally published by *MEL* magazine, November 2016

# The True Crime Story Behind a 1970s Cult Feminist Film Classic

## BY SARAH WEINMAN

They met in New Orleans just before Mardi Gras, in 1959. He was part owner of a French Quarter bookshop. She was looking for a job. He was 30. So was she, though she claimed to be three years younger. He said his name was Don Reisinger. She gave hers as Alma Malone. His name was fake. Hers was, too, in a way; she hadn't used her birth name, Stephens, in a long time.

She didn't get the job. She did, however, get the guy.

Alma and Don made a strange couple. He was short—five foot four without his customary elevator shoes, and 110 pounds on a good day. He tended to squint at the light or when something didn't suit, but was rarely photographed with glasses on. She was taller, rangier: a natural brunette with an elegant neck.

Don tended to disappear for days or weeks at a time. Alma never had warning before he'd take off, and even less when, in early September, he told her they were leaving for Cleveland. She didn't have anyone to alert, anyway, being estranged from her family.

That family included a mother and a younger sister, back in her hometown of Salina, Kansas, both of whom she refused to write. Her father played no part in her life; his repeated molestation of her had driven her to juvenile delinquency, a stint in a Kansas City convent, and a permanent grudge against her mother. She wasn't in contact with her 11-year-old son, Robert—who lived with his father—either, nor with any of her four ex-husbands, the first of whom she married when she was only 14 years old.

Alma and Don arrived in Cleveland on September 7, 1959. Once there, Don revealed that his real name was William Ansley. (He also operated under the aliases Shannon Ansley, William Shannon, and Robert Shannon.) He had drifted into New Orleans two years earlier, after finishing up probation and a suspended sentence in Philadelphia for armed robbery.

That sentence stemmed from an earlier, more serious one in Boston, when William decided to hold up the Northeast Airlines offices at the Statler Hotel. It didn't go well. William bungled the robbery, nearly killed a cab driver, and received a 9- to 12-year sentence for both crimes.

But William had a new plan, as he explained to Alma: the newspapers were full of reports about someone who had tried to heist the Lorain Avenue branch of the Cleveland Trust Company bank. William would do one better. "He said if I would help him he could do it successfully, but if anything did go wrong, we could die," Alma later told reporters. "I kept stalling the job. I suppose I wanted to live, even though I didn't have much to live for."

Alma and William spent the next two weeks planning the job. She bleached her brown hair blond and pretended at pregnancy, thanks to a maternity dress and foam-rubber padding. William bought a blond wig of his own to conceal his bald head, as well as all the equipment they would need for a successful bank heist.

By the morning of September 23, William and Alma were ready. He affixed the wig on his head. She threw on a shabby blue gabardine dress and a pair of faded black loafers. He made a list of 15 steps to follow to the letter, and put the list in his pocket.

What happened in no way resembled what they had planned. It did, however, end up immortalized on film.

WATCHING *WANDA*, BARBARA LODEN'S 1970 DIRECTORIAL debut, is a revelation. The pace is languid, until it isn't. Grimy and washed-out, the film makes a point of being naturalistic.

Wanda Goronski, played by 38-year-old Loden herself, is drabness personified—a Rust Belt housewife barely awake, listless about cooking, cleaning, and her employment status. She lies on the couch, absorbing her sister's pointed criticism about her state of apathy. She drifts into bars and mediocre sex. She is robbed while asleep in a movie theater and barely reacts.

"I'm just no good," Wanda declares in court as she loses

custody of her two children to the husband she's divorcing. She soon takes up with Mr. Dennis, who she meets in a bar, endures his physical abuse, and goes along with his criminal plans, because she has nowhere else to go.

The filmmaker herself could relate. "I used to be a lot like that," Loden explained to the *Los Angeles Times* a few months after *Wanda* was released. "I had no identity of my own. I just became whatever I thought people wanted me to become."

Loden was an ex-Copacabana showgirl with a heavy North Carolina accent who was transformed by Method lessons into an actress of note. (Her Marilyn Monroe–inspired performance in Arthur Miller's *After the Fall* won her a Tony Award.) She landed juicy film roles, including one as Warren Beatty's sister in *Splendor in the Grass*, and a famous director husband, Elia Kazan, to whom she was married until her premature death in 1980 at the age of 48.

Loden's marriage to Kazan came after she spent years as his mistress, an affair begun while she was still married to the father of her two sons, Leo and Marco. She endured a heavy dose of public humiliation from Kazan's depiction of her in his 1967 roman à clef *The Arrangement*, made even worse when Loden was passed over for a role in the film adaptation in favor of Faye Dunaway. Kazan later tried to take credit for *Wanda*'s initial script—though he claimed, with mock gallantry, to have stayed out of his wife's way as she shot the film in and around Scranton, Pennsylvania.

Loden's internal strife provided the emotional motivation for her to write, direct, and act in the film. But the seed for

*Wanda*—which manifests, in the second half of the film, in a bank robbery that goes awry—was planted a decade before the film's limited release: Loden had chanced upon a March 27, 1960, newspaper story called "The Go-for-Broke Bank Robber," which described a duo's failed bank heist in Cleveland that led to the death of the lead robber. Loden seized upon the story of the accomplice, a woman who later thanked the judge for her long prison sentence.

The French film theorist Nathalie Léger, in her brilliant 2012 book *Suite for Barbara Loden*, a hybrid of biography, memoir, fiction, and criticism, identified the woman as Alma Malone. ("She might have been the daughter of Samuel Beckett's Malone, the one who says at the beginning of the book, 'I shall soon be quite dead at last in spite of all.'")

Léger found the discovery of Loden's real-life inspiration deflating: "All the thrill of the quest evaporated. An overwhelming sense of sorrow overtook me during the exhausting period of going through these pages and I immediately lost all interest in the subject for a period of several weeks, filled with regret for ever having allowed myself to be overtaken by the urge to pinpoint the source of the story."

For Léger, finding out about Alma detracted from her own work, opening up questions she knew she wouldn't have time to investigate. But had Léger persisted, she'd have discovered a remarkable tale of a woman more like Loden's creation than the filmmaker herself had ever realized. One whose story has never been fully told.

THE DOORBELL RANG AT SEVEN A.M. HERBERT FOX WENT to answer. The bank manager's two daughters, 18-year-old Marilyn and 10-year-old Bonnie, continued to eat breakfast. His wife, Loretta, was washing the dishes.

William Ansley and Alma Malone were at the door.

"Our car broke down. May we use your telephone?" said William. Alma, the taller of the two, peered over Ansley's shoulder.

"Why, uh—"

William thrust his foot into the doorway. Then, pointing a .45 at Fox, he went inside with Alma. Fox grabbed at William. Alma set down a hatbox and pulled an automatic handgun from her red handbag. "Let him go!" she cried.

Loretta Fox stuck her head out from the kitchen. "What is it, dear?"

"Come in here!" cried Alma. The girls appeared in the doorway. "You too!"

The Fox family assembled in the living room. Alma pulled some cord from her handbag and began to tie them up, one by one. William pointed to the hatbox.

"See that? That's a bomb. A real, live bomb. You cooperate with us and we'll be back here to disarm it before the time it's set to go off." William turned to Fox. "You are going to take me to the bank."

"Wh-wh-wh-what for?"

William chuckled.

"To rob it, of course."

No one said anything further. A ticking sound came from the hatbox.

"You just sit still," Alma said. "If you joggle around trying to go free, the bomb will go off."

William motioned for Fox to get his coat and hat. Fox put a rosary beside Bonnie, still tied up. "Pray for all of us," he said, and walked out of his home with William and Alma following behind. "Go to your car," ordered William. "Act natural." Fox obeyed.

As they got into Fox's car, Alma got into a blue Ford with a white top, intending to follow them. But when the men arrived at the bank, she was no longer behind them.

EDDIE LEE WAITED AT THE ENTRANCE TO THE LORAIN Avenue branch of the Cleveland Trust. He greeted Fox with a smile that evaporated when he saw William, who spirited both men into the bank.

William gave the same spiel to Eddie that he recited to the other dozen or so employees filing into the Lorain Avenue branch: there was a bomb at Fox's house that would go off if they didn't follow instructions. Fox was then ordered to fill a cardboard box with money.

He was about to hand off the box stuffed with bills to William, when a policeman appeared at the window.

"Stall him off!" said William. "Get out there, at the center of the floor." Fox moved slowly, wondering if his family would survive because of his decisions.

Then he saw a second cop.

———

THE FICTIONAL RELATIONSHIP BETWEEN WANDA AND Mr. Dennis is quite faithful to what Loden knew of the relationship between Alma and William. The film version of the heist stays true to the details of what happened at the Fox residence, down to the ticking hatbox. Wanda's existential ennui could have, and likely did, come straight from what Alma later told reporters.

So one could imagine the real Alma reacting to William as Wanda does to Mr. Dennis when he says this on how to dress and act, and how to stop being so passive: "If you don't want anything, you won't have anything, and if you don't have anything, you're as good as dead."

Or when Mr. Dennis slaps Wanda, and it takes her several beats of quiet shock before responding with a tepid, plaintive, "Hey, that hurt."

"COME ON, WE'VE GOT TO HELP DADDY!"
Marilyn Fox had broken free of the cord that kept her tied up. She untied her mother, Loretta, and sister, Bonnie. The hatbox kept on ticking. For 15 minutes, the trio prayed. Then they ran over to a neighbor's house. It was 8:20 a.m. The radio reported "some kind of disturbance" at the Lorain Avenue bank branch.

Patrolmen James Gatter and Thomas McNamara were on duty that morning. They heard the police scanner and stopped their car near the bank. Gatter grabbed a shotgun. McNamara fetched his service revolver. They were at the entrance when Eddie Lee ran out the door.

A hand holding an automatic gun rose over the bank counter.

The robber fired. Gatter fired back. They exchanged fire two more times, as glass shattered around them. Gatter first aimed at the wood near the top of the counter. The next time he aimed at the floor.

He reached for more ammunition and found it gone—William's shot had ripped a hole in his pants, right at the ammunition belt.

Gatter got ready to draw his revolver again when a third policeman rushed in. "After that," Gatter later recalled, "just about every policeman in town came up behind us. It was just like a movie thriller."

Police swarmed up to nearby rooftops by the dozens, dropping tear gas into the bank through an open window. "Come out in ten minutes or we're coming in," Cleveland police chief Frank Storey intoned through a megaphone. "It's your funeral."

William fired more shots. A bank employee jumped through a window, shouting, "Hold your fire! He's letting us out!"

The bank staff streamed out. This included Fox, who learned—to his relief—that his family was safe and the bomb had not gone off in his house. The hatbox turned out to be harmless: it held two dry cell batteries, a timer, and fuses of coal dust. That was it. Nothing explosive.

Detective Jack Hughes entered the bank. He saw William

on the floor, clutching an automatic. Hughes kicked away the gun from the robber's hand. That's how he learned William was dead. A shot had gone right through his temple, which had blown off his blond wig and exposed the bald head underneath.

THE CLEVELAND POLICE SEARCHED FOR ALMA AND found her rented blue Ford, abandoned on the city's east side. In it, cops discovered a picture of her with William from a New Orleans nightclub. They also found an ID card with the name Billy Jean Carroll, a blond wig, and her maternity-dress disguise. There was also a book on child care, some food, a cosmetics case, and men's and women's clothing.

Alma knew something had gone terribly wrong. Following Fox and William, she would later say that she had "made a wrong turn somewhere"—and by the time she got near the bank, "there were so many people around, a traffic cop directed me away."

Alma figured William had committed suicide as planned. "It was understood that if anything went wrong, Mr. Ansley would kill me and then himself," she later told local reporters. "I wouldn't have had the courage to kill myself. With us, it was either make the job good or die, because Mr. Ansley said he would never go back to jail if anything went wrong."

After being directed away from the bank, Alma ditched the car and found a nearby bar. As she drank a beer, the television came on with a news flash. Alma fled as soon as she could.

For "three cold days and nights," she slept under a bridge in the woods near Baldwin Reservoir, about a mile from where she abandoned the getaway car, at East 105th Street and Euclid Avenue.

On the third day, she decided to walk back into town and get a room at a rooming house—where, once she saw her own face on TV, she resolved to stay put. For the next two weeks, she didn't leave the building. She also managed to make a few phone calls to her younger sister, who did not tell anyone else—not their mother, and certainly not the FBI agents looking for Alma. "They are listening in. Your phone is probably tapped," Alma told her sister. "But I'm okay."

Alma might have remained at the rooming house even longer had she and a fellow tenant (and local drug dealer) not argued, their voices so loud it disturbed the other occupants. A tip went out to the police department. When they arrived, there was Alma.

"Thank God it's over," she reportedly said, "I'm so tired of hiding."

THE CASE MADE HEADLINES ACROSS THE COUNTRY, EVEN the world. Alma's past as an accessory to another heist came to light—she had been asleep in a car when a boyfriend and two accomplices robbed an inn in New York State in 1954, eventually getting a year in prison. Cleveland police deemed her a "very disturbed person."

On November 25, 1959, Alma was indicted for armed robbery, kidnapping, conspiracy to kidnap, and "malicious entry into a financial institution." Six weeks later, on January 7, 1960, she pleaded guilty to the last charge, while the others were dropped as part of a deal made with the prosecutor, John T. Corrigan, to reduce her prison sentence.

Judge Joseph Artl sentenced Alma to 20 years in prison, which she began on January 21, 1960, at the Ohio Reformatory for Women in Marysville. The newly minted prisoner number W-7988 expressed relief to reporters afterward: "Oh, I'm very happy. I really expected him to lower the boom!"

TWO MONTHS LATER, LODEN READ ABOUT ALMA IN RUTH Reynolds's Justice column in the *New York Sunday News*. She saw the bones of a great movie—"That's what struck me: Why would this girl feel glad to be put away?" she told an interviewer in 1974—but, after years of rejection by prospective studios and directors, Loden told the *Los Angeles Times* in 1971, "If I wanted to get it done, I'd have to [direct] it myself . . . It was like being a housewife. You do everything—you don't differentiate."

A producer friend, Harry Shuster, put up the $115,000 budget, an amount Loden felt she must not exceed. Nick Proferes, the cinematographer, and Michael Higgins, who played Mr. Dennis, were the only professionals Loden hired. The others were amateurs, nonunion workers, or both. "It's not a new wave . . . It's the old wave," Loden told the *New York Times* in 1971. "That's what they used to do. They took a camera and they went out and shot. Around that act this

whole fantastic apparatus grew up—the Hollywood albatross. They made a ship out of lead. It won't float anymore."

Loden disdained most Hollywood films as "too perfect to
be believable" and wanted to stay far away from them. "The
slicker the technique is, the slicker the content becomes,"
she said, "until everything turns into Formica, including the
people."

When it was finally time to start shooting *Wanda*, Loden
reached out to the prison warden at Marysville to ask for
permission to interview Alma. It had taken Loden many
years to find out where Alma was housed, but the warden refused the request. "No, I don't think it would be interesting,"
said the warden, according to Loden. "I don't think that you
should be interested in this story. I'm the person who gives
permission for everything here, and that I will not allow."

SHORTLY BEFORE DYING OF THE BREAST CANCER THAT
would consume the last two years of her life, Loden gave an
interview in the late '70s for a German television documentary
about herself and *Wanda*. "There's so much I didn't achieve, but
I tried to be independent and to create my own way," she said
in the posthumously released broadcast. "Otherwise, I would
have become like Wanda, all my life just floating around."

Loden didn't spend her final decade floating around. She
did, however, run into difficulty after finishing her film.
Though it received critical acclaim—a warm reception at the
Venice International Film Festival, a rave from *Times* film

critic Vincent Canby (*"Wanda's* a Wow")—that didn't translate into commercial success. Loden, Higgins, and Proferes were then attached to a film to be called *Love Means Always Having to Say You're Sorry*, about a housewife involved with three men at the same time, but it never got made. Nor did Loden's adaptation of Kate Chopin's classic story *The Awakening*. She did direct and produce *The Boy Who Liked Deer* (1975), an educational short film broadcast on PBS, which was about the horrific consequences of vandalism.

*Wanda*, for Loden, was a declaration of filmic independence. But because she found no way to make more features—a struggle too many female directors still face—it ended up as her own albatross.

Criticized by feminists upon its release for its passive nature—which Loden took in stride, feeling she came too late to the movement—the film is now justifiably lauded as a second-wave landmark. But *Wanda* was more or less forgotten soon after its release, until its revival began in earnest when Bérénice Reynaud wrote an essay about it in 2002. *"Wanda's* historical importance [is that] Loden wanted to suggest, from the vantage point of her own experience, what it meant to be a damaged, alienated woman—not to fashion a 'new woman' or a positive heroine," argued Reynaud. Since then, *Wanda's* cult appeal has only grown; its influence is evident in directorial and acting work by Chantal Akerman, Isabelle Huppert (who spearheaded a French DVD release in 2004), and Deb Shoval.

———

ALMA WAS RELEASED ON PAROLE FROM MARYSVILLE ON April 8, 1970, ten years into her prison sentence. She did not go back to Salina, as she had after her previous incarceration, but instead to the Denver suburb of Commerce City, Colorado, where her younger sister, Dixie, lived with her then-husband and six sons, the youngest not even old enough for school.

Alma, now 37 years old, tried to settle in. Her nephews enjoyed her company. Dixie, three years younger, was thrilled to have her sister back in her life. The one time she'd visited Alma in Marysville, taking her mother and one of her sons along, it nearly broke her heart. The years of incarceration had taken a toll on Alma's psyche and appearance.

Dixie knew what others thought of Alma. They judged her for her actions, for being a convicted bank robber. They saw a lithe figure with a five-foot-six frame (although she had gained weight in Marysville, she slimmed down upon being released), and found her beauty dangerous. They grew weary of her lies, of which there were many.

They couldn't see her as Dixie did: as the older sister who had taken care of her, who had tried to look out for her when they were young. The sister who bore the brunt of their father's abuse, shielding and protecting Dixie, while also refusing to condemn her for loving the man and wanting some semblance of a good relationship with him. The sister who knitted sweaters for the people she loved best. And the person responsible for the best tomato soup recipe Dixie had ever tasted. "She could be anyone she wanted to be and be very convincing," Dixie said in a telephone interview last month. "I was in awe of that!"

Alma could still attract men. "She did not like men, but she could get one and control him," said Dixie. She met them at dance studios or bars. One, named Glenn, had a mother who lived in a nearby suburb.

Dixie didn't recall exactly how Glenn and Alma met, but she remembered, vividly, one of the last times she saw him. She was cooking in the kitchen; Alma and Glenn sat at the table. "Daddy," said Alma, "show this Dixie what you have." Dixie had never heard her sister talk like that. Alma's eyes were all snappy. "Show him your baby," Alma said.

Glenn stood up, opened his jacket, and revealed a gun tucked in his waistband.

Dixie wasn't afraid of such displays; maybe it was her innocence, or because she hadn't been around guns much. She said, "Oh. That's nice." It was the last time the subject, or the object, ever came up.

But Dixie remembers the scene well because, soon after, Alma and Glenn disappeared. Alma jumped parole on August 28, 1970, just four months after her release from prison. Dixie paid a visit to Alma's parole officer, with no luck.

Years went by. Then decades. Dixie thought Alma would get in touch eventually. It was her way to go underground for long stretches of time without contact. And if Alma was back in prison, perhaps she couldn't phone or even write.

Eventually, Dixie divorced her husband, remarried, and moved back to Salina. She hoped that eventually, Alma would find her. She hoped Alma would figure it out and find her. But then her mother, Helen, died of cancer on Christmas Eve 1981, at the age of 66. In 2015, Alma's son, Robert, died, also at the age of 66.

Still nothing from Alma.

"I always wondered," Dixie told me. "I always thought she would get a hold of me. And then I knew, after all those years not hearing anything, that she was dead. Don't know why, but I did. Deep down inside, I think she would have contacted me if she could."

Dixie's voice, a melodic, midrange Kansan lilt, broke periodically during our 90-minute conversation. She would cry as if she hadn't let herself do so for years. "I'm sorry I didn't think about what happened to her sooner. Now I feel ashamed of myself. I just tucked it away."

Dixie celebrated her 82nd birthday last August. Alma, if still living, would be 85. So much time has passed. "I just want to know where she's buried," Dixie said.

*WANDA* ENDS IN A BAR, NOT LONG BEFORE CLOSING TIME. The title character arrives in the aftermath of the failed robbery. She sits down among a group of men. The lighting is coarse and claustrophobic. Fiddle music plays as she drinks her beer and scarfs down a hot dog. Wanda lifts her head, eyes downcast as a cigarette reaches her lips. Her mouth alternates somewhere between a smile and a grimace. Despite the crime, trouble, and tragedy, there is an aura of quiet possibility about her.

The likelihood is that Alma Helen Stephens Malone came to a bad end, not long after jumping parole in Colorado. She may be buried somewhere, waiting to be identified. The Ohio Bureau of Prisons lists an "administrative release" from parole of February 23, 1990, but it's not clear if that was paperwork shuffling or if they had some contact with Alma.

Dixie never thought to report her older sister missing. So much time passed, and the shame seemed too great to overcome. But she plans on doing so soon.

Perhaps Alma, like Wanda, found some aura of quiet possibility, too. Maybe she did not, as one would expect, heed the wrong call. Perhaps she is still out there, in a disguise of her own making.

Originally published by *Topic*, October 2017

PART III

# *JUSTICE AND SOCIETY*

# What Bullets Do to Bodies

BY JASON FAGONE

The first thing Dr. Amy Goldberg told me is that this article would be pointless. She said this on a phone call in summer 2016, well before the election, before a tangible sensation that facts were futile became a broader American phenomenon. I was interested in Goldberg because she has spent 30 years as a trauma surgeon, almost all of that at the same hospital, Temple University Hospital in North Philadelphia, which treats more gunshot victims than any other in the state and is located in what was, according to one analysis, the deadliest of the 10 largest cities in the country until 2016, with a homicide rate of 17.8 murders per 100,000 residents in 2015.

Over my years of reporting here, I had heard stories about Temple's trauma team. A city prosecutor who handled shooting investigations once told me that the surgeons were able to piece people back together after the most horrific acts of violence. People went into the hospital damaged beyond belief and came walking out.

That stuck with me. I wondered what surgeons know about gun violence that the rest of us don't. We are inundated with news about shootings. Fourteen dead in San Bernardino, six in Michigan, 11 over one weekend in Chicago. We get names, places, anguished Facebook posts, wonky articles full of statistics on crime rates and risk, Twitter arguments about the Second Amendment—everything except the blood, the pictures of bodies torn by bullets. That part is concealed, sanitized. More than 30,000 people die of gunshot wounds each year in America, around 75,000 more are injured, and we have no visceral sense of what physically happens inside a person when he's shot. Goldberg does.

She is the chair of Temple's Department of Surgery, one of only 16 women in America to hold that position at a hospital. In my initial conversation with her, which took place shortly after the mass shooting in Orlando, where 49 people were killed and 53 injured by a man who walked into a gay nightclub with a semiautomatic rifle and a Glock handgun, she was joined by Scott Charles, the hospital's trauma outreach coordinator and Goldberg's longtime friend. Goldberg has a southeastern Pennsylvania accent that at low volume makes her sound like a sweet South Philly grandmother and at higher volume becomes a razor. I asked her what changes in gun violence she had seen in her 30 years. She said not many. When she first arrived at Temple in 1987 to start her residency, "It was so obvious to me then that there was something so wrong." Since then, the types of firearms have evolved. The surgeons used to see .22-caliber bullets from little handguns, Saturday-night specials, whereas now they see .40-caliber and 9mm bullets. Charles said they get the occasional victim of a long gun, such as an AR-15 or an AK-47, "but what's remarkable is how common handguns are."

Goldberg jumped in. "As a country," she said, "we lost our teachable moment." She started talking about the 2012 murder of 20 schoolchildren and 6 adults at Sandy Hook Elementary School. Goldberg said that if people had been shown the autopsy photos of the kids, the gun debate would have been transformed. "The fact that not a single one of those kids was able to be transported to a hospital, tells me that they were not just dead, but really really really really dead. Ten-year-old kids, riddled with bullets, dead as doornails." Her voice rose. She said people have to confront the physical reality of gun violence without the polite filters. "The country won't be ready for it, but that's what needs to happen. That's the only chance at all for this to ever be reversed."

She dropped back into a softer register. "Nobody gives two shits about the black people in North Philadelphia if nobody gives two craps about the white kids in Sandy Hook . . . I thought white little kids getting shot would make people care. Nope. They didn't care. Anderson Cooper was up there. They set up shop. And then the public outrage fades."

Goldberg apologized and said she wasn't trying to stop

me from writing a story. She just didn't expect it to change anything.

THE HOSPITAL'S MAIN BUILDING IS A NINE-STORY TOWER on North Broad, the street that traces a north-south line through Philadelphia. If you think of Broad as the city's spinal column, the hospital is about level with the heart. Stand on the sidewalk outside the hospital and look south on a clear day and you can see the pale marble and granite of City Hall, about four miles away, near Philly's pelvis.

You can go to Temple for high-end elective surgery, like getting a knee replacement, same as at any other major teaching hospital in the country. As Jeremy Walter, Temple Hospital's amiable director of media relations, reminded me more than once, "Temple isn't just a hospital that treats drug addicts and gun victims." Still, it was founded 125 years ago by a Samaritan to provide free care, and that public-service mission persists. Some of the most violent blocks in the city are within a four-mile radius of the hospital, and crime victims funnel in.

I first met Goldberg one summer weekday, in the hospital lobby. I had arranged to stay and observe for 24 hours, accompanied every moment by Walter, who carried a trauma pager and a yellow folder of consent forms. The rule was that I could observe a surgery if the patient or a family member consented, and if I wanted to do an interview, the patient had to sign a form. Goldberg is five feet two inches tall, with a runner's build. She wore a gray mock-turtleneck sweater with no sleeves. Her hair is short, and there was a little gel in it that made it spiky. She explained that there are two main categories of trauma: blunt and penetrating. Blunt trauma is like a beating, a fall. Penetrating is a gun or stab wound. "Unfortunately we get a lot of penetrating traumas," she said. Temple sees 2,500 to 3,000 traumas per year, around 450 of which were gunshot wounds in 2016.

The trauma pager buzzed shortly after noon. LEVEL 1 PED, it said—a pedestrian struck by a car. I followed Goldberg to the ER, and she disappeared behind a windowless set of double doors, into the trauma resuscitation area. A few moments later, she emerged and waved me inside.

The trauma area is a rectangular room with three bays, each of which can accommodate two patients side by side when it's busy. It's an organized place—there are small trays on wheels for different surgical procedures, each tray holding a particular complement of instruments—but the tubes and cables snaking from poles and machines make it feel a bit chaotic to the untrained eye. The goal of a trauma surgeon is to limit the amount of time that a patient spends in a trauma bay, to stabilize the patient until he can be transferred for a CT scan or to the OR for surgery. The temperature in the room feels about five degrees hotter than in the rest of the hospital. The air doesn't seem to move.

The pedestrian was awake but silent. This concerned Goldberg because by all rights he should have been screaming in pain. He looked to be in his late 20s. He had black hair and his shirt had been removed. He spoke Spanish. There was a laceration above his right eye and a small amount of blood on the sheets near his head. Goldberg and about 20 other doctors and nurses in blue scrubs clustered around him, checking vital signs, asking questions. Goldberg wore purple latex gloves. She tapped lightly on the patient's left forearm with one hand. The arm was broken.

*"No dolor?"* she asked in Spanish. No pain? He shook his head. "Really?" she said. "No?"

Goldberg walked over to another doctor and said, "So are you troubled by the fact that he's not screaming? He has an arm that's so freaking broken and he's not screaming." She frowned. "I'm troubled by that."

The patient's vital signs appeared stable, but Goldberg was worried about internal bleeding. A lack of pain could indicate a hidden injury. He needed a CT scan.

Staff wheeled the patient out of the trauma unit and into a nearby procedure room for the scan. Goldberg took off her latex gloves and threw them in a biohazard trash can. Two police officers had been observing from a distance with pens in hand and notepads open. One of the cops, a large man with a buzzcut, got Goldberg's attention by saying, "Doc."

"I'm Goldberg."

The officer asked what the police should put down in their report for the patient's condition. She said "critical." This has been Goldberg's policy for years, she explained to me as she exited the trauma bay and walked down a hallway toward the CT scanner. "I always make the patients critical until I know they're fine. It's a jinx thing."

Goldberg is superstitious. On days when she's on call, she shaves her legs. She can't say why, she just started doing it years ago and now she will not deviate. She's been wearing the same style of tan Timberlands for 15 years; her current pair, given to her by a colleague when she became chair of surgery, has the Temple logo inked on the heels. She parks her gray BMW in the same spot every time. "It's so hard to take care of patients without making mistakes that you need every edge." She recently hired a sports psychologist to talk to the residents about strategies for peak performance. Visualization. Positive self-talk. Breathing. For most of her career, she has stopped at the same Dunkin' Donuts to order a large coffee with cream and two Sweet'N Lows. A few years ago, the store stopped carrying Sweet'N Low, so she bought a box and left it there; they keep it under the counter for her. "It's pink," she told me once. "Sweet'N Low is pink, Equal is blue, Splenda is yellow. And that is how you have to build a good system, believe it or not. So nobody makes a mistake."

In the hallway next to the ER, she opened a door, and I followed her into a small, darkened room where six young doctors sat at computers. A window looked into the bay next door that held the CT scanner. "Billie Jean" played at low volume from a tinny speaker. Goldberg watched through the window as staff moved the patient from his gurney onto the bed of the machine. He cried out. Goldberg said, "That seems more appropriate." Now they gave him some pain medicine. She looked at me and winced. "He has a broken humerus. I mean, you can feel it." She streaked the thumb of her right hand against her fingers. "It's one of my least favorite injuries. You can feel the bones rubbing together." The CT scan showed some clotted blood in the patient's head, appearing on the screen as patches of white. Goldberg ordered some additional scans.

When a shooting comes across the trauma pager, the code is GSW. There were no GSWs that night, only assaults. One patient was an older man who had been beaten up and complained of stomach pain. Another had been stabbed in the abdomen during a fight. His assailant was brought in, too, in handcuffs, a white-haired man in a red T-shirt, his left eye bloodied and swollen shut.

The injuries weren't life-threatening. Goldberg attended to the patients in the trauma unit. When she wasn't there, she went on rounds, taking the elevator up to the eighth and ninth floors to check in with patients recovering from earlier traumas. She walked fast from one place to the other and I would lose her sometimes behind corners and doors and she'd have to double back for me. These are busy shifts even when there aren't a lot of fresh traumas coming in. During a down moment, Goldberg mentioned that she was thinking about scaling back her call schedule now that she's chair of surgery, with large administrative and educational responsibilities. "I've been doing this 30 years," she said. "Do I need to be on call? Do I need to do Saturdays?"

The pager stayed quiet overnight and through late morning, when Goldberg's call shift ended. I arranged to return and shadow her again on her next shift, in two days. I left the hospital before lunch. The following morning the trauma pager blew up. LEVEL I GSW TO CHEST. LEVEL I MULTIPLE GSW TRANSFER FROM EPISC [Episcopal Hospital]. LEVEL I SECOND GSW MALE.

GOLDBERG DIDN'T KNOW MUCH ABOUT GUNS OR GUN violence until she got to Temple. She grew up in the quiet Philadelphia suburb of Broomall. Her father owned a dairy business in the city; her mother was a schoolteacher. She was an intense kid who really believed the religious ideas she was learning at Jewish summer camp "in a big, bad way." When she was 11, she woke up to see a light through her window and feel a tremor underfoot, and she wondered if it was God's doing.

She went on to study psychology at the University of Pennsylvania and medicine at Mount Sinai in New York. She particularly loved anatomy. "It's a miracle," she told me. "The creation of a person, you know. It's the heart beating and the lungs bringing air. It is so miraculous." Surgery, for Goldberg, was a way of honoring the miracle. And trauma surgery was the ultimate form of appreciation, because a surgeon in trauma experienced so much variety. She might be operating on the carotid artery in the neck, or the heart in the chest, or the large bowel or small bowel in the abdomen, or the femoral artery in the thigh, at any given moment, on any given night.

In her first or second year of residency at Temple, when she was in her mid-20s, she helped treat a young boy who had been shot in the chest by his sibling who picked up a loaded gun that was lying around. The doctors couldn't save him. The senselessness made her so angry. Goldberg listened as a senior resident informed the boy's mother. "I'm sorry," the resident said, "he has passed." The mother didn't react; she didn't seem to understand what she had just heard. Goldberg spoke up. "He died. We're so sorry. He died." It was a lesson: be direct. "You have to find a very compassionate way of being honest," she said.

She finished her residency in 1992 and decided to stay at Temple, and the feeling of wrongness only intensified. There was a teenage boy in August 1992 who was shot in the heart. His heart stopped beating. Goldberg revived it. He lived. But some weeks later he came in again, with a shooting injury to his brachial artery, in the upper arm. He almost bled out, almost died again, but the surgeons got him back, again. "And then of course the third time he came in, he was shot through the head, and he was dead," Goldberg said.

She started thinking that Temple should find a way to intervene—to try to talk to patients while they're in the hospital so they would never need to come back. But she didn't have the authority yet. She was just a trauma surgeon, a good one, and getting better. She had good hands and good judgment and a methodical approach to the craft. And as 5 years stretched into 10, and 10 into 20, Goldberg built up a deep well of experience in doing the things that are necessary to save the lives of gun victims, the things that are never shown on TV or in movies, the things that stay hidden behind hospital walls and allow Americans to imagine whatever they like about the effects of bullets or not to imagine anything at all. "You think you know what happens here?" Scott Charles asked me. "Because I thought I knew. But there's nothing that can prepare you for what bullets do to human bodies. And that's true for pro-gun people also."

The main thing people get wrong when they imagine being shot is that they think the bullet itself is the problem. The lump of metal lodged in the body. The action-movie hero is shot in the stomach; he limps to a safe house; he takes off his shirt, removes the bullet with a tweezer, and now he is better. This is not trauma surgery. Trauma surgery is about fixing the damage the bullet causes as it rips through muscle and vessel and organ and bone. The bullet can stay in the body just fine. But the bleeding has to be contained, even if the patient is awake and screaming because a tube has just been pushed into his chest cavity through a deep incision without the aid of general anesthesia (no time; the patient gets an injection of lidocaine). And if the heart has stopped, it must be restarted before the brain dies from a lack of oxygen.

It is not a gentle process. Some of the surgeon's tools look like things you'd buy at Home Depot. In especially serious cases, 70 times at Temple last year, the surgeons will crack a chest right there in the trauma area. The technical name is a thoracotomy. A patient comes in unconscious, maybe in cardiac arrest, and Goldberg has to get into the cavity to see what is going on. With a scalpel, she makes an incision below the nipple and cuts six to 10 inches down the torso, through skin, through the layer of fatty tissue, through the muscles. Into the opening she inserts a rib spreader, a large metal instrument with a hand crank. It pulls open the ribs and locks them into place so the surgeons can reach the inner organs. Every so often, she may also have to break the patient's sternum—a bilateral thoracotomy. This is done with a tool called a Lebsche knife. It's a metal rod with a sharp blade on one end that hooks under the breastbone. Goldberg takes a silver hammer. It looks like—a hammer. She hits the top of the Lebsche knife with the hammer until it cuts through the sternum. "You never forget that sound," one of the Temple nurses told me. "It's like a tink, tink, tink. And it sounds like metal, but you know it's bone. You know like when you see on television, when people are working on the railroad, hammering the ties?"

"It's just the worst," Charles told me. "They're breaking bone. And everybody—every body—has its own kind of quality. And sometimes there's a big guy you'll hear, and it's the echo—the sound that comes out of the room. There's some times when it doesn't affect me, and there are some times when it makes my knees shake, when I know what's going on in there."

Now the chest is open, and Goldberg can work. If the heart has stopped, she can try to get it beating again. This may involve open cardiac massage—literally holding the heart in her hands and massaging it to get blood flowing up to the brain again. If there's bleeding in the cavity, she can control it by putting a metal clamp on the heart or on the lung. She can also clamp the aorta, the largest artery in the body, so that instead of the blood going down into the bowels, where it's needed less, the blood goes up to the brain.

"These crossing bullets are just so challenging," she said. "Where is the injury? Is it in the chest? Is it in the abdomen? You're down there, looking, and sometimes you find it, and sometimes you don't. And sometimes it just really hurts as you work your way through." She meant that it hurts when patients suffer. Hurts them and hurts her.

There are some gun victims who die quickly, right there in the trauma bay, or soon after being transferred up to the OR. Others develop cascades of life-threatening complications in the following days that surgeons race to manage.

Goldberg said she saw a movie a few years ago that captures what it's like to operate under these conditions. It was a documentary about the 33 Chilean miners who were trapped underground for months in 2010. "They interviewed them all. And the miner that had the hardest time down there was the youngest guy. Not the oldest guy. It was the youngest guy. And they said, why? Why did you have such a hard time? And he said, God and the Devil were with me." Goldberg thought that was perfect. "That's what I had been searching for, for years, in how you feel in the operating room. God and the Devil are with you. You start a case. A young person. Shot. They come in talking. You go upstairs. They have this devastating injury. The Devil. You suck. You're gonna kill this guy. You call yourself a good trauma surgeon. You're the worst. And you just plow ahead and plow ahead and plow ahead. You find what's injured. You control it. God. Oh, you are the best. You've done a great job. Then you're working. You find another injury you didn't expect. You suck, you suck, you suck."

It's possible for a surgeon to get distracted by the wrong wound. The most dangerous wounds don't always look the worst. People can get shot in the head and they're leaking bits of brain from a hole in the skull and that's not the fatal wound; the fatal wound is from another bullet that ripped through the chest. One patient a few years ago was shot in the face with a shotgun at close range over some money owed. He pulled his coat up over his mangled face and walked to the ER of one of Temple's sister hospitals, approaching a nurse. She looked at him. He lowered the coat. The nurse thought to herself what you might expect a person to think in such a situation: *Daaaaaamn.* He was stabilized, then transferred to Temple. He lived.

The price of survival is often lasting disability. Some patients, often young guys, wind up carrying around colostomy bags for the rest of their lives because they can't poop normally anymore. They poop through a "stoma," a hole in the abdomen. "They're so angry," Goldberg said. "They should be angry." Some are paralyzed by bullets that sever the spinal column. Some lose limbs entirely. During trauma surgery, when the blood flow is redirected to the brain and heart by an aortic clamp, blood goes away from other areas, and tissue in the lower extremities can die, causing gangrene, in which case surgeons must amputate the leg at higher and higher points, first at the shin, then at the knee, then at the thigh, to stay ahead of the necrotic tissue as it spreads. The femur bone may have to be disarticulated—removed entirely from the socket, and discarded. There was a woman several years ago whose boyfriend shot her in the leg. The bullet clipped the femoral artery and she bled. Goldberg was on call that day. She had to amputate the woman's legs to save her life. "I'm so haunted by that," she said.

Eighty percent of people who are shot in Philadelphia survive their injuries. This statistic surprises people when they hear it. They tend to think that when people get shot in the belly or the chest or the face, they die. But the reality is that people get shot and then they are going to survive, because trauma surgeons are going to save them, and that's when the real suffering begins.

RAFI COLON WAS SHOT ONCE IN THE ABDOMEN WITH A 9mm handgun while defending himself from home invaders in September 2005. The bullet tore through his intestines. Trauma surgeons at Temple had to open his abdomen to repair the injuries, but fistulas developed, holes that wouldn't heal, and until they healed, the incision couldn't be closed. He spent the next 11 months in the hospital, immobilized in bed, with an open wound down the front of him that had the circumference of a basketball. It got to the point where it was a normal thing for him to look down and think, *Oh, those are my intestines; there they are.*

"It became second nature," he told me recently over lunch at a Panera Bread in the Philly suburbs. "It wasn't like a gruesome thing." The holes in his intestines leaked stomach acid and burned away the surrounding tissues and skin, leaving less skin available to eventually stretch over the wound and close it. Colon learned to sop up the excess acid from his exposed intestines with gauze pads and later with a machine that sucked the acid through a tube. When his friends came to visit, they had a hard time looking at him. He messed with them once by asking a buddy to get him a Rita's water ice, Philadelphia's version of a snow cone. He knew what would happen when he ate it. The water ice was red, the Swedish Fish flavor from that summer, and 30 seconds after he swallowed it, the red water ice came oozing out of the hole in his intestine. His friends bolted.

Over the course of his long recovery, from the fall of 2005 into the spring and summer of 2006, Colon got a feel for the rhythms of the Trauma Service. Lying there in the bed, he occupied himself by counting the number of times each day that trauma codes were announced over the PA system. It seemed like the busiest times were Thursday, Friday, and Saturday nights. He'd ask the doctors, how many yesterday, was it 17? "They'd say, 'No, 18.'" He could tell when the residents were stressed out by how many Diet Cokes they drank. There were days when the doctors were so busy with fresh traumas that they didn't make rounds until 7 or 8 at night. "They would say, 'Yeah, it was a busy day.' I'd be like, 'Yeah, I heard.'"

It ultimately took 14 surgeries to repair the damage done by one bullet. Temple's surgeons stretched his abdominal wall closed with the help of some muscle from another part of his body and an artificial mesh. If you see Colon today, the only way you can tell he was wounded is that he walks with a minor tilt; he calls it "my Keyser Söze limp."

Goldberg was part of the team of doctors who cared for him. They talked about muscle cars and sports. (She liked the Eagles; his team was the Giants.) He remembers that she was the doctor who would notice when he was feeling despair and let him eat a little something that the nurses wouldn't necessarily allow, like a small chip of ice, or sometimes a piece of candy. He couldn't eat normally—he was being fed intravenously—but "the fact that I could get a piece of ice, it was like heaven."

She has gotten more sensitive over the years, she said. When you're a young trauma surgeon, you're developing skills, like how to put a bowel back together. Her medical training was all about learning to operate, to recognize the kinds of patterns that she now teaches to students and young doctors. I once saw her give a lecture to 11 medical students who had just completed their surgical rotation. Goldberg diagrammed anatomy and formulae on a whiteboard and asked questions about how the students would diagnose various hypothetical patients. But she also asked the students to share their experiences with patients and their feelings about those cases. One student spoke about stitching together the chest of a young shooting victim who had died after surgeons attempted to resuscitate him in the trauma area; the student's first thought was that he was excited to practice stitching a chest, then he felt guilty for being excited. Another student recalled being surprised when a patient asked for his business card even though he was just a lowly medical student. "Yeah," Goldberg said. "He trusted you."

Often when Goldberg meets a shooting victim, it turns out she once treated a sibling, parent, cousin, or friend. "I'm a family doctor, a little bit, because I've been here so long," she said. One day at the hospital, I saw her go on rounds, meeting with patients in the Surgical Intensive Care Unit (SICU) on the ninth floor. A sign on a bulletin board said WELCOME TO SICU! YOUR HEALING STARTS HERE! The letters were surrounded by gold stars.

Talking to patients seemed to energize Goldberg. She was alternately lighthearted and serious. The patients were uniformly docile and tired. They were on pain medication that slowed their speech. The first patient, shot in the neck, was a young man accompanied by his girlfriend, who sat next to him on the bed with an expression of concern. "When I was shot, I fell on my face," he said. The second patient was older. A tube to drain fluids was snaking out of his chest. He held out a trembling left hand and smiled. "A little bit of the shakes," he said. Goldberg told the man he was scheduled to be released the following Monday. He had been caught in some kind of cross fire. "We will miss you," Goldberg said, "but there comes a day."

"Cut the umbilical cord, huh?" he said, and laughed softly.

Goldberg descended to the eighth floor to meet with another gun victim. She knocked on his door and said hello in her friendly voice. There were two large men inside the room in T-shirts and shorts. She assumed they were his family, but when she entered, the men rushed over to her and said that the patient was a suspected shooter himself. They were plainclothes cops, guarding him.

"I don't want to know," she said. "It's better if I don't know."

She went over to the side of the patient's bed as the cops watched. She said she was Dr. Goldberg and she wanted to explain what was happening and help him if he needed anything.

He looked young. He seemed afraid. There was an open wound in his chest, a vertical incision from below his nipples to his belly button, rising and falling with his breath. Surgeons had needed to remove one of his kidneys, his spleen, and part of his stomach to repair the damage of the bullet and save his life. After the surgery, the tissue swelled, which happens sometimes, and they couldn't immediately stitch the incision closed, so they had to leave it open. The edges of the wound were pink and raw.

Goldberg reached out and held his left hand in her hand while telling him what organs he'd lost.

"You don't need your spleen. You do need your kidney," she said. "But luckily, God gave us two."

He nodded slightly. She asked how he was feeling. All he said was, "Pain."

Goldberg said they would try to help with that and rubbed her fingers across his hand in a gesture of tenderness.

THE KEY DISTINCTION FOR GOLDBERG ISN'T INNOCENT or guilty, it's rational or irrational. Gun violence is irrational; there's no pattern to it. Police statistics show that shootings decrease in the cold winter months and pick up when the weather warms, but any given trauma shift in the winter can be busy and any shift in the summer perfectly quiet.

Goldberg has always found the senselessness of violence frustrating, and when she was promoted to chief of trauma 15 years ago, she started thinking about how to engineer some control, to help patients "above and beyond just being a trauma surgeon." She imagined a comprehensive approach to prevent shootings and keep patients from showing up in a trauma bay in the first place. She knew this would involve talking to people in the community, but she also knew she was a flawed messenger. "Who's going to listen to this white Jewish girl say that guns in the inner city aren't good for you? Nobody's going to listen to me say that. I wouldn't listen to me." She went looking for help, and found Scott Charles.

A big, energetic guy with glasses and a master's degree in applied positive psychology from the University of Pennsylvania, Charles has been working to reduce youth violence since 1988. When he was growing up in Sacramento, two of his older brothers were shot and his sister committed suicide with a gun, and at 19 one of his best friends was shot and killed. He moved to Philadelphia when his sociologist wife got hired by Penn, and two years later, he joined a nonprofit that designed service-learning projects in public schools. Some of his students from North Philly started collecting the stories of families who had lost children to gun violence, which is how Charles made the connection to Goldberg— Temple had treated one of the victims, Lamont Adams, a 16-year-old from North Philly who was shot and killed in 2004 after a false rumor was spread about him.

Goldberg hosted a tour for Charles and his students, inviting them into the trauma unit and explaining what gun patients experience there. She was immediately impressed by the way he dealt with the kids. She told him she'd create a new outreach position for him at Temple, that she'd get up "in people's faces" until she made sure it happened.

"She said, 'Don't go anywhere else,'" Charles recalled. "'I'm going to write you a check for one year of your salary. If I don't get this position for you, you can cash the check, it's yours, and take another job.' And I was like—this white lady's crazy. My wife was like, who's this lady who keeps calling you at eleven o'clock at night? 'It's this crazy doctor.'"

Charles accepted, joining Temple in August 2005, and since then he and Goldberg have developed a suite of ambitious programs in collaboration with other Temple doctors and staff. "The thing that allows us to do so much of this is she carries a big stick," Charles said. "Who was going to get in her way?"

There are three programs aimed at preventing violence

before it happens. Cradle to Grave is an expansion of that first tour Charles took at Temple. He brings groups of kids and adults into the trauma area and shows them how surgeons save gun patients. He has his own copies of the various surgical instruments for demonstration purposes, removing them from a travel bag: chest tube, rib-spreader, hammer, Lebsche knife. He introduces the visitors to Goldberg if she's available. He tells the story of Lamont Adams, asking a volunteer to pretend to be Lamont and then placing a circular red sticker on the location of each of Lamont's 24 bullet wounds (entry and exit). On his chest. His abdomen. His thigh and arms. And most disturbing of all, the two bullet wounds on his hand, a sign that Lamont was trying to shield his face from the bullets at close range.

Charles also runs the Fighting Chance program, a series of training sessions for community members, where doctors show people in neighborhoods how to give first aid to gunshot victims, to apply tourniquets and stop blood loss in the seconds immediately following a shooting, before the EMTs or police arrive. Recently, Charles has also become a sort of Johnny Appleseed of gun locks, handing them out to parents who want to keep their children from getting hurt in accidents. He keeps boxes of them at the hospital and distributes the locks with no questions asked. Sometimes he lugs them to subway stations and offers them to commuters.

That's prevention. Temple has also created an intervention component, called Turning Point, where shooting victims get extra counseling while they're still in the hospital. "They come in, they're very scared," Goldberg said. "'Am I gonna die? Where's my mom?' Then, as soon as they would recover, they would not be so scared anymore, which maybe wasn't good." So if a victim is between 18 and 30 years old, he's offered a series of supports in addition to the usual visits with Charles and a social worker. Temple asks the patients if they want to talk to a trauma survivor. And they are given an opportunity to view a video of their own trauma-bay resuscitation. (The surgeries in the trauma area are videotaped for quality control.) About half say yes. Charles shows them the video. They get psychological counseling for any PTSD symptoms, as well as case management services to help them get high school diplomas or jobs.

Turning Point was initially controversial within the hospital. Some doctors thought it was cruel to show patients videos of their own surgeries, especially patients who had done nothing wrong. But Goldberg argued that she wasn't judging anyone's past or even asking about it. "The only way I know how to deal with a problem is, let's break it down. Let's try to educate," she said.

Breaking it down has involved doing science. Goldberg and her team have needed to gather data about questions that have never been rigorously answered, a common situation when it comes to gun violence. For instance, when a paramedic first finds a gun or stabbing victim, nobody knows if it's better to administer IV fluids and put a tube down the victim's throat on the spot, or if the medic should simply race the victim to the hospital. Trauma surgeons have long suspected that the latter option is preferable—most shooting victims actually arrive at Temple in the back of police cruisers, a practice the cops call "scoop and run"—but there has never been a long-term randomized study.

So Temple launched one. It's called the Philadelphia Immediate Transport in Penetrating Trauma Trial (PIPT), an elaborate undertaking that has involved close coordination with emergency personnel and also dozens of community meetings where doctors explained how the study works (over the next five years, some victims of penetrating trauma will receive immediate transport and some won't) and how people can opt out of the study (by wearing a special wristband). In that same spirit, Goldberg has been gathering data on the Turning Point program. For years, patients have been randomized into a control group and an experimental group. One group gets typical care and the other gets Turning Point, and then patients in both groups answer a questionnaire that quantifies attitudes toward violence.

In November the hospital published its first scientific results from Turning Point, based on 80 patients. According to Temple's data, the Turning Point patients showed "a 50% reduction in aggressive response to shame, a 29% reduction in comfort with aggression, and a 19% reduction in overall proclivity toward violence." Goldberg told me she was proud of the study, not only because it suggested that the program was effective, but also because it represented a rare victory over the status quo. Turning Point grew out of her experience with that one patient in 1992, the three-time shooting victim who died the third time. It took her that long to get the authority, to gather the data, to get it published, to shift the system a little bit.

Twenty-four years.

EACH TIME I WENT TO THE HOSPITAL, I ASKED GOLD-berg what else was going on with her aside from work. She usually talked about running. She likes to run along the Schuylkill River while listening to music and thinking about nothing at all. She competes in a few half marathons a year.

I never learned much about Goldberg's personal life. She lives alone in an apartment in Center City. She has a rowing machine there and access to a treadmill in the building's gym. Her religious faith is still strong—it's not that she goes around talking about it, she told me, it's just that she has worked for 30 years in trauma and seen a lot of death, and it's hard to do that and not feel something about God. I noticed one day she was wearing a white Lokai bracelet, a ring of plastic capsules said to contain mud from the Dead Sea and water from Mount Everest. "The highs and the lows, to stay even-keeled," she said. "I probably need ten of them, five on each hand."

The major nonrunning events in her life tend to be awards ceremonies. She has reached the point in her medical career where people gather and say nice things about her, and there are plates of olives and prosciutto. Her med-school alma mater, Mount Sinai in New York, recently invited her to give a special lecture at Grand Rounds, a hallowed medical tradition.

On March 16, Temple threw a party for her "investiture," a ceremony where she passed from being merely the chair of surgery to being the George S. Peters, MD, and Louise C. Peters Chair of Surgery. Endowed chairs at universities are a big deal. Past colleagues from all over the country came to speak about her qualities. One compared her to Teddy Roosevelt's famous Man in the Arena, "whose face is marred by dust and sweat and blood . . . who spends himself or herself in a worthy cause." ("Or herself" is not actually a part of Roosevelt's quote, but the guy modernized it for Goldberg.) She gave a brief acceptance speech focusing on the importance of teamwork to medical excellence. She said she used to dream about being a sports coach, and now she's coaching the next generation of surgeons. As she once put it to me, "One of us can't give perfect care. But together, maybe, we can give perfect care."

One of the speakers at the investiture called Goldberg a "realistic idealist," and when I saw her later, she said she'd been thinking about the phrase. At first it surprised her that people saw her that way, but she realized it captured something true. "When I get angry, and hurt," she told me, "it's because I can still be a little naïve." Even after all this time, the sense of horror she first experienced as a resident treating gun patients has never completely gone away.

One evening when I was at the hospital, I saw what she meant. Two shooting victims came in, a man and a woman, about two hours apart, and were quickly patched up. The man was shot twice, in a wrist and a thigh—four holes, not life-threatening. The woman was shot once in the thigh with a small entry wound but no exit wound—a stray bullet that struck her while she was walking down the street. In the trauma bay, the surgeons taped a paper clip over the entry wound so they could identify that spot on the X-ray. Goldberg wheeled the monitor over to show me the X-ray image: paper clip and bullet. "Very small," she said, pointing to the slug, "like a .22." As so many other patients do, the patient asked the trauma surgeons if they were going to take the bullet out, and the surgeons explained that they fix what the bullet injures; they don't fix the bullet.

They left the wound open to prevent infection and put a dressing on it. "We'll probably send her home tonight," Goldberg said. "Isn't that awful?"

She meant it as a strictly human thing. There's no medical reason for a patient to be in a hospital longer than necessary. The point was the ridiculousness of the situation. A woman gets shot through no fault of her own, she comes to the hospital scared, and if she's okay, Goldberg says, "It's like, here, take a little Band-Aid." The woman goes home, and for everyone else in the city, it's as though the shooting never happened. It changes no policy. It motivates no law. In a perverse way, the more efficiently Goldberg does her job inside the hospital, the more invisible gun violence becomes everywhere else.

Which is why she pours so much of herself into the outreach programs, the scientific studies, and any other method she has of finding control and making the problem visible.

Then, as always with Goldberg, she does her call shifts. "We care," she told me once. "We're gonna be here. We're gonna be here. We're gonna be here, and then you know what, we're still gonna be here. And then we're still here. That kind of thing."

The last time I saw Goldberg, I was eating breakfast in the hospital's basement cafeteria, one corridor away from the morgue, where bodies are kept, pending transport. It was at the end of a relatively quiet overnight call shift in late March. She walked in with a coffee, looking calm and fresh. The forecast showed rising temperatures. The crust of snow on the sidewalks would soon melt, the days would lengthen, people would leave their houses to enjoy the weather. Spring was coming, and the shootings would pick back up.

Originally published by *Highline* for HuffPost, April 2017

# Checkpoint Nation

### BY MELISSA DEL BOSQUE

aura Sandoval threaded her way through idling taxis and
men selling bottles of water, toward the entrance of the
Cordova International Bridge, which links Ciudad Juárez,
Mexico, to El Paso, Texas. Earlier that day, a bright Saturday in December 2012, Sandoval had crossed over to Juárez
to console a friend whose wife had recently died. She had
brought him a few items he had requested—eye drops, the
chimichangas from Allsup's he liked—and now that her care
package had been delivered, she was in a hurry to get back to
the Texas side, where she'd left her car. She had a three-hour
drive to reach home, in the mountains in New Mexico, and
she hated driving in the dark.

Sandoval took her place in the long line of people waiting
to have their passports checked by US Customs and Border

Protection (CBP). When it was her turn, she handed her American passport to a customs officer and smiled amicably, waiting for him to wave her through. But the officer said she had been randomly selected for additional screening. Sandoval was led to a secondary inspection area nearby, where two more officers patted her down. Another walked toward her with a drug-sniffing dog, which grew agitated as it came closer, barking and then circling her legs. Because the dog had "alerted," the officer said, Sandoval would now have to undergo another inspection.

She was taken to a fluorescent-lit, windowless room inside the port of entry office. Two female officers entered and announced that they were going to search her for drugs. They patted her down again, but found nothing. At that point, Sandoval assumed they would release her, but instead they told her they were going to conduct a strip search. The officers put on latex gloves, picked up flashlights, and asked Sandoval to remove her clothes and bend over so they could look for signs of drugs in her vagina and rectum.

By the time they finished, Sandoval had been detained for more than two hours in the stifling room. Her passport and cell phone had been confiscated; her husband and children had no idea where she was. Sandoval begged to be released. "I was shaking and I was in tears," she told me. Saying nothing, the officers put her in handcuffs and led her to a patrol car waiting outside. They left the international bridge and drove north into Texas. Frightened, Sandoval asked the officers if they had a warrant for her arrest. "We don't need a warrant," one of them replied.

CBP IS THE AGENCY TASKED WITH GUARDING AMERICA'S borders, as opposed to Immigration and Customs Enforcement (ICE), which investigates, arrests, and deports undocumented people throughout the country. Over the past 18 months, as resistance to President Trump's immigration crackdown has grown, most of the criticism has been directed at ICE, whose interior enforcement mission often targets long-term residents without criminal records. Immigrant rights groups have begun a campaign to defund or abolish the agency. "ICE is terrorizing American communities right now," Angel Padilla, national policy director of the Indivisible Project, told the *Nation*. "They're going into schools, entering hospitals, conducting massive raids, and separating children from parents every day."

Increasingly, Padilla's description applies to CBP as well. It turns out that the legal definition of "the border" is troublingly broad. Some 200 million people—nearly two-thirds of all Americans—live within the "border zone," which is defined by the Department of Justice as the area up to 100 air miles from any US land or coastal boundary. Nine of the country's 10 largest cities lie within the zone. It touches 38 states and encompasses all of Connecticut, Delaware, Florida, Hawaii, Maine, Massachusetts, Michigan, New Hampshire, New Jersey, and Rhode Island.

Within the border zone, Congress has granted CBP powers far beyond those of other law enforcement agencies. CBP, which largely consists of customs officers at ports of entry and Border Patrol agents who monitor the highways, has the authority to set up checkpoints almost anywhere within the 100-mile zone, and to search and detain people without a warrant as long as they feel they have "probable cause" to suspect that someone is in the country illegally or smuggling contraband. The Fourth Amendment of the Constitution protects citizens from "unreasonable searches and seizures," but CBP operates with wide discretion, often using alerts from dogs as a reason to pull people aside for secondary inspection. Within 25 miles of any border, Border Patrol agents have even more expansive powers; they can enter private land without a warrant or the owner's permission.

Being a US citizen doesn't protect you from harassment by CBP. Even if you never leave the United States, you can encounter Border Patrol at the 35 fixed checkpoints and dozens of temporary checkpoints they operate deep in the interior. The locations of these checkpoints are not made public, but the Cato Institute, a libertarian think tank, has developed a project to track them. In a recent report, Cato mapped checkpoints as far as 80 miles from the border.

Agents at these checkpoints interact with more than 27 million people annually, the vast majority of them US citizens or legal residents, and conduct thousands of searches and seizures. Latinos in particular are routinely stopped and searched, in what has come to be known as the "Southwest stop-and-frisk." Over the past 10 years, advocacy groups have seen complaints about harassment and abuse at these checkpoints rise, and they have raised concerns that CBP is slowly creeping farther into the interior of the country. "In court cases, we've seen roving patrols 200 miles beyond the border," said Chris Rickerd, a policy counsel at the American Civil Liberties Union. "People are surprised to see CBP in Los Angeles or in Houston, but it's a consequence of the agency not having any limits."

A CBP spokesperson, responding to written questions, insisted that Border Patrol does not have significant operations in major coastal cities north of Los Angeles or in the Mid-Atlantic region. "We are a border security agency, not an interior enforcement agency," she wrote. But she also noted that CBP's activities "are not geographically restricted by law." Even beyond the border zone, the spokesperson asserted, Border Patrol agents have the authority to question individuals and make arrests.

Any political coalition seeking to reform immigration enforcement in the United States will not only have to rein in ICE; it will also have to halt CBP's inward expansion and push its agents back to the borders. But Trump has emerged as the agency's greatest defender. He has pledged to add 5,000 more Border Patrol agents to the force while signaling with his rhetoric about "bad hombres" and "animals" how they should treat those they stop.

———

IN MARCH, I MET SANDOVAL AT A SMALL CAFE IN DOWN-town Albuquerque, New Mexico. A slender woman in her 50s with pale green eyes, Sandoval wore a tailored gray business suit and sat down apprehensively at a table in the corner. Before our interview, she had never spoken publicly about her experience with CBP.

Sandoval, whose name has been changed to protect her privacy, told me that after the officers forced her into the squad car, they drove her to University Medical Center, a public hospital in El Paso. The officers found an empty room and shackled her to the examination table. A nurse entered and asked her to swallow a laxative so they could observe her bowel movement. Then a group of doctors came in. Sandoval pleaded with them to let her go. "A nurse told me to calm down," she said. "That this was something they did any time Border Patrol brought people in." One of the doctors conducted a vaginal and rectal search using a speculum and his hands. "The agents kept saying that they knew I had drugs," Sandoval told me. Still not satisfied, the doctor ordered an X-ray and a full-body scan. Again they found nothing. "The only thing left was to cut me open," Sandoval said.

After more than four hours, the officers called off the search. One of them asked Sandoval to sign some government forms. "She wanted me to give my consent," Sandoval explained. "She said that if I signed the papers, they would take care of the hospital bill. They would be 'good guys' and pay, because it would be expensive." Sandoval pushed the papers away.

Finally, the officers drove her back to the bridge. At the port of entry, a third officer tried again to persuade her to sign the consent forms. He let her smoke a cigarette. "He said I probably needed it after what I'd been through." Sandoval still refused to sign. By the time she got back to her car, it was eight o'clock at night—six hours after her encounter with CBP began.

Sandoval tried to forget about what had happened to her. She figured it would be too costly to fight the government. But then the bills from the hospital started to arrive. For the cavity searches, the X-ray, and the CT scan, the hospital was charging her $5,488. "I pay all my bills, but I was not going to pay these," she told me. "So I started looking for a lawyer."

Sandoval went to the ACLU to seek help with her medical bills, and they agreed to take her case. Edgar Saldivar, a staff attorney, explained to her that CBP appeared to have violated its own policies. CBP mandates that body cavity searches, which must be conducted by medical personnel, be ordered only "under the most exceptional circumstances," and requires agents and officers to obtain a warrant from a judge, or a person's consent. "It still baffles me why they kept going even though each exam came out negative," Saldivar told me. "My client feels she was a victim of sexual assault."

In December 2013, the ACLU filed a civil suit on Sandoval's behalf against the customs officers and the hospital staff who had conducted the exams. From interviews the ACLU conducted with hospital staff, Saldivar got the sense that what had happened to Sandoval wasn't out of the ordinary. "The reaction of the nurse was that these kinds of searches were normal," he told me. "The doctors felt compelled to follow the orders of the law enforcement officers with guns." CBP says that only 21 such searches were carried out nationwide in 2016, the most recent year for which complete data was provided, but Saldivar suspects that many others have experienced similar searches and are too ashamed or traumatized to come forward.

Even though CBP has a policy requiring that records be kept of all body cavity searches, the agency said it had nothing to send me when I filed a FOIA request for drug searches that did not result in an arrest, detention, or deportation. That admission suggests that, in fact, the agency does not keep consistent records of searches like Sandoval's, which turn up nothing. "There's just no telling how many other illegal searches of American citizens go unreported," Saldivar told me. "We have no way of holding CBP accountable."

THE LAW THAT GIVES CBP ITS EXTRAORDINARY CONTROL over the lives of Americans, documented and undocumented, was in part a response to Cold War paranoia. In the first half of the 20th century, the United States employed fewer than 1,600 border agents, almost all of them stationed along the perimeter of the country. But in the mid-'40s, fear of a communist invasion began to grow in the nation's capital. At the White House, President Truman ruminated on the Soviet threat in his personal diary: "The Reds, phonies and the Parlor Pinks seem to be banded together and are becoming a national danger," he wrote. "I am afraid they are a sabotage front for Uncle Joe Stalin." In the summer of 1946, Congress passed legislation giving federal border agents the "power without warrant to arrest any alien who in his presence or view is entering or attempting to enter the United States." The authority would extend "within a reasonable distance from any external boundary of the United States." Congress did not define at the time what it meant by a "reasonable distance."

Border agents would soon use this new authority, but not against communists. During the Second World War, thousands of Mexican farm laborers had been brought to the United States under the Bracero Program, a binational agreement aimed at providing a much-needed supply of agricultural workers during the wartime boom. Many Mexicans not authorized to enter the United States also crossed the border looking for work. Less than a decade later, as a recession hobbled the US economy, these unauthorized workers became convenient political scapegoats. In 1954, President Eisenhower appointed a retired general, J. M. Swing, to run what was then called the Immigration and Naturalization Service and look into the illegal immigration problem. In his first report to Congress, Swing compared the migration of undocumented Mexicans across the border to an "invasion" and warned of "mounting waves of people, always reaching further inland with each incoming wave."

A year earlier, the Department of Justice had adopted the regulation that defined a "reasonable distance" as up to 100 air miles from the border. Swing proposed that a permanent "special mobile force" of border agents be dispatched by land and air to carry out mass deportations of Mexicans. The mission grew out of Operation Wetback, during which Latino farming communities in California, Arizona, and Texas were terrorized by raids, which then expanded north to cities such as Chicago and Spokane, Washington. ("Wetback" is an ethnic slur that originally referred to people who came to the United States by swimming or wading across the Rio Grande.) As historian Kelly Lytle Hernández describes in her book *Migra!*, federal border agents set up temporary detention facilities surrounded by barbed wire in public parks in Los Angeles. At least 300,000 people were deported during the operation, including a small number of US citizens who were mistakenly swept up. Several people drowned while being transported in vessels that a congressional investigation would later compare to "eighteenth-century slave ships," and others died from heat exposure after being abandoned in the Mexican desert.

Operation Wetback expanded the concept of immigration enforcement from something that took place on the border to something that could happen anywhere. But it was September 11 that most profoundly transformed the role of border agents. A year and a half after the attacks, the Bush administration merged the Customs Service and Border Patrol into one agency called US Customs and Border Protection, and put it under the jurisdiction of the massive new Department of Homeland Security (DHS). As the country embarked on its global war on terror, the ranks of CBP surged to more than 44,000, making it the largest federal law enforcement agency in the nation. Today, CBP consists of more than 23,000 customs officers and nearly 20,000 Border Patrol agents.

During CBP's rapid expansion, the agency ramped up its use of interior checkpoints, subjecting ever more Americans to warrantless searches, seizures, and detentions near their schools, in their neighborhoods, and on public roads. CBP's own data suggests that its interior checkpoints do little to catch what it calls "unauthorized entrants" and instead ensnare US citizens on minor drug charges. (Forty percent of its seizures were one ounce or less of marijuana taken from citizens.) From 2013 to 2016, interior checkpoints accounted for only two percent of CBP apprehensions of undocumented immigrants. In May, a circuit court judge in New Hampshire threw out charges against 16 people who were arrested for possessing small quantities of drugs at a checkpoint manned by local police and Border Patrol agents, about 90 miles south of the Canadian border. "While the stated purpose of the checkpoints in this matter was screening for immigration violations," the judge wrote, "the primary purpose of the action was detection and seizure of drugs," which he ruled unconstitutional.

The Trump administration has been aggressively promoting further cooperation between immigration agencies and police departments. Border Patrol agents often accompany officers during routine traffic stops and serve as backup or sometimes as interpreters, but their involvement in domestic policing has had lethal consequences. In 2011, a man in Washington state called 911 because his son, 30-year-old Alex Martinez, who had a history of mental illness, was smashing the windows of their home. Border Patrol accompanied local sheriff's deputies to the residence, likely because the call was made in Spanish. When they arrived, Martinez stepped out of his house holding something in his hand. Law enforcement say it was a hammer; the family alleges it was a flashlight. A local deputy and a Border Patrol agent, who said they felt threatened, shot Martinez 13 times. Since 2010, watchdog groups have counted 77 CBP-related fatalities— at least one-fifth of them US citizens.

CBP operates with less oversight than your local police department, despite having one of the largest federal budgets in Washington. The agency doesn't reveal the names of agents or details of its internal proceedings in fatality or misconduct investigations. Until four years ago, CBP even kept its use-of-force policies secret; they were made public only after a congressional inquiry into a wrongful death resulted in an independent review. CBP hasn't widely adopted dashboard or body cameras, although it began a six-month pilot project in May. In 2015, the Homeland Security Advisory Council, a panel of law enforcement experts formed by DHS, warned that CBP had no effective process to root out corruption and that its internal affairs office was woefully understaffed. "The true levels of corruption within CBP are not known," the council warned. "Pockets of corruption could fester within CBP, potentially for years."

POLITICIANS HAVE BEGUN TO TAKE NOTE OF CBP'S CUL-ture of impunity. In 2008, Patrick Leahy, a senator from Vermont, was stopped at a temporary immigration checkpoint in New York—125 miles from the border. Agents ordered Leahy to get out of his car and asked him to prove that he was a US citizen. When Leahy asked under what authority the Border Patrol agent was acting, the agent pointed to his gun and said, reportedly, "That's all the authority I need."

In 2013, Leahy sponsored legislation to limit the northern border zone to 25 miles for vehicle stops and 10 miles for searches of private land without a warrant. His language was attached as an amendment to an immigration reform bill that passed in the Senate but failed to make it through the House. (Leahy reintroduced the measure in June. "The need for this legislation has never been clearer," he said in a written statement, accusing the Trump administration of "aggressive yet wasteful use of immigration enforcement resources" and subjecting citizens to "needless and intrusive searches at Customs and Border Protection checkpoints far from the border.")

Meanwhile, in the House, Beto O'Rourke, a third-term congressman from El Paso who is challenging Ted Cruz for his Senate seat, has proposed a bill that would attempt to restrain CBP. O'Rourke, a Democrat, is running a tough campaign in Texas, where Democrats haven't won a statewide race in 24 years. He supports a legal path to citizenship for Dreamers, opposes Trump's border wall, and believes that reform is needed at both CBP and ICE. (Cruz has called O'Rourke's views "radical," and a spokesperson for his campaign said that O'Rourke would let "criminal aliens run wild around Texas." Cruz supports Trump's call for more Border Patrol agents and has been endorsed by their union, the National Border Patrol Council.)

Like Leahy's, O'Rourke's opposition to CBP's sweeping powers stems in part from his own encounter with border agents. In 2009, he and his two-year-old son were detained at a checkpoint more than 70 miles from the border while agents pulled his truck apart. "They don't have to explain why they're holding you," he said, "and you're not given the right to an attorney." O'Rourke told me that he and his son were held in a cell for close to 30 minutes before they were allowed to leave. "It was a strange feeling to be held against my will and to have my car searched," he said. "I hadn't committed any crime. I hadn't even crossed the border."

O'Rourke's El Paso district includes University Medical Center, where Laura Sandoval was held. "At that point you are miles into the United States," he said, "but she was not able to benefit from Miranda warnings or have an attorney." O'Rourke's legislation, called the Border Enforcement Accountability, Oversight, and Community Engagement Act, is cosponsored by Steve Pearce, a Republican congressman from New Mexico—Sandoval is his constituent. It calls for a slew of changes at CBP, including the establishment of an

independent ombudsman to investigate complaints, an oversight committee, and subcommittees made up mostly of residents from the northern and southern borders to weigh in on
how the agency is conducting itself in their communities. The
legislation would also require the US Government Accountability Office to issue a report on CBP's interior enforcement
practices—including at its checkpoints—and their practices'
impact on civil, constitutional, and private-property rights.

Most importantly, CBP would have to reveal how far into
the United States its current activities extend. The agency
divides the United States into 20 sectors, and each sector
chief has the authority to set up checkpoints anywhere up
to the 100-mile limit as long as they sit along a route that
ultimately leads to a border crossing. But the chiefs are not
required to report where they deploy resources, so the exact
boundaries of enforcement are impossible to know.

O'Rourke's bill has languished in committee; he hopes
that in November, voters in Texas will give him a new man-
date to press the issue on the national stage. But he faces
an uphill battle. Despite the evidence proving otherwise,
CBP officials continue to argue that their interior enforcement efforts are crucial to America's safety. In 2016, Mark
Morgan, then the chief of Border Patrol, defended the use
of interior checkpoints before the House Subcommittee on
Border & Maritime Security. "The security of the border
cannot be achieved by only enforcement activities located at
the physical border," he testified. "Checkpoints greatly enhance our ability to carry out the mission of securing the

nation's borders against terrorists and smugglers of weapons, contraband and unauthorized entrants."

SINCE IT HAS THUS FAR PROVED IMPOSSIBLE TO REFORM CBP through political consensus, critics of the agency are increasingly turning to the courts. Over the decades, judges have repeatedly upheld the constitutionality of CBP's warrantless searches and seizures. In a 1985 case, *United States v. Montoya de Hernandez*, the Supreme Court ruled that the detention, observed bowel movement, and cavity search of a Colombian woman would be justified if "customs agents, considering all the facts surrounding the traveler and her trip, reasonably suspect that the traveler is smuggling contraband." In an earlier case, *United States v. Martinez-Fuerte*, the justices ruled that CBP could stop anyone at its checkpoints across the country without cause. (These have become known as "suspicionless checkpoints.")

But there are some limits. In a 1973 case, *Almeida-Sanchez v. United States*, the Court found that random stops and searches by agents on patrol—as opposed to those at checkpoints—were unconstitutional. Most recently, a federal judge in Massachusetts rejected the Trump administration's bid to dismiss a lawsuit filed last year by 11 people who had their laptops and cell phones seized by officers at airports and border crossings around the country. That case will most likely be the next challenge to CBP's authority to reach the Supreme Court.

The newest front in the legal battle over the border zone is located in Michigan. CBP considers the Great Lakes a maritime border, which means that all of Michigan lies within the 100-mile border zone, and anyone can be subjected to a warrantless search at any time. Miriam Aukerman, a senior staff attorney at the Michigan chapter of the ACLU, remembers being stunned when she discovered that CBP was operating throughout the state. "This exceptional power was given based on the idea that they patrol the border, not the whole state, which we think is unconstitutional," she said.

In 2015, Aukerman started inquiring with CBP to find out more about the scope of their practices in Michigan, but the agency refused to answer any of her questions. "Their position is, 'We might be operating anywhere in Michigan, but we won't tell you,'" she said. "The residents of Michigan have the right to know whether they're going to be subjected to warrantless searches regardless of where they are in the state."

Since then, Aukerman has sued CBP for a broad range of information relating to its authority within the 100-mile zone, from citizen complaints to incident reports and policy materials. "We want to know who they're stopping and where, and we're really interested in seeing how far from the border it's happening," Aukerman said. She expected it would take years before CBP handed over all the documents the ACLU had requested, but her resolve was buoyed by what they'd uncovered so far.

I visited Aukerman at her office in Grand Rapids. A preacher's daughter with a wide, earnest expression, Aukerman clicked through a spreadsheet on her computer, showing me the hundreds of pages of CBP apprehension logs they had obtained. Already the data was revealing a troubling pattern, she said. Instead of using its vast resources to protect America's boundaries from illegal activity and terrorists, as officials so often claim the agency is doing, Border Patrol is stopping American citizens and legal residents far from the border. In Michigan, Aukerman said, Border Patrol often worked in tandem with the police. Traffic stops for speeding or other infractions often lead to inquiries about citizenship status and a call to CBP. Of the people stopped by agents whose immigration status was recorded, nearly one-third were US citizens. Of the people who said they were foreign citizens, only 5 percent had crossed the border in the past 30 days. At least 82 percent of the foreign citizens apprehended were Latino, she said. "There's a real concern about how this turns into racial profiling."

Similar practices had already been uncovered in New York, where CBP has ramped up its interior enforcement over the past decade. In 2011, Families for Freedom, a nonprofit immigrant rights organization, obtained documents through FOIA litigation showing that agents at a single Border Patrol station in Rochester had wrongfully arrested nearly 300 US citizens and legal immigrants during a four-year period. The only way that CBP measured its effectiveness, the group found, was through its apprehension rates. Agents in Buffalo were offered cash bonuses, prizes, and extra vacation time if they boosted their arrest numbers, fostering a dragnet approach to enforcement that targeted people of color.

Among the documents she had obtained from CBP, Aukerman was disturbed to find a complexion code chart, which categorized skin color on a scale from "white to sallow to olive and black." The document raises real questions, she said, about what CBP is doing with racial data. "It's the fact that they're thinking in those categories at all," Aukerman said. "Because immigration is really about national origin and what your citizenship is. We're a very diverse country, and whether or not you are here lawfully doesn't depend on the color of your skin, but what's on your paperwork." (CBP confirmed that complexion is one of several "appearance annotations" that are entered into their system.)

Ultimately, what Aukerman is fighting for is the geographic data—CBP has refused to turn it over so far—so that she can map where Border Patrol is targeting people, along with their racial background and citizenship status. Aukerman told me that after she gets what she needs from the FOIA lawsuit, she and her colleagues will decide on the next legal step. She would like to see agents' authority limited to enforcement at the border, as it was before the Second World War.

But the constant presence of CBP has already had a profound impact on Latino communities in Michigan. Elvira Hernández, Aukerman's office manager, no longer leaves home without her US passport. Hernández, who is in her

40s, was born in Mexico, but grew up in a small farming community outside Grand Rapids; she became a US citizen in 1995. For many years before taking the job with the ACLU, she assisted seasonal farmworkers in Michigan with legal defense. Because of the heavy profiling by police and immigration enforcement in communities like Grand Rapids, Hernández said, she is afraid that if she were stopped by CBP or ICE, she would be detained until she could prove her citizenship. "I'm brown with dark hair," Hernández said. "They're not going to take my word for it."

OUTSIDE THE CAFE IN ALBUQUERQUE, THE SUN HAD BEgun to dip behind the mountains. Sandoval and I had been talking for nearly two hours, and an employee had started stacking chairs around us, preparing to close up. Sandoval pulled her cup of coffee closer and frowned. "I don't know why this is so difficult for me to get past," she said. "I've become a different person, a reclusive person." In 2014, University Medical Center agreed to a settlement of $1.1 million for its role in Sandoval's cavity search. Two years later, CBP settled for $475,000 without admitting guilt. The agreement mandated that CBP personnel in El Paso receive training on searches and Fourth Amendment law to combat abuses. (A CBP spokesperson said that the agency "takes all its responsibilities with training seriously and complied with all provisions in the settlement.")

Shortly after the agreement was reached, the ACLU sent out an advisory letter to more than 100 hospitals and medical facilities near the southern border, clarifying that medical personnel cannot be forced to conduct such searches. "While courts may afford somewhat more latitude on searches within border regions, all such searches are still bound by constitutional limits," the letter read. A spokesperson for University Medical Center said the hospital no longer conducts searches or X-rays for CBP without informed consent or a warrant from a judge.

Sandoval said she was glad to hear that the hospital had changed its policy, but she still worried that CBP would subject others to similar treatment. She has not been back to Juárez. "It's not because I'm afraid to go to Mexico," she told me. "I'm afraid of coming back to my own country."

This article was published by the *Texas Observer* in October 2018, in partnership with *Harper's* and the Investigative Fund at the Nation Institute.

# How a Dubious Forensic Science
# Spread Like a Virus

## BY LEORA SMITH

The prosecution's star witness—a forensics specialist named Herbert MacDonell—set out an array of props before the jury: a medicine dropper, a mirror hastily yanked from the wall of the courthouse bathroom, and a vial of his own blood, drawn that day at a nearby hospital.

It was a strange sight in the 1985 Texas courtroom, and the jurors, the judge, and even the defense attorneys watched, rapt, as MacDonell laid the mirror flat and then climbed up on a chair, holding the vial and dropper.

MacDonell's expertise lay in an obscure discipline known as bloodstain-pattern analysis. He claimed he could reconstruct the events of a crime by reading the bloodstains left behind.

Like a professor performing a classroom demonstration, he dipped the dropper's tip into the blood and, with a practiced hand, released a single drop onto the mirror. It landed with a muted thud, forming a perfect crimson circle.

Blood landing on a flat surface should not spatter, MacDonell told the jurors with satisfaction. He let another drop fall onto the white shirt he was wearing. Blood lands differently on fabric, he showed them.

A defense attorney shot up from his chair in protest. This was a murder trial. There was no mirror at the crime scene. No medicine dropper. The demonstration was not reliable science, he argued. The judge disagreed.

MacDonell's testimony would be pivotal to proving the Fort Bend County prosecutor's theory that 21-year-old Reginald Lewis had murdered his family, shooting his mother and two brothers and setting his father on fire. MacDonell had identified dozens of minuscule blood spots on Lewis's clothing, and he said they placed Lewis at the scene during the crime.

The jurors gave Lewis four 99-year sentences.

"MacDonell kind of took over the courtroom," Lewis's attorney, Donald Bankston, recalled, his disbelief still fresh. "It was almost like having Mr. Wizard."

But MacDonell's testimony that day did more than mesmerize the jury. It gave bloodstain-pattern analysis its first toehold of legitimacy in Texas courts, spreading it quietly, but surely, further into the justice system.

Two years later, Texas's First Court of Appeals ordered a retrial because of evidentiary flaws (two retrials ended in hung juries), but it expressly rejected Lewis's argument that bloodstain-pattern analysis was a "novel technique" that should never have been admitted and was not "scientifically recognized" or reliable.

"MacDonell's studies are based on general principles of physics, chemistry, biology, and mathematics, and his methods use tools as widely recognized as the microscope; his techniques are neither untested nor unreliable," Judge James F. Warren wrote for the court. To support his decision, Warren cited four other states—Tennessee, California, Illinois, and Maine—that had already affirmed bloodstain-pattern analysis's use at trial. Two of those states had based their decisions on court testimony by MacDonell.

Warren's hearty defense of MacDonell and his methods percolated through Texas's courts, reassuring hundreds of the state's judges that bloodstain-pattern analysis was reliable enough to be admitted at trial. They would allow it, again and again.

Over time, a parade of spatter experts, often trained by MacDonell—or by someone he trained—dazzled juries across the country with their promise of scientific surety, often tying bows of certainty on circumstantial evidence. Judges in Minnesota, Idaho, and Michigan would rely on the Texas court's decision when deciding to admit blood spatter in their own states in the 1990s. Those decisions, in turn, would be relied upon by other states.

Blood-spatter testimony spread through courtrooms across the country like a superbug.

Its path—the steady case-by-case, decision-by-decision

acceptance of a new forensic science by the justice system—is one that's rarely, if ever, been retraced. But it reveals the startling vulnerability of judges, and juries, to forensics techniques, both before and after they've been debunked.

Although the reliability of blood-spatter analysis was never proven or quantified, its steady admission by courts rarely wavered, even as the technique, along with other forensic sciences, began facing increasing scrutiny.

In 2009, a watershed report commissioned by the National Academy of Sciences cast doubt on the whole discipline, finding that "the uncertainties associated with bloodstain pattern analysis are enormous," and that experts' opinions were generally "more subjective than scientific."

Still, judges continued allowing spatter experts to testify.

Subsequent research, funded by the Department of Justice, raised questions about experts' methods and conclusions. But little changed.

All along, attorneys like Bankston continued challenging the admission of bloodstain-pattern analysis. But they came to learn that a forensic discipline, once unleashed in the system, cannot easily be recalled.

[ THE BIRTHPLACE OF BLOOD SPATTER ]

About a four-hour drive northwest of New York City, down a quiet winding road, a house with bright red siding peeks through the trees, nondescript except for its fitting hue. At first glance, the home is typical. A side door opens into an overstuffed kitchen, where a stairwell descends to the lower level.

Down those steep stairs, in a sprawling warren of rooms, forensic history was launched more than a half century ago.

Modern American blood-spatter analysis didn't originate in a federal crime laboratory or an academic research center. It started in Corning, New York, in MacDonell's basement. Decades before blood-spatter analysis gained fame in TV series like *CSI: Crime Scene Investigation* or *Dexter*, MacDonell spent countless hours in his home laboratory, incubating and refining the technique.

Then he spent a lifetime helping it spread.

MacDonell built his first basement laboratory in 1935, when he was seven, setting up some test tubes on a marble slab by the furnace in his childhood home.

But it wasn't until the 1950s, when he was pursuing a graduate degree focusing on analytical chemistry, that he got a firsthand taste of real forensics while working in a Rhode Island state crime laboratory. After graduating, MacDonell took a stable job as a chemist for the local corporate giant Corning Glass Works, best known for its CorningWare casserole dishes. But in his off hours, he taught forensics at a nearby community college and began moonlighting as a consultant.

In 1968, the focus of MacDonell's career began to narrow when he testified for a defendant in a New York murder trial. Steven Shaff, a veterinarian, had shot a former employee but claimed it was an accident. The prosecution said the man was sitting in his car when Shaff shot him. Shaff said the victim had thrown open the car door and knocked the muzzle of Shaff's gun, discharging it accidentally.

When MacDonell studied the crime scene, he found blood spattered along the inside edge of the car door—an area only exposed when the door was open. It was proof, MacDonell testified, that Shaff's story was true. The jury still found Shaff guilty of manslaughter. MacDonell was disappointed, but the case was a revelation: he could decipher a crime through blood left behind—and it whetted his appetite for more.

A year later, MacDonell successfully applied for a Department of Justice grant to continue his study of bloodstains. In 1971, the DOJ published his findings in a report titled "Flight Characteristics and Stain Patterns of Human Blood." It would come to be known as the founding text of modern American bloodstain-pattern analysis, and its author the preeminent expert.

MacDonell described blood spatters as a long-overlooked well of information. With a trained eye and a "natural scientific attitude," he believed, investigators could analyze bloodstains at crime scenes to determine critical evidence such as where the victim was standing during the bloodshed and the kinds of blows—punches, shots, stabbings—inflicted. He documented his work in pages and pages of photographs of blood spattering on different surfaces: neat circles on a plastic wall tile, sprawling splotches on a kitchen towel.

In his report, MacDonell openly acknowledged the accuracy of his methods could not be quantified. "Final conclusions should be considered from the legal viewpoint of 'proof within a reasonable scientific certainty,'" he wrote in the introduction. "Little attempt has been made to express data in this report in a statistical manner."

The uncertainty did not slow his momentum.

Propelled by the report's publication, MacDonell traveled to conferences and industry meetings presenting his research. He piqued the interest of prosecutors, defense attorneys, and police officers, who heard him, then hired him. Satisfied customers spread the word of his unnerving but seemingly useful techniques.

Soon MacDonell quit Corning Glass Works to work full-time as an instructor and forensic expert for hire. He branded his unaccredited basement lab with an impressive title, "The Laboratory of Forensic Science," and named himself its director. In time, MacDonell would testify and publish books and articles using this official-sounding moniker. Few realized the limited scale of the operation.

A grainy VHS recording of a 1980s TV appearance showed MacDonell in a pristine white lab coat speaking with casual confidence about his grisly specialty. "Herbert MacDonell says he doesn't work at home," a local TV reporter said, "but rather lives where he works."

The cameras captured charts covering the laboratory walls and a battery of expensive-looking scientific equipment resting on white countertops. A sign reading EVIDENCE DO NOT REMOVE mostly obscured a pair of shoes in an open cardboard box. Differently shaped and sized bottles of chemicals filled the shelves along with a tiny, humanlike skull.

In 1973, the Mississippi office of a DOJ-funded agency invited him to Jackson to spend a week teaching police officers how to analyze bloodstain patterns. MacDonell quickly realized police departments liked having their own in-house experts. "I must've got good reviews," MacDonell recently recalled, "because they kept asking me, 'Would I teach this for them?'"

He began crisscrossing the country teaching 40-hour "Bloodstain Evidence Institutes" to groups of mostly law enforcement officers who trekked from small towns like Estherville, Iowa; Gulfport, Mississippi; Appleton, Wisconsin; and Sanford, Florida, to attend his courses. Although Mac-Donell would emphasize his own scientific education when acting as an expert witness, his advertisements assured students there were "no minimum educational requirements to be accepted into the class."

By 1982, MacDonell had taught 19 institutes in eight states (Mississippi, New York, Florida, Alabama, Indiana, Illinois, Louisiana, and Colorado), turning out scores of newly minted blood-spatter experts. He also gave single-day seminars in Germany, Italy, England, Switzerland, and Canada.

At the end of each course, MacDonell administered an exam, handing out certificates to students who passed. He would eventually teach for 38 years and recalled only five students who failed.

Then he expanded his offerings. He began teaching advanced courses to students who had already passed his basic course. Graduates of his first advanced class formed a new professional society—the International Association of Bloodstain Pattern Analysts—in 1983. The following year, IABPA published the first issue of the *Journal of Bloodstain Pattern Analysis*. MacDonell was named IABPA's sole "distinguished member" in honor of his contributions.

In the span of about a decade, MacDonell had created an industry in which he became the reigning expert.

[ A GROWING FAME IN COURTROOMS ]

As he forged legions of bloodstain-pattern experts, MacDonell's star continued to rise. A steady stream of cases poured into the Laboratory of Forensic Science. With his help, a savant-like mythos developed around him.

In 1987, Corning's local ABC news affiliate ran a three-part series about MacDonell. "Herbert MacDonell," the first episode began, "has been described as an American Scotland Yard, all by himself." It was a line straight from the back cover of *The Evidence Never Lies: The Casebook of a Modern Sherlock Holmes*, a highly flattering book MacDonell coauthored about himself. Interviewers and attorneys often compared him to Holmes. MacDonell happily leaned into the image, adopting a curved pipe and deerstalker hat for the cover of a self-published book.

Old courtroom footage, collected on VHS tapes by MacDonell, documented the deference he was shown. At a coroner's inquest, a coroner introduced MacDonell's testimony by waving one of his books before the jury and saying, "We have not called another expert of your caliber because we don't have another expert of your caliber that we know of." The coroner provided autographed copies of MacDonell's book as a "nice memento" for each juror.

Over time, MacDonell was called to testify in increasingly high-profile cases.

During the hugely publicized 1981 trial of Jean Harris, a private-school headmistress accused of killing her ex-lover, "Scarsdale Diet" creator Herman Tarnower, MacDonell provided dramatic testimony for the defense. Holding Tarnower's spattered bedsheets up before the jury, he explained the choreography of Tarnower's death from the blood left behind. Harris was, nevertheless, convicted.

In 1994, O.J. Simpson's defense team hired MacDonell, in part to demonstrate that the notorious glove found at the murder scene did not shrink after being soaked in blood, a theory the prosecution suggested to explain its ill fit on Simpson's hand. On the stand, MacDonell recounted how he'd placed an identical glove on a photocopier to record its size, then saturated it in blood drawn from his own arm. When the blood dried, he measured it again. The glove, he said, holding up ghoulish pictures for the jurors, had hardly shrunk at all.

Lead prosecutor Marcia Clark cross-examined Mac-Donell for three days about the glove and his other testimony. She questioned the scientific rigor of his methods,

suggesting he had inflated his résumé. Yet even these asper-
sions, cast on national TV, did not slow the acceptance of
bloodstain-pattern analysis.

Along the way, MacDonell's reputation for eccentricity
also grew. In his books, he described shooting dogs to record
the resulting spatter and drenching a female student's hair in
human blood then having her shake it around to photograph
the patterns. For decades, MacDonell collected his own
fingernail clippings, preserving and pressing them between
glass slides to study their striations, developing expertise in a
field he called "fingernail identification."

These macabre experiments only added to his intrigue.

"He's the kind of guy that likes to have an audience," recalled Martin A. Sells, a former DA in Columbia County,
Oregon, whose testimonial once appeared on advertisements
for MacDonell's institutes. "He likes impressing you. But I
never had a single doubt in my mind that he knew what he
was talking about."

Judges, too, were impressed. They regularly allowed Mac-
Donell to testify in their courtrooms, based on his expertise
and the industry he himself had built.

Eventually, defense attorneys began appealing convictions
that relied in part on MacDonell's testimony. They argued
that MacDonell and his field were unscientific. But appellate
judges almost never agreed. Again and again, they affirmed
MacDonell's right to testify as an expert. "His background
and experience were formidable," the Supreme Court of Tennessee wrote in 1982.

In time, MacDonell's students, many of whom only had 40 hours of training, started testifying as experts, too. Then the students of his students. They modeled their testimony after his. They invoked MacDonell's name as evidence of their expertise. They borrowed his phrases, his descriptions, his experiments, to support their analysis. Judges borrowed the reasoning of other judges who had admitted MacDonell when they ruled to admit his students.

In this way, over time, MacDonell's testimony laid the legal bedrock for a field whose roots hardly reached farther than the lower level of his home.

## [ WINNING OVER JUDGES ]

For a new forensic discipline to grab hold, it needs to get past the court system's gatekeepers: the judges.

Trial judges can refuse to hear evidence they deem unreliable. At the appellate level, judges review decisions made at trial and can deem an individual expert unqualified or label a whole field unreliable, banishing it from trial courts below.

Around the turn of the last century, judges rejected precursors to modern bloodstain-pattern analysts. Mississippi's Supreme Court and the California Court of Appeal both affirmed decisions to exclude blood-spatter experts—in 1880 and 1927, respectively—on the grounds that their analysis added nothing to the jury's own common-sense inferences.

But courtroom attitudes shifted as MacDonell's brand of expertise seeped in.

In 1957, California's Supreme Court accepted blood-spatter testimony from Paul Kirk, a man MacDonell cited as an inspiration. Kirk, a professor of biochemistry and crimi nalistics at the University of California, Berkeley, had worked on the Manhattan Project and was an early practitioner of bloodstain-pattern analysis. The court wrote that Kirk's "inferences required knowledge and experience beyond those of ordinary jurors."

Kirk became the technique's first flag-bearer. Nine years later, he would use blood-spatter analysis to help exonerate Sam Sheppard, a doctor who had been convicted of killing his wife in a trial so aggressively covered by the news media that the US Supreme Court condemned the "virulent pub-licity" surrounding it. That same year, the Alaska Supreme Court accepted bloodstain-pattern analysis.

Then came a lull. Kirk died a few years after the Shep-pard trial. Appellate courts mostly stopped talking about bloodstain-pattern analysis. Then MacDonell came along.

In 1980, Iowa's Supreme Court became the first to review MacDonell's testimony. The judges didn't examine the ac-curacy of his technique. Instead, they cited his "status as the leading expert in the field." Finding his testimony reliable, they noted MacDonell's discipline had "national training programs"; "national and state organizations for experts in the field"; "the holding of annual seminars"; and "the exis-tence of specialized publications."

With seals of approval from some of the country's highest courts, bloodstain-pattern analysis continued its spread.

It moved east, gaining acceptance in an Ohio court of appeals, where both the defense and prosecution presented blood-spatter experts. Then south, as Tennessee's highest court affirmed a trial judge's decision to admit MacDonell as an expert. "Mr. MacDonell's testimony was clear, understandable, and accompanied by demonstrations to the jury," the court wrote. "He obviously knew whereof he spoke."

MacDonell's students carried the technique west to Oklahoma and Illinois. When a defendant argued a police officer who studied with MacDonell did not have a sufficient understanding of science to testify as an expert, an appeals court in Illinois responded, "We again reject the defendant's argument that this area of expertise requires substantial training in physics."

In Minnesota, a court affirmed expert testimony that bloodstains could reveal whether a victim was crouching or standing; in Idaho, that the stains showed a victim was walking away when shot.

After a while, some judges facing the issue for the first time simply cited the decisions of their counterparts in other states.

Acceptance of bloodstain-pattern analysis became almost inevitable.

Throughout, a handful of judges expressed concern. In 1980, Judge Mark McCormick of Iowa's Supreme Court singled out MacDonell in writing. "I am unable to agree," he wrote, "that reliability of a novel scientific technique can be established solely on the basis of the success of its leading proponent in peddling his wares to consumers."

Judge Stephen Bistline of Idaho's Supreme Court, in a vehement dissent in 1991, wrote: "The danger presented by expert testimony interpreting blood-spatter evidence is that the prosecution is provided with an expert who appears to be able to reconstruct precisely what happened by looking at the blood left at the scene of a crime. However, a quick review of the 'science' relied upon by the expert suggests that we would be better off proving guilt beyond a reasonable doubt without the help of such experts."

But the skeptics' dissents and uneasiness could not contain the spread.

By 2004, a Texas court of appeals wrote: "Have any courts held blood-spatter analysis to be invalid? The short answer is no."

Over time, growing layers of legal precedent protected bloodstain-pattern analysis, allowing it to flourish unhindered.

Attorneys on both sides began presenting competing experts, assured they would be admitted. Some forensic scientists grew concerned by the number of police officers qualifying as experts based on a mere 40 hours of formal training.

MacDonell deflected responsibility in one of his books. "The fault for permitting such individuals to testify as an expert must rest with the opposing attorney," he wrote, adding that "a judge should be able to recognize unqualified charlatans."

MacDonell ran his last Bloodstain Evidence Institute in 2011. By then, he had taught 75 workshops and over 1,000 students. Some of them replicated his business model, running 40-hour workshops of their own. This new wave of blood-spatter entrepreneurs established fiefs in different corners of the country, advertising their services through the IABPA.

In 2012, MacDonell, then 84, retired. That same year, two girls alleged he had sexually abused them when they were 11 and 16. One said the abuse occurred while she was a student at a summer forensics program taught in his home. MacDonell was charged in Corning town court with forcible touching, two counts of endangering the welfare of a child, exposure of a person, and aggravated harassment in the second degree. He pleaded guilty to the harassment and the remaining charges were dropped. MacDonell said recently that he'd done nothing wrong and pled to the charges on "the bad advice of my attorney."

Afterward, no lawyer could reasonably present MacDonell at trial as he was too easy to undermine on the witness stand. His career as an expert witness was over.

But by that time, the field hardly noticed his absence. Others, many members of law enforcement who'd gotten their start as MacDonell's students, had taken his place at the forefront of the discipline. And while the technique's earliest experts, MacDonell and Kirk, had impressed judges with their extensive scientific backgrounds, many of the new wave of experts had little to no scientific education at all.

[ A TECHNIQUE PUTS DOWN TENACIOUS ROOTS ]

In 2006, federal judge Nancy Gertner handed down a sentence that still haunts her.

A jury in her courtroom convicted a man named James Hebshie of burning down his convenience store to fraudulently collect insurance money. Gertner thought the prosecution's most damning piece of evidence—that a state trooper's accelerant-sniffing dog identified where Hebshie started the fire—was bogus. But Hebshie's defense attorney never objected, even when Gertner interjected three times, offering him the chance.

Without arguments before her, Gertner could not exclude the evidence. The mandatory minimum sentence was 15 years, and she had to impose it. "I was appalled," she said.

Before her 1994 appointment to the bench, Gertner worked for years as a defense attorney, scrutinizing and challenging forensic evidence presented against her clients. She later taught law students about the risks of forensics as a professor of evidence at Boston College Law School. But as a judge, she realized cases like Hebshie's could render her powerless.

So, when the National Academy of Sciences' groundbreaking report on forensics came out in 2009, Gertner saw an opportunity.

The report was a rigorous examination of the forensics widely used in the nation's courts and revealed troubling inadequacies with virtually every technique. It included a harsh assessment of bloodstain-pattern analysis and questioned the abilities of experts in it. A capable analyst, it said, must possess an understanding of applied mathematics, significant figures, the physics of fluid transfer, and the pathology of wounds—subjects that aren't covered in depth in the field's 40-hour workshops.

Using the National Academy of Sciences report as a launching pad, Gertner published instructions for attorneys arguing cases in her courtroom, the gist of which were: "If the evidence at issue is challenged in the NAS report, I will automatically hold a hearing."

"If the courts routinely admit junk science," Gertner said recently, "the lawyer with a finite amount of resources is not about to say I will spend this dollar on a challenge if it's not going to make a difference."

Other judges on the US District Court for Massachusetts did not follow her lead. "Everybody thought I was crazy," she recalled with a wistful laugh. Gertner was used to being an outsider. She was one of a few women litigating criminal cases in the 1970s. Among her judicial peers, defense attorneys were a rarity.

Still, she was disappointed to see how few judges—on the federal bench or in state courts where the majority of spatter cases arose—saw the National Academy of Sciences report as a call to action.

Gertner, who retired from the bench in 2011 and now teaches at Harvard Law School, said the failure of the report to take hold in courts "was an institutional failure." Lawyers failed. Trial judges failed.

Appellate judges failed.

She saved her strongest criticism for appellate judges who, she insisted, could raise the stakes of admitting bad science by shaming trial judges who do.

"If you were reversed by the court of appeals for allowing in junk science," she said, speaking as a former trial judge, "you are bound to be more critical the next time you have this issue." But appellate judges are loath to overturn forensic-related precedent, even in the face of advancing scientific understanding.

"Precedent is like a child's game of telephone," Gertner said. "You start off saying something. You whisper it down the line and you continue to whisper it even though it no longer makes sense."

For attorneys, convincing appellate judges to break ranks has proven Sisyphean.

Last year, Geneva Williams, a defense attorney in Iowa, used the concerns raised in the National Academy of Sciences report to argue that her client's former lawyer was ineffective for failing to challenge the admission of bloodstain evidence at his trial. Her client's conviction, she said, should be overturned. The court rejected her argument.

"The admissibility of such evidence is determined by the Iowa Rules of Evidence," Judge Richard Blane wrote for the Court of Appeals of Iowa, "not a research journal."

The expert who testified at the trial was a former IABPA officer who studied with MacDonell.

[ QUESTIONING THE REAL-WORLD VALUE OF RESEARCH ]

While the National Academy of Sciences report fell flat in the courts, its findings roused the Department of Justice. The department and other federal agencies began doling out millions to researchers to enhance the scientific bona fides of forensic disciplines like bloodstain-pattern analysis.

Starting in February 2010, the DOJ's research arm, the National Institute of Justice, offered a pool of grant money for a study of the fluid dynamics of blood.

The call for proposals landed in the inbox of Daniel Attinger, a fluid dynamics specialist at Columbia University in New York. Attinger, who wears round, frameless glasses and sneakers with his suits, had been training computers to recognize fluid stains: first, to differentiate between Coke and Diet Coke, then between cabernet and merlot.

But "bloodstains," he recalled thinking, "had more important stories to tell." He just didn't know anything about them.

So Attinger read everything he could and then, like so many before him, made the trek to Corning to learn from the man who had propagated the very technique the National Academy of Sciences report now questioned. He went to MacDonell's house.

The two men huddled in MacDonell's kitchen, talking about Attinger's research ideas, MacDonell's methods, and the practical needs of investigators in the field. "What he knew, he was able to explain clearly," Attinger said of Mac-Donell. "He also had a clear understanding of what he did not know." In the unknowns, Attinger saw potential.

That summer, Attinger attended one of MacDonell's final 40-hour workshops. By fall, Attinger's team won a grant of just over $632,000 from the DOJ to start their studies.

In 2013, Attinger published his first blood-spatter paper in the journal *Forensic Science International*. One of his three coauthors was a now-retired Canadian police officer who had been an assistant teacher in MacDonell's workshop.

The paper showed that the hypotheses that underpin bloodstain-pattern analysis remained largely untested. And, it said, analysts' assumptions and errors could make their conclusions rife with uncertainty. Analysts failed to properly account for gravity when using bloodstains to calculate victims' locations. They assumed things about how speed influences blood patterns that had never been scientifically proven.

But Attinger's paper had a solution: It posited fluid dynamics research as a promising way to refine the accuracy of bloodstain-pattern analysis.

Once published, the article didn't attract widespread concern, but it did attract more funding.

Today, Attinger, now at Iowa State University, has been studying the technique for eight years and has received over $1.3 million in federal grants. Other scientists have received grants, too. The NIJ alone dedicated $175 million to forensic research between 2009 and 2017.

A review of Attinger's research reveals some investigation of fundamental questions, like trajectories of blood in flight. But his experiments are highly simplified and extremely specific when compared with the complex problems faced at crime scenes. "The key in doing meaningful experiments," he said, "is to start from the simple, understand it and then go to the complex." A recent paper, for example, examined distortions of bloodstains on perfectly flat-lying military fabrics, results that Attinger and his coauthors said could be generalized to any woven fabric that had been laundered four or more times.

Such studies frustrate forensic experts like Ralph Ristenbatt, an instructor of forensic science at Pennsylvania State University and a 15-year veteran of the Office of Chief Medical Examiner in New York City. "These are great academic studies," he said, "but what do they lend to real-world problems?" Ristenbatt said he isn't sure researchers will ever be able to model lab experiments as complex as real life, so they may not be the best way to address the chasm between analysts' training and the conclusions they draw at crime scenes.

"There's this belief out there that you can look at the patterns of blood at a crime scene and it's the be-all end-all," he said, "when in reality bloodstain-pattern analysis is just one tool in the toolbox of what we call crime-scene reconstruction." The very idea that bloodstains will "tell the story for us," he said, is "misguided."

Attinger freely admitted that his years of work have had little impact on practices of blood-spatter experts at crime scenes. "I would say there's been no change," he said. But he saw no reason for law enforcement to hit pause until techniques improve.

"I have trust in the US justice system," he said. The technique's limitations, he said, "are known by both the prosecution, the defense and, hopefully, the judge."

Attinger now appears to be a part of the very industry he was hired to scrutinize.

In 2015, he co-taught an advanced bloodstain-pattern analysis course to members of the Las Vegas Metropolitan Police Department. His partner was Craig Moore, the retired officer who coauthored his first blood-spatter article. Attinger taught an introduction to ballistics and the fluid dynamics of bloodstain-pattern analysis, while Moore taught the practical application of the discipline. "An advanced class is designed for a person who will be testifying in court," Moore said. Attinger said he had "no opinion" as to whether the students were qualified to act as expert witnesses after completing the course.

He is also a dues-paying member of IABPA. In June, Attinger spoke at the first South American IABPA conference. "A whole continent is eager to do #forensics with bloodstain patterns," he tweeted afterward. "Go for it!"

One month later, Attinger settled a lawsuit with Iowa State University, whom he had sued after student complaints about verbally abusive conduct led to an internal investigation and sanctions against him. He claimed the process violated school policy and his constitutional rights. Attinger denied the allegations, saying he is "very articulate and honest in the feedback" he provides to students. "Some people do not like to receive honest feedback and not everyone is called to be a researcher."

The settlement allowed Attinger to remain at Iowa State and work full-time on research and related activities, but only until 2021, when a current grant expires.

Today, Attinger talks a lot about his new idea: he'd like to develop a computerized, handheld device that analysts could use to read bloodstains at crime scenes—even if they didn't understand the complex science behind them.

Ristenbatt said the justice system would be better served by more educated investigators who could grasp the limitations of different forensic techniques. Ristenbatt also used to teach introductory blood-spatter courses, but said he stopped when he realized his students were holding themselves out as experts. "The easiest way to control it is not to do it anymore," he said.

In 2016, the Texas Forensic Science Commission—a state panel consisting of seven scientists, one prosecutor, and one defense attorney—opened an inquiry into two cases that turned on bloodstain-pattern analysis. At the center of one is Joe Bryan, a beloved high school principal who has been in prison for 31 years over the killing of his wife. The bloodstain-pattern analyst in that case, a local police officer who took a 40-hour class with one of MacDonell's former students, recently acknowledged that his conclusions were wrong.

Ristenbatt gave an impassioned speech to the commission,

calling for mandatory educational requirements for analysts, including a four-year degree in natural or forensic science. In February, the commission announced it would require accreditation for all bloodstain-pattern analysts testifying in court starting in May 2019. Commission decisions only affect Texas courts, but have influence across the country.

In the meantime, experts in the old methods—the ones that got their start all those years ago in Corning—keep testifying.

"I think if you were to do a study," Ristenbatt said in an email, "of all the people who call themselves bloodstain-pattern experts and you looked at the genealogy, if you will, of how they've obtained their training, it'll all likely come back to Herb MacDonell through some means."

### [ "I AM VERY SATISFIED." ]

MacDonell still lives in the big red house in Corning. He is 90 and uses a stair lift to descend to his laboratory. It takes, he said with characteristic precision, exactly 31 seconds to reach the last step.

The stairs lead to a long hallway lined, floor to ceiling, with fading photographs of MacDonell's students, their changing hairstyles and glasses a vivid timeline of his decades of teaching.

The laboratory now has the fluorescent-lit feel of a high school chemistry classroom. The rows of bottles, still there, are covered in layers of dust. The whole room has a yellowed tint to it, like stepping into one of the old photographs on the wall.

Behind the lab, in a large office, MacDonell carefully catalogs his legacy. A thick book details every student who attended a Bloodstain Evidence Institute. A glass display case showcases mementos from police departments across the country. Stacks of VHS tapes chronicle courtroom triumphs and TV appearances.

Today, MacDonell's demeanor is much the same as it was in his earliest videos. He is confident, sometimes curt. Little gets under his skin as much as people who refer to his field as "blood splatter" instead of "blood spatter," a phrase he said he coined ("Splatter is splash. Spatter is not splash," he said). He is keenly aware of his impact.

"Overall," MacDonell said, "I am very satisfied with my life's accomplishments and have few regrets."

When asked to pinpoint the proudest moment of his long career, MacDonell's answer comes easily: Susie Mowbray's exoneration. Mowbray was imprisoned for nine years over the killing of her husband. At her retrial, MacDonell used blood spatters to reconstruct the crime, testifying her husband's death was a suicide and discrediting the expert who testified for the prosecution at her first trial. The expert was MacDonell's former student.

MacDonell has testified against his own students numerous times. Asked recently whether he ever considered changing his course structure, or certification process, after seeing students give faulty testimony, MacDonell answered in the negative. "You can't control someone else's thinking," he said. "The only thing you can do is go in and testify to the contrary."

Leave it to the lawyers to cross-examine, to the trial judges to exclude, to the appellate judges to overturn.

According to MacDonell, this June marked 50 years since he first testified about blood-spatter analysis. To honor the occasion, he planned to pour himself a glass of single-malt scotch and toast Shaff, the client whose case unleashed modern American bloodstain-pattern analysis on the world. Sitting in a home maintained as a shrine to his accomplishments, MacDonell could rest assured his legacy would be protected in the courts for years to come.

Herbert MacDonell died on April 11, 2019, five months after this story was originally published by *ProPublica* in December 2018.

# "I Am a Girl Now," Sage Smith Wrote.
# Then She Went Missing.

BY EMMA COPLEY EISENBERG

On the late afternoon of November 20, 2012, just a few weeks shy of her 20th birthday, Sage Smith stepped out of the neon pink–walled apartment in Charlottesville, Virginia, she shared with two friends. After a tough and tumbling childhood, things finally seemed to be falling into place: She had moved out of her grandmother's house, was taking classes, had just reconciled with her dad. And she had just started openly identifying as a transgender woman.

At night and on the weekends, Sage and her roommates gussied up and went out to dance at Charlottesville's only queer club or to the strip of bars near the University of Virginia. Her friend Shakira had started taking estrogen injections, and Sage wanted to start, too. Sage changed her gender on Facebook to "female." "I am a girl now #Respect it," she wrote to a friend on Facebook on November 9, 2012, and to a family member on November 18: "Look I am transitioning and I am your niece."

Sage walked toward the 500 block of Main Street. She stopped to talk to a friend and told them she was going to meet a man. She didn't come home that night, nor the next morning, nor the day after that.

Sage has been missing for more than four years and is now considered murdered, but the Charlottesville Police Department says they're no closer to knowing what happened to her—or if they have any new information, they're not sharing it. The prime suspect was the man she was supposed to meet, who skipped town just days after Sage's disappearance, before police could interview him in person.

After years of trying to locate him, police suddenly cleared him of suspicion in 2015, only to change their minds again. The CPD says it has aggressively pursued the case, which has been difficult, and if people have information they haven't shared it with police. A new police chief took office last year and he promises the case is getting a fresh look—but if anything new has come to light, Sage's friends and family certainly don't know it.

"There's a bigger issue there," said Lieutenant James Mooney, the detective who's stayed with the case the longest, and who blames the lethargic pace of the case on the fact that Sage was black and trans and poor. "Only a very small fraction of our community has taken interest in Sage."

Sage was memorable, and stories about her abound. Like

how she ended up doing a *Vogue*-style shoot with a UVA student on the Route 7 bus. Like how she once helped carry an old man's groceries to his car while wearing a miniskirt and three-inch heels. Like how every clubgoer leaned closer when Sage spoke, as if they were campers pulled to a fire, according to Jason Elliott, Mr. Pride of America. But Sage's family and friends say, unlike those afforded to missing white girls, the investigation into her disappearance was slow, slap-dash, and followed a zigzagging logic that makes little sense to anyone. And they're in search of a better story.

THE UNIVERSITY OF VIRGINIA IN CHARLOTTESVILLE WAS built by the enslaved and worships Thomas Jefferson, a pragmatic and brutal slave owner. Charlottesville's public schools closed for five months in 1958 rather than comply with the federal order to desegregate. In the mid-1960s, a middle-class black neighborhood called Vinegar Hill was razed—under the guise of "urban renewal"—because of its proximity to downtown, which developed into a commercial corridor that would put the city on the map for education, culture, and tourism. What were once black-owned homes are now a major roadway, hotel, and Staples that border a brick-paved pedestrian shopping mall.

These days, Charlottesville can claim the titles of one of the top 10 best American cities for book lovers and the "happiest city in America." But happy for whom? This past May, a crowd led by noted white nationalist and UVA alum

Richard Spencer gathered in Charlottesville's Lee Park to protest the removal of a statue of the park's namesake, chanting, "You will not replace us."

Home values and rents are high, but the number of affordable housing units is low. The median income in Charlottesville is about $50,000 a year, yet nearly a third of its residents do not earn a wage that allows them to pay for food, clothing, housing, and transportation. Just 20 percent of Charlottesville's population is black, but they make up 80 percent of those stopped and frisked by police. Just 6 percent of UVA students are black, yet people of color make up the vast majority of staff in UVA's on-campus cafes and cafeterias.

In 2011, the author of a report on poverty put it plainly: "When you look in the middle of the city of Charlottesville, you see a big orange dot, and that's where all the poor people live."

Sage grew up in that orange dot, raised from the age of three by her grandmother, Miss Cookie, in her apartment in what was then called Garrett Square, an affordable housing complex. Miss Cookie was a dedicated parent and a prominent community figure, serving on the tenants' association board and resident patrol.

When Sage was 12, a wrought-iron fence went up that made the complex residents feel like prisoners, so Miss Cookie moved Sage to a house in Charlottesville's Fifeville neighborhood. That's when they met Shakira Washington, who lived two doors down, and who would soon call Miss Cookie "grandma," too.

"[Sage and I] got into an altercation," Shakira said. "Our families came out of the house and stopped it. We were together every day after that." Shakira is trans and was already asking her middle school teachers to use female pronouns.

One day, Sage came to Miss Cookie and said there was something she needed to confess—then asked Miss Cookie not to be mad.

"And she said, 'Grandma, I'm gay.' And I said, 'You aren't telling me anything that I don't already know.'" They sat there hugging for a long time.

Although she often struggled in school, Sage became the first in her family to graduate high school. She took cosmetology classes, braided out of her home, and swept hair at a salon. Foster care—where she had been since Miss Cookie returned her to her mother, who was subsequently deemed unfit—paid for her to have her own apartment, so she asked Shakira and another childhood friend, named Aubrey Carson, if they would move in and share it with her.

Sometimes they went to parties that catered to men on the down low. They also hosted parties at the apartment on Harris Street and invited men and other friends over. They had a tight friend crew that also included Aubrey and three women named Alexis, Tiffany, and Chelsea. Sometimes they hooked up for fun, other times for money. The guys they met came from all walks of life; many of them were married. If either Sage or Shakira was going to hook up, they would text the other. One time, Shakira recalls, a UVA professor arranged for her to come over to his house in a fancy neighborhood and when the man left the room, she heard a knock on the window. It was Sage, outside in the bushes, watching her to make sure she was okay.

Shakira didn't hold a high school diploma, and getting a job without one wasn't easy; potential employers seemed nervous when she mentioned she was trans, then didn't call. Sage and Aubrey were harassed on the street, called slurs, once chased by a crowd. Sage's jobs paid minimum wage, and neither Miss Cookie nor Sage's dad, Dean, had a lot of cash to spare.

Dean had been incarcerated for several years on a drug charge when Sage was young, but now he was eager to play a bigger role in Sage's life. He struggled to accept Sage, first as a gay man and then as a trans woman, but a Lifetime movie called *Prayers for Bobby* changed his mind. "Dude was like that and his family dropped him. I just felt I couldn't do that to my child," Dean said. "When she walked by on the street and I was at the barbershop with my boys, I would say, 'Come here, I want you to meet my child.'"

Sage wasn't a stranger to interpersonal trouble. Her Facebook account shows messages from March 2012 in which a friend is telling her to "watch her back," that people on the street had it out for her because she'd contacted the wife of a man she'd hooked up with. Occasionally, Sage also placed Casual Encounters ads on Craigslist, a practice Shakira didn't approve of. This is how police believe Sage met Erik McFadden.

———

NOVEMBER 19, 2012, WAS A MONDAY, AND SHAKIRA'S 19TH birthday. The friend group celebrated Shakira in style at the apartment. But then a girl came busting through the door wanting to start a fight with one of Sage's friends over a man. The fight migrated outside. There were cars parked all the way up Sage's street. Then car doors opened and a crowd of people tumbled out. In the fray, Sage ended up fighting with a man named Jamel Smith, an acquaintance whom Sage had seen around town. Things escalated and someone called the police.

Police responded at about 11:20 p.m. and Jamel Smith filed a report that Sage damaged his car, but no one was arrested. Shakira said fights were not unheard-of in their circle, but that something about this one felt different.

"Where did it come from? It didn't start with Sage or me," she said. "So it was kinda weird how it ended up on Sage."

Later that night, Jamel Smith tweeted: "Been disrespected to the point of no return."

After the cops left, Shakira called a couple of friends from her hometown of Norfolk, Virginia, and they came at dawn and drove her back with them to the coast. Shakira didn't intervene on Sage's behalf in the fight; Sage felt let down and angry.

"Her last words to me were 'I hate you,'" Shakira said. "We never got to make it right."

Sage woke up late the next day and called her dad. She congratulated him on the anniversary of his getting out of jail and asked him for money to get her hair braided.

Sage's other roommate, Aubrey Carson, said that Sage woke him up from a nap when she left and told him simply that she was off to meet a man. When Aubrey woke again around eight p.m., the house was black. He called Sage's phone, but it went straight to voicemail.

"Major red flag," Aubrey said. "Sage would charge [her] phone anywhere." In the morning, Sage still was not back.

When the phone rang at around nine a.m., Shakira thought it was Sage calling to apologize. But it was Aubrey. Shakira told Aubrey to call Miss Cookie, who told Aubrey to call the police.

Miss Cookie remembers receiving this call, which detonated a bomb at the center of her life.

"The police came to the house and talked to us," she said. "I told them what I have been saying all along: Sage would never leave her family right before Thanksgiving and not tell anyone. Somebody must have taken her."

Aubrey called the Charlottesville Police Department on the afternoon of Wednesday, November 21. He said the officer on the line sounded calm, simply asked for Sage's name, birth date, and a picture.

"From the start, it seemed like they didn't see it very seriously," Aubrey said.

Detectives began investigating on Thursday, November 22—Thanksgiving Day. The case was originally assigned to Detective Sergeant Marc Brake, who has not returned multiple requests for comment.

Dean and Latasha Grooms, Sage's mother, both confirmed that it was extremely out of character for Sage's phone to go to voicemail and for her not to have been in touch with family or friends for 36 hours. Detectives also spoke to the friend who confirmed she had seen Sage walking west on Main Street just after 6:30 p.m. on November 20, that the two had stopped to chat, and that Sage had said she was "going to meet a man."

Two additional detectives were brought on board who would stay with Sage's case for years. Lieutenant James Mooney is a big man just a few years shy of retirement with a close-shaven head who favors logo-free gray sweatshirts, belted blue jeans, and black sneakers. Detective Ronald Stayments is a second-generation cop but with a slicker look—pink tie on pink shirt, handcuffs that dangle from his dress pants.

Six CPD officers conducted a "grid search" of the busy commercial corridor, checking trash cans, dumpsters, open lots, parking lots, and fields for any signs of Sage, as well as checking nearby businesses for any surveillance footage. The only camera was a traffic camera, but it only monitors, it doesn't record.

On Friday, with Sage missing for 72 hours, Mooney got ahold of Sage's cell phone records, which showed that Sage talked to a friend from northern Virginia for about 20 minutes on the day of her disappearance, but the last call Sage's phone received was at 6:36 p.m. from an unidentified number. After that call, all activity on Sage's phone stopped.

To identify the unknown number, the detectives gave it to

Sage's family. Dean posted it to his Facebook page, and before long he received a message from an acquaintance named Yami Ortiz, a trans woman who moved in similar circles as Sage. I know that number, she said. That's Erik McFadden.

Sage's phone records reveal that the two had been exchanging texts and calls for several weeks before Sage's disappearance, that they had met multiple times for sex, and that McFadden may have already given Sage some money in exchange for Sage not outing him to his girlfriend.

Years of living in Charlottesville and being stopped, sometimes seemingly at random, by the CPD had left a bitter taste in Dean Smith's mouth, and the slow start out of the gate made Dean suspicious.

"I felt they were lying to us on the whole," Dean said. "I did my own investigation."

Dean learned that McFadden worked at a Sherwin-Williams paint store and lived in downtown Charlottesville with his girlfriend. Dean also posted McFadden's picture to Facebook.

"That really set us back a long way," said Mooney, who believes that Dean posting that picture spooked McFadden into fleeing. "If we'd have had a chance to find him without his picture being out there, we might be talking to him instead of looking for him."

At the same time, Sage's family wonders why they as civilians had more information about the case than the police did at that point.

"All their information came from us," Miss Cookie said,

also referring to efforts undertaken by Sage's aunt Tonita Smith, who found McFadden's Facebook profile and, being able to access Sage's Facebook and Twitter, began checking them for clues. "It began to feel like we were doing their job for them."

On Saturday, November 24, after conducting a search of Sage's neighborhood, the Charlottesville Police Department got another call about a missing person. This time, it was a young woman named Esther Ayeni. She said she had not heard from her boyfriend, Erik McFadden, who had been staying in her apartment while she was out of town for Thanksgiving. CPD detectives told Ayeni that they were actually already looking for McFadden to question him about his role in Sage's disappearance. McFadden's job confirmed he had not shown up to work in several days with no explanation and no warning.

The investigation seemed to have gone dark over the weekend. "I don't think they really did enough at that time," Shakira said. "Instead of calling people, they should have been getting people in investigating rooms and interrogating them."

On Monday, CPD officers talked at length with Ayeni. She had finally gotten a call and emails from McFadden the previous night, Sunday, November 25—he told Ayeni he was in Washington, DC, and needed money. She told him that the police wanted to speak to him about Sage Smith and gave him contact information for the detectives.

Police entered Ayeni's apartment looking for McFadden.

He wasn't there, but they collected McFadden's stuff from her apartment, including his laptop computer and clothes. A receipt from CVS showed that he had been in Charlottesville until as recently as the evening of Thursday, November 22, two days after Sage went missing.

On Tuesday, November 27, with Sage missing for a week, detectives got a call from McFadden himself. Yes, McFadden explained, I was supposed to meet Sage near the Amtrak station that day, but she never showed up, and I don't know what happened to her. He was in New York now, he told detectives. Why? "Because I've never been to New York before," McFadden responded. Detective Marc Brake told McFadden that he should to return to Charlottesville. McFadden hung up.

On Wednesday, November 28, Charlottesville police officers searched the streets and wooded areas along West Main street, where Sage was last seen, and then they expanded their search to include the area around where McFadden had been living.

The next day, Esther Ayeni told police that McFadden was taking a bus to Charlottesville arriving the next evening and that he expected to be picked up by police. The police affidavit reads, "Brake reasonably assumed, based on the email communication, that McFadden would be speaking with him at that time to explain his absence from Charlottesville and his relationship with Smith."

But that's not how it turned out. On Friday, November 30, while coming back from a visit to a trash expert that helped them determine that the dumpsters behind McFadden's apartment went to a landfill some 60 miles away in Henrico County, near Richmond, detectives heard again from Esther Ayeni. McFadden was going to run.

"[I]m heading out," McFadden wrote to Ayeni in an email on November 30. "This is what happened i never did anything sexual with that guy and he was blackmailing me, he wanted me to give him money not to lie from saying we did and i did and he agreed to stop and then the next time he hit me up for money i said no . . . we did meet up but he had alot of enemies me and him were walking and some people sowed up and i kept walking not looking back."

In other words, McFadden did in fact meet up with Sage. Police obtained warrants for McFadden's computer, email accounts, cell phone apps, Twitter, and bank records. Another email to Ayeni in May of 2013 from an untraceable email address is the last anyone has heard from Erik McFadden.

That December, police made two more efforts to find Sage. On the first, Charlottesville police, in conjunction with officers from the Virginia Department of Emergency Management and cadaver-sniffing dogs from the Virginia Search and Rescue Dog Association, again searched the areas around Main Street and McFadden's house as well as nearby railroad tracks and near a deep sediment pond. A dog made a "slight indication" that they picked up Sage's scent.

A dive team was called in to search the pond, but nothing turned up. The final attempt was a large-scale search of that Henrico landfill that involved Charlottesville police officers as well as officers from Henrico County, forensic and hazmat personnel, and a retired special agent specializing in landfill searches. But they found nothing.

Over the past four years, Sage's case has stayed "under active investigation." In January of 2013, detectives met with agents from the FBI and US Marshals Service to see if they might be able to consult or provide assistance. In May of 2013, they got in touch with the National Center for Missing and Exploited Children. Later that month, dental records for Sage were obtained and placed into a national registry. A few tips came in that Sage might be living in the Tidewater area or in the Carolinas. They went nowhere.

ON SEPTEMBER 13, 2014, A WHITE UNIVERSITY OF VIRginia sophomore named Hannah Graham went missing from Charlottesville's Downtown Mall. Within 24 hours, the Virginia State Police had taken over the case.

By September 15, nearly every law enforcement office in central Virginia knew Graham's name and dozens of officers were searching. Then the FBI came on board, as well as the Albemarle County Sheriff's Office, the Blue Ridge Mountain Search Group, and the Virginia Department of Emergency Management. More than 5,000 tips flooded in, necessitating a separate Hannah Graham tip line. Police announced a $50,000 reward for information, $10,000 of which came from the city of Charlottesville itself (the reward pool would later total $100,000). A massive volunteer search drew more than 1,000 participants from all over the state.

In the early hours and days of Hannah Graham's disappearance, Charlottesville police chief Tim Longo gave several press conferences during which he shook his fist, banged the lectern, and wiped away tears.

Communications Officer Captain Gary Pleasants was sending 146 members of the international press updates more than once per day.

Detective Mooney was also the lead detective on Graham's abduction case. Law enforcement officers from all over the country were calling offering help—did Mooney need trucks? Helicopters? A drone? The CPD declined to disclose the total amount spent on the search, but it has been called the most extensive and intensive in Virginia state history. "Ungodly amounts of overtime dollars," Mooney said.

The suspect in Hannah Graham's case fled as well, triggering a national manhunt that located the fugitive in Texas in three days. Hannah's remains were found after 36 days, and the suspect pleaded guilty in spring of 2016. He will spend the rest of his life in jail.

"HOW DO YOU THINK I FEEL?" DEAN SMITH WANTS TO know. "I watched the helicopters come right up and over the field there behind my house. They didn't do that for my child."

Hundreds of thousands of people are reported missing each year, but most of them are found. Key factors distinguish these ordinary missing from the truly gone, and it falls to law enforcement, who have finite time and resources, to tell the difference, and quickly. Every expert says that the choices law enforcement makes in the first 72 hours determine the outcome. In Hannah's case, every choice was made correctly. In Sage's, many of them were not.

The Virginia Department of Criminal Justice Services has clear protocol as of 2015 for high-risk missing persons cases (though no such document existed in 2012; when called for comment, the CPD declined to do so). The protocol includes making requests for search and rescue and other external support "in the early hours of the investigation."

Yet the detectives did not make requests for substantive external support in this case until December 1, 2012, 11 days after Sage went missing. Detective Mooney said the Virginia State Police and the US Marshals were consulted, and that the FBI offered technical assistance to find McFadden. When contacted this February, the first two agencies said they never had any agents working on Sage's case nor are they actively assisting on it now.

Protocol also advises police officers to contact local government and trash companies to request a delay in trash collection near where the subject was last seen or might have been abducted. CPD did not request any such delays. Finally, protocol advises detectives to get consent or obtain search warrants for emails, chats, and "other online communications" for clues relevant to the disappearance and to communicate frequently and openly with the victim's family.

Police did file for a warrant to search the email files associated with Sage's phone as well as the laptop they seized from McFadden's apartment—but not until March 11, 2013, nearly four months after Sage's disappearance. Miss Cookie states that she had to call and leave messages for several days, even during the first week of the investigation, in order to receive a return phone call from lead CPD detective Marc Brake.

Aubrey Carson, who called about Sage's disappearance, was not contacted until "three or four days, maybe longer" after Sage went missing. Aubrey was staying with his grandmother 20 minutes north of town. Detectives asked Aubrey to come down to the police station. Aubrey agreed, but because he didn't have a car, he asked to be picked up at his grandmother's home. The detective agreed. But no officers ever showed. Aubrey was not interviewed for nearly two more weeks.

When interviewed in January of 2016 in her home on Chincoteague Island, Virginia, Shakira said detectives had never talked to her beyond a short factual phone call. Mooney said he and Stayments had been meaning to go up to see her but that his desk duty, which he had for most of 2015 due to a knee injury, had prevented it.

A final point of misstep was police communication with the public. On November 28, with Sage missing for eight days and detectives searching the areas around McFadden's apartment, CPD Lieutenant Ronnie Roberts called the first press conference about Sage's case.

"It's not a criminal case," the lieutenant told the gathered reporters, nearly all local or regional. "We have nothing at this point in time that indicates it being a criminal case, which makes it difficult to get warrants and things of that sort, because you have to have a criminal case to go in that direction."

"I don't know why he said that," Mooney said recently. "He was our public information officer. He should have asked for the public's help."

Mooney said the case was clearly criminal since November 30 when McFadden sent the email to his girlfriend admitting to meeting with Sage. "At that point, this obviously wasn't a missing persons case anymore—something had happened," Mooney said. In the police affidavit for a warrant to search McFadden's computer, Lieutenant Mooney wrote, "These facts when considered together present probable cause to believe that [Sage] Smith has been abducted, is either being held against [her] own will or has met with harm." The search warrant was granted; the charge was criminal abduction.

But Lieutenant Roberts must have not gotten the memo. An NBC29 article from December 1 read, "At this point, police do not suspect foul play." And on December 7, Roberts responded to Sage's family's public pleas that the department request help from the Virginia State Police or the FBI by saying that the city would refrain from seeking investigative assistance unless it was deemed necessary, which in this case, he said, it was not. In another article from December 2014, in the *C-VILLE Weekly*, Mooney said police were still treating Smith's disappearance as a missing persons case, not a criminal investigation.

"I don't know why I would have said that," Mooney said. "Maybe it was for a strategy."

Leading up to the third anniversary of Sage's disappearance, in 2015, the police department held a press conference to announce that the CPD no longer believed McFadden was responsible for abducting Sage.

"He didn't have the means to get rid of anybody," Mooney said. "He didn't have a car, he was living in a suite with other people, it's very unlikely that he would have done that. And he stayed in town until his picture popped up on Facebook. He was here for almost three days after [Sage] went missing."

It seems then that all of the information that led investigators to believe Sage had been abducted and that McFadden was responsible, Mooney acknowledged, was available to police investigators within the first days of Sage's investigation. Yet the public was allowed to believe otherwise.

"What happened?" Miss Cookie asked. "How did this go so wrong?"

Mooney doesn't see it that way. When asked what the protocol is for a missing person, Mooney answered, "There's no standard there. The facts kind of dictate your actions."

Detective Stayments agreed, adding that the CPD receives a missing persons case nearly every other day. Charlottesville is a hub for Virginia youth from around the state in the midst of juvenile detention proceedings.

"Juveniles run away from these community detention homes all the time," Stayments said. "A lot of times those kids show up within a few hours, they just wanted to leave the home for a while and do whatever they wanted to do and then come back."

Many of these cases involve young people who are black and poor. Is it possible that since Sage is also black and poor, detectives assumed Sage was one of these itinerant youths? Mooney says no. But Natalie Wilson, cofounder of the Maryland-based Black and Missing Foundation, who worked with the Smith family, said police more often classify minority children as runaways rather than victims of crimes, and that the reverse is true for white children.

Aubrey said that when detectives finally interviewed him, they brought up a time the year prior where Sage and Aubrey had left Charlottesville for several days to go to the beach, but Aubrey said they had been clear with their family where they went. Aubrey said that police asked, "Well, wouldn't Sage run away again if she had done it before?"

Furthermore, the detectives had a history with the Smith family. Detective Stayments was the officer who responded to the call about the fight the night before Sage disappeared and took Jamel Smith's statement against Sage.

"I had run-ins with Detective Mooney because I wasn't no angel in the streets," Dean Smith said.

"Yeah, I know Dean," Mooney confirmed.

The Charlottesville Police Department is no stranger to racial controversy. From 2003 to 2004, as part of a rape investigation, Mooney and other officers stopped black men on the street, showed up to their homes and workplaces, and demanded cheek swabs; all told, officers collected swabs from 190 black men. There was widespread outrage, and one man filed a 2004 lawsuit against the CPD that specifically named Detective Mooney for assault and battery and racial discrimination.

Then there are the facts that Sage is trans and had moved within the queer community. In official police documents, the person the police are looking for has always been "Dashad Laquinn Smith," Sage's birth name. Sometimes "Sage Smith" is added in quotes or referred to as an alias. Mooney and Stayments have said they understand what it means to be trans, yet in all email and phone correspondence with Splinter they have used "he" and "his" as well as "Dashad." In police affidavits and statements to media, Mooney repeatedly refers to the fact that McFadden had gay sex as his "alternative lifestyle."

One night in the winter of 2013, Sage's father, Dean, and his partner, Latasha Gardner, said they got a call from Detective Stayments. Stayments had gone to Charlottesville High School with Dean, and the two families knew each other a little bit.

"He sat right there on that couch," Dean said. "He dropped his handcuffs on that table. He said, 'We dropped the ball. We weren't prepared for something like this.'"

Miss Cookie said she also received a home visit from Stayments around the same time. "He said his conscience was eating away at him," she remembered. "And he just couldn't sit by."

Detective Stayments doesn't deny that he has been to both Miss Cookie's and Dean's homes on several occasions. "My heart went out to them, and I did talk to them," Stayments said, "but I never said anything that would imply that our officers didn't do everything they possibly could have done in this case.

"I can tell you my detectives bust their ass on every case they get," Mooney said. "The frustrating part is that instead of helping us find Sage, people want to argue about gender issues and things like that. I don't think it should matter."

Still, Mooney admits that the police could only do so much in a city that was more inclined to sympathize with victims that look like them—and that sympathy controls resources and response.

"When Hannah went missing, people were beating down the door to help," he said. "In [Sage's] case when you ask for help it wasn't an easy process. It was like pulling teeth."

Police captain Gary Pleasants said that the Hannah Graham case and the Sage Smith case are different because in Hannah's case, she and Matthew were seen together, plus Matthew had access to a car, but Erik McFadden didn't. Still, it's hard not to compare the demeanor of Charlottesville's police chief Tim Longo while talking about Hannah versus Sage.

When asked by a local activist if he had ever cried for Sage, Chief Longo admitted he had not. By explanation,

Longo told a reporter from the local alt-weekly, "I think, I felt as if I were in the shoes of [Hannah's] parents, as a dad having a 15-year-old girl who is growing up too quickly," he said. "I'm a human being and I can't always control how I react to things."

In early 2013, the Smith family requested an interview with Chief Longo because they felt their concerns weren't being taken seriously by detectives. But they say it was nine months before Longo consented to sit down for a face-to-face meeting.

"He just told us, 'I'm sorry but I don't think there's going to be a good outcome,'" Miss Cookie recalled.

Detective Mooney and now-former chief Longo have both expressed that they felt some hostility and antipolice sentiment coming from the Smith family in a way that hampered communications.

"Miss Cookie very quickly came out publicly and blasted the police department before she met with anybody," Mooney said. "That didn't sit right with a lot of people." Mooney specifically recalled an incident at a vigil for Sage held at Miss Cookie's house in which those congregated chanted, "Fuck the police."

Another point of contended inequality is the difference in money spent on the two cases. All told, the police department spent $127,000 to find Sage Smith, the lion's share of which was spent on the fruitless Henrico County landfill search.

And then there is the reward money that the city of

Charlottesville gave in Hannah's case within a week of her disappearance. By comparison, in Sage's case, on December 18, nearly a month after Sage went missing, an anonymous donor gave $10,000. The city contributed nothing until Miss Cookie inquired about the discrepancy. Charlottesville City Council member Kristin Szakos responded that the $10,000 had indeed come from the city.

This wasn't true. The city council, who gave that information to Szakos, claim they genuinely thought the money for Sage had come from them. But as it turns out, it hadn't. Confronted with their mistake in 2012 and their mistaken public statement in 2014, the City of Charlottesville rectified the error and donated $10,000 to Sage's reward, two years after Sage went missing, bringing the total reward to $20,000.

In November 2015, Mooney and Stayments took to the streets to distribute flyers to local businesses and along the corridor where Sage was last seen. Some of the businesses flat-out refused to let the detectives hang the posters, Mooney recalled. One reluctant business owner told Mooney, by way of explanation, "It's kind of a downer, isn't it?"

"I know some of what the family's experiencing because I see it, too. Racial problems. Gender issues," Mooney said.

Fellow queer people of color in Virginia and nationwide have stepped forward to raise awareness for Sage at rallies, conferences, and city council meetings as well as through fund-raising campaigns—groups like the Black and Missing Foundation, the Lavender Kitchen Sink Collective, and the Richmond chapter of Southerners on New Ground. CeCe

McDonald visited Charlottesville to do an event in honor of Sage. "Just know that it could have been you," she said in a video from the event. "Put yourself in the shoes of this family. Think about what you would do if it was your child . . . We are all equal, we are all valid, and we need to show support and get active."

SINCE SAGE WENT MISSING, MISS COOKIE'S BODY HAS SIM-ply shut down. Her heart is quite literally broken—she's been diagnosed with chronic obstructive pulmonary disease, and during her triple bypass surgery, doctors had to take a vein from her leg and put it in her chest to keep her alive. She's also struggled with breast cancer and congestive heart failure. Oxygen tanks line the kitchen walls of her apartment. Sitting outside on the sidewalk in a wheelchair, neighbors smile and greet her. (Her health problems persisted; she died in May 2019.)

One question that still plagues Miss Cookie is why the detectives didn't get a warrant for McFadden's arrest. Such warrants would have allowed CPD to track him across state lines and get access to other national resources, as was done in Hannah Graham's case.

"I probably could have gone out and gotten a warrant for Erik McFadden but we didn't have enough to prosecute him," Mooney said. "Down the line, a judge could determine that we didn't have probable cause and then throw out the results of a search or interrogation. I didn't want to jeopardize the case."

For better or worse, law enforcement spent the early days

of Sage's disappearance investigating McFadden, and only McFadden.

But Sage's father wishes other leads had been explored, too. "In my gut, it's the friends," he said. "I think [Aubrey] had something to do with it. They all disappeared." (Aubrey denies this, claiming he was home.)

When Dean went over to Sage's apartment on Wednesday, all of Sage's wigs were gone. He believes Aubrey took many of them, though Aubrey vehemently denies that, too. Another of Sage's friends was wearing a locket on a chain that had belonged to Sage. When asked, the friend said, "My boyfriend gave it to me."

Aubrey was caught on video on Wednesday, November 21, at a gas station, using Sage's EBT card.

"Your friend is missing and you're using her food stamp card?" Dean Smith said in disbelief. "No."

Was Aubrey indeed home at the time of Sage's disappearance? Maybe, but no one can verify it. Aubrey's phone was indeed pinging off a cell tower near the Harris Street apartment, but Mooney said in a small town like Charlottesville where cell towers are far apart this isn't necessarily conclusive.

As a possible motive, Dean suggests jealousy. "[Sage] had her own crib, she had family support, she didn't want for anything. To see your friend thriving and you're not. When they went out, Sage would get all the attention."

Shakira reiterates her concerns about the fight and Jamel Smith. After Jamel Smith tweeted that he'd been "disrespected" on November 19, the night before Sage went missing, he didn't post anything for a month, even though he had been tweeting almost daily up to that point. Later, on May 11, 2013, he retweeted, "I can't stand a nigga that wants to be a woman. I want a man who's a man, not a man who's a woman."

"It's a scenario we considered," said Mooney, who acknowledges that Jamel Smith didn't have an alibi. Where is Jamel Smith now?

"Is it Richmond or is it Florida? I can't remember," Mooney said. "One of them's in Florida. But without evidence, we couldn't really investigate."

CHARLOTTESVILLE HAS A NEW POLICE CHIEF NOW. HIS name is Al Thomas Jr., and he's the first black man to ever hold the position in Charlottesville. (At the time of this printing, there is now a new police chief, RaShall Brackney; Chief Thomas resigned after only a year and a half on the job.) Chief Thomas met with the Smith family in August 2016, and initially seemed attentive to their concerns.

But future inquiries from Miss Cookie went unanswered. Then, in late March, Miss Cookie read online that the case had been reclassified as a homicide. (Neither Chief Thomas nor the departmental spokesperson could comment on the reasoning behind this change.) A petition to Chief Thomas was started to urge him to ensure the CPD continues to aggressively investigate Sage's case and communicate openly with Miss Cookie. When that failed, Miss Cookie and her community supporters staged a protest outside CPD headquarters.

In mid-April, Miss Cookie finally sat down with the new police leadership team. They informed her that Sage's case had been assigned to a new detective, Regine Wright-Settle, that she was working solely on Sage's case and had undergone training in homicide and cold cases to prepare for it. She is also approaching the case with new eyes, reinterviewing witnesses rather than relying on Mooney's and Stayments's notes.

When Miss Cookie asked why it had taken four years for Sage's case to be classified as a homicide, the new investigation team blamed the old, saying they could not speak to frustrations with actions in the past nor disclose details of what specifically the new detective was doing due to the case being an ongoing criminal investigation. CPD leadership agreed that it was suspicious that Erik McFadden continues to be missing and that his family in Maryland has not filed a missing persons report.

"So y'all gonna bring the FBI in or what?" Miss Cookie asked. "What is being done to find this man?"

A captain told her that Sage's case now being classified as a homicide gives them the ability to bring in the FBI "if and when" they are needed.

But the family and police leadership still struggle to work together. Lieutenant Joseph Hatter asserted that it was necessary for CPD to continue to refer to Sage by her birth name in order to get the best information from the public, and Chief Thomas said that in the eyes of science, the department was still looking for a male (Sage's birth mother agrees). Plans for the Charlottesville Police Department to undergo transgender sensitivity training may be in the works, but nothing is definitive yet.

At a recent vigil, Miss Cookie appeared in a wheelchair, wearing a huge faux-fur coat, a loan from a supporter to block out the freezing wind in Lee Park.

"We need some closure," she said in front of the small crowd, who stand holding balloons marbled pink and purple. "What makes one life more valuable than another? That's how it makes our family feel, that we don't matter."

Dean Smith was there, too. His face and beard were buried into the collar of his North Face jacket, and he was stamping his feet to shake off the cold. His voice was clear and loud. "I miss my child," he said. "I'll be sitting at home eating and I stop eating and think, is my child eating? I don't sleep. Never cut my phone off. I haven't changed my number. I usually change it every couple of years. Sage was taken from me just as we were getting to know each other. I'll never get to truly know my child."

The CUE Center for Missing Persons was there to support the family. They even had a bench made in Sage's honor. Miss Cookie asked the city if she could place the bench in a city park and plant a tree in Sage's memory.

"They told us, 'Sure,'" Miss Cookie said, "but that it would cost us $1,000."

Originally published by *Splinter News*, July 2017

# ACKNOWLEDGMENTS

*Unspeakable Acts* was several years in the making, and it would never have come into being without the tireless efforts of my editor, Zack Wagman, a true partner in crime (projects, that is!). Deepest thanks to my agent, David Patterson, as well as Aemilia Phillips, Hannah Schwartz, Ross Harris, and everyone at SKLA; to my wonderful publisher, Ecco, and especially Dominique Lear, Norma Barksdale, Miriam Parker, Martin Wilson, Meghan Deans, Sonya Cheuse, Rachel Kaplan, and Ashlyn Edwards; to Sara Wood for the brilliant cover; to the HarperCollins sales force and library marketing team for championing my work to larger audiences; to the booksellers, particularly independent stores, who share in my passion and excitement for crime stories; to Patrick Radden Keefe, for the insightful introduction; to all the talented and dynamic contributors included in this anthology; and to family, friends, and writers who provided untold support as I put together this project.

# OTHER NOTABLE CRIME STORIES

*What to Read, Listen To, and Watch*

ESSAYS AND FEATURES

"Remembering the Murder You Didn't Commit" by Rachel Aviv (*New Yorker*, June 19, 2017)

"The Indispensable Guide to Early American Murder" by Casey Cep (NewYorker.com, June 2016)

"The Girl Detectives" by Marin Cogan (Topic, August 31, 2017; originally appeared in *Pop-Up Magazine*)

"The Mystery of Leslie Arnold" by Henry Cordes (*Omaha World-Herald*, September 3–5, 2017)

"Improbable Cause" by Amy Dempsey (*Toronto Star*, April 2018)

"An Odd, Almost Senseless Series of Events" by Thomas Dybdahl (The Marshall Project, June 2018)

"The Strange, Spectacular Con of Bobby Charles Thompson" by Daniel Fromson (*Washingtonian*, March 2017)

"'I Killed Them All': The Life of One of America's Bloodiest Hitmen" by Jessica Garrison (*BuzzFeed*, May 2018)

"Framed" by Christopher Goffard (*Los Angeles Times*, September 3, 2016)

"Home Free" by Jennifer Gonnerman (*New Yorker*, June 20, 2016)

"The Making of Dylann Roof" by Rachel Kaadzi Ghansah (*GQ*, September 2017)

"A Positive Life" by Justin Heckert (*GQ*, April 28, 2016)

"The Fugitive, His Dead Wife, and the 9/11 Conspiracy That Could Explain Everything" by Evan Hughes (*GQ*, June 28, 2016)

"Accused" by Amber Hunt (*Cincinnati Enquirer*, 2016)

"The Final, Terrible Voyage of the 'Nautilus'" by May Jeong (*Wired*, February 2018)

"Murder, He Calculated" by Bob Kolker (*Bloomberg Businessweek*, February 8, 2017)

"The Encyclopedia of the Missing" by Jeremy Lybarger (Longreads, January 2018)

"The Murder House" by Jeff Maysh (Medium, October 2015)

"Finding Lisa: A Story of Murders, Mysteries, Loss, and, Incredibly, New Life," by Shelley Murphy (*Boston Globe*, May 2017)

"How an Aspiring 'It Girl' Tricked New York's Party People" by Jessica Pressler (*New York*, May 2018)

"Bad Boys: How 'Cops' became the most polarizing reality TV show in America" by Tim Stelloh (The Marshall Project, January 2018)

"Ted Bundy's Living Victim Tells Her Story" by Tori Telfer (*Rolling Stone*, March 2019)

## BOOKS: NARRATIVE NONFICTION

Shane Bauer, *American Prison* (Penguin Press, 2018)

Maureen Callahan, *American Predator* (Viking, 2019)

Casey Cep, *Furious Hours* (Knopf, 2019)

Kate Winkler Dawson, *Death in the Air* (Hachette Books, 2017)

David Grann, *Killers of the Flower Moon: The Osage Murders and the Birth of the FBI* (Doubleday, 2017)

Monica Hesse, *American Fire: Love, Arson, and Life in a Vanishing Land* (Liveright, 2017)

Bill James and Rachel McCarthy James, *The Man from the Train: The Solving of a Century-Old Serial Killer Mystery* (Scribner, 2017)

Kirk Wallace Johnson, *The Feather Thief* (Viking, 2018)

Patrick Radden Keefe, *Say Nothing* (Doubleday, 2019)

Jill Leovy, *Ghettoside* (Spiegel & Grau, 2015)

Wesley Lowery, *They Can't Kill Us All* (Little, Brown, 2017)

Michelle McNamara, *I'll Be Gone in the Dark* (Harper, 2018)

Hallie Rubenhold, *The Five* (Houghton Mifflin Harcourt, 2019)

Eli Sanders, *While the City Slept* (Viking, 2016)

Kate Summerscale, *The Wicked Boy* (Penguin Press, 2016)

Sarah Weinman, *The Real Lolita: A Lost Girl, an Unthinkable Crime, and a Scandalous Masterpiece* (Ecco, 2018)

Albert Woodfox, *Solitary* (Grove, 2019)

## BOOKS: MEMOIR, ESSAYS, CRITICISM

Alice Bolin, *Dead Girls: Essays on Surviving an American Obsession* (William Morrow, 2018)

Leah Carroll, *Down City* (Grand Central, 2017)

Myriam Gurba, *Mean* (Coffee House Press, 2017)

David Kushner, *Alligator Candy* (Simon & Schuster, 2016)

Rachel Monroe, *Savage Appetites: Four True Stories of Women, Crime, and Obsession* (Scribner, 2019)

Carolyn Murnick, *The Hot One* (Simon & Schuster, 2017)

Sarah Perry, *After the Eclipse* (Houghton Mifflin Harcourt, 2017)

Tori Telfer, *Ladykillers* (Harper, 2017)

Piper Weiss, *You All Grow Up and Leave Me* (Harper, 2018)

## PODCASTS

*Accused* (*Cincinnati Enquirer*)

*Bear Brook* (New Hampshire Public Radio)

*Bundyville* (Oregon Public Radio/Longreads)

*Crimetown* (Gimlet Media)

*Crime Writers On* (Partners in Crime Media)

*Criminal* (Radiotopia)

*Dirty John* (*LA Times*/Wondery)

*Dr. Death* (*ProPublica*/Wondery)
*Headlong: Running from COPS* (Pineapple Street Media/Topic Studios)
*In the Dark* (American Public Media)
*Serial* (WBEZ/*This American Life*)
*S-Town* (WBEZ/*This American Life*)
*Someone Knows Something* (CBC)
*The Ballad of Billy Balls* (Cadence 13/Crimetown Presents)
*The Clearing* (Pineapple Street Media)
*Uncover: The Village* (CBC)

## FILM AND TELEVISION

*American Crime Story* (Season 1: *The People v. O.J. Simpson*; Season 2: *The Assassination of Gianni Versace*)
*American Vandal*
*Evil Genius*
*Making a Murderer*
*Mindhunter*
*Mommy Dead and Dearest*
*O.J.: Made in America*
*Tales of the Grim Sleeper*
*The Jinx*
*The Keepers*
*The Last Resort*
*Unbelievable*
*When They See Us*
*Wild Wild Country*

# CONTRIBUTORS

ALICE BOLIN is the author of *Dead Girls: Essays on Surviving an American Obsession*, a *New York Times* Notable Book of 2018. She is an assistant professor of creative nonfiction writing at the University of Memphis.

PAMELA COLLOFF is a senior reporter at *ProPublica* and a staff writer at *The New York Times Magazine*. She was previously a staff writer and executive editor at *Texas Monthly*. Colloff has been nominated for six National Magazine Awards, more than any other female writer in the award's history, and won for feature writing, for "The Innocent Man," in 2013. The Nieman Foundation for Journalism at Harvard University awarded her the Louis M. Lyons Award for Conscience and Integrity in Journalism the following year. Her oral history, "96 Minutes," about the 1966 University of Texas shootings, served as the basis for the 2016 documentary "Tower," which was short-listed for an Academy Award in Best Documentary Film. She lives in Austin, Texas.

MICHELLE DEAN is the author of *Sharp: The Women Who Made an Art of Having an Opinion* (Grove Press) and cocreator of *The Act*, which aired on Hulu in May 2018 and was adapted from her *BuzzFeed* feature, reprinted in this anthology. Dean received the National Book Critics Circle's Nona Balakian Citation for Excellence in Reviewing in 2016, and her work has appeared in *The New York Times Magazine*, *The New Yorker*, *The New Republic*, *The Nation*, and *Elle*. She lives in Los Angeles.

MELISSA DEL BOSQUE is an investigative reporter based in Mexico City. Her work has appeared in ProPublica, the *Wall Street Journal*, the *Texas Observer*, the *Guardian*, *The Intercept*, and *Harper's Magazine*, among other publications. In 2016 del Bosque won the Hillman Prize for "Death on Sevenmile Road." In 2015 del Bosque's four-part series with the *Guardian* on migrant deaths in South Texas won an Emmy and a National Magazine Award. Her 2012 investigative feature "Valley of Death," about the drug war and massacres in Juarez Valley, Mexico, was a finalist for the National Magazine Award. Del Bosque is also the author of *Bloodlines: The True Story of a Drug Cartel, the FBI, and the Battle for a Horse-Racing Dynasty* (Ecco, 2017).

EMMA COPLEY EISENBERG is the author of *The Third Rainbow Girl: The Long Life of a Double Murder in Appalachia*, published by Hachette Books in 2020. Her fiction, essays, and reportage have appeared in *McSweeney's*, *The Paris Review* online, *Granta*, *Virginia Quarterly Review*, *Tin House*, *Guernica*,

*AGNI*, the *Los Angeles Review of Books*, *American Short Fiction*, Electric Literature's Recommended Reading, *The New Republic*, *Pacific Standard*, *Slate*, *VICE*, 100 Days in Appalachia, and others. She is the recipient of fellowships or awards from the Tin House Summer Workshop, the Elizabeth George Foundation, the Helene Wurlitzer Foundation, the Millay Colony for the Arts, and Lambda Literary. She lives in Philadelphia, where she directs Blue Stoop, a hub for the literary arts.

JASON FAGONE is an investigative reporter at the *San Francisco Chronicle* and the author of *The Woman Who Smashed Codes* (Dey Street Books). Previously a contributing editor at *Huffington Post Highline*, his work has also appeared in *The New York Times Magazine*, *Wired*, *GQ*, *Grantland*, *Washingtonian*, and NewYorker.com.

ELON GREEN is the author of *Last Call*, forthcoming from Celadon Books. He lives in Port Washington, New York.

KAREN K. HO is a business and culture reporter based in New York City. She has been published in *Time*, *GQ*, *Glamour*, *The Globe and Mail*, Vox, Refinery29, *Interview*, and *The Walrus*. "Jennifer Pan's Revenge" was her first magazine story, and *Toronto Life*'s first story translated into another language.

PATRICK RADDEN KEEFE is a staff writer at *The New Yorker* and author of the *New York Times* bestseller *Say Nothing: A True Story of Murder and Memory in Northern Ireland*, which won the 2019 Orwell Prize for Political Writing, as well as two previous books, *The Snakehead* and *Chatter*.

ALEX MAR is a writer based in her hometown of New York City. Her first book, *Witches of America*, was a *New York Times* Notable Book in nonfiction, a *New York Times* Editors' Pick, and included in multiple year-end lists for 2015. Some of her work has appeared in *The Believer*, *Wired*, *New York*, *The New York Times Book Review*, *The Guardian*, *Elle*, *Virginia Quarterly Review*, *Oxford American*, and *The Best American Magazine Writing 2018*. She was nominated for a 2018 National Magazine Award (ASME) for Feature Writing. Formerly an editor at *Rolling Stone*, she is also the director of the feature-length documentary *American Mystic*, now streaming on Amazon. Mar is currently at work on her second nonfiction book, for Penguin Press.

SARAH MARSHALL grew up in Oregon and Hawaii and earned an MFA in fiction at Portland State University. Her writing has appeared in *The New Republic*, *BuzzFeed*, and *The Believer*, among other publications, and she cohosts *You're Wrong About . . .*, a podcast on misremembered history.

RACHEL MONROE is the author of *Savage Appetites: Four True Stories of Women, Crime, and Obsession*. She was a 2016 finalist for a Livingston Award for Young Journalists and was named one of the "queens of nonfiction," along with Susan Orlean, Rebecca Solnit, and Joan Didion, by *New York*. Her essay about murder fandom and adolescence, "Outside the Manson Pinkberry," originally published in *The Believer*, is anthologized in *The Best American Travel Writing 2018*. She is a contributing writer at *The Atlantic* and regularly writes for *The New Yorker*, *The New York Times Magazine*, *Texas Monthly*, *The Guardian*, *Bookforum*, and elsewhere.

LEORA SMITH is a lawyer and writer living in Toronto. Her research and writing have appeared in *ProPublica*, *The New Yorker*, *The New York Times Magazine*, the Canadian Broadcasting Corporation's *The Fifth Estate*, and *The Harvard Civil Rights–Civil Liberties Law Review*.

SARAH WEINMAN is the award-winning author of *The Real Lolita: A Lost Girl, an Unthinkable Crime, and a Scandalous Masterpiece*, and editor of the anthologies *Women Crime Writers: Eight Suspense Novels of the 1940s & 50s* and *Troubled Daughters, Twisted Wives*. Her work has appeared in *The New York Times*, *Vanity Fair*, *The Washington Post*, *New York*, and *CrimeReads*, where she is a contributing editor and columnist. Weinman also publishes the "Crime Lady" newsletter, covering crime fiction, true crime, and all points in between. She lives in New York City.

# PERMISSIONS